A realistic depiction of the duality between good and evil that our Brothers and Sisters in Blue see every day. The book entails real life scenarios that exhibit the daily experiences that police officers choose to deal with and accept as a responsibility as part of "the job".

The book highlights the despicable treatment of man that the normal citizen does not witness. Therefore, the book is an excellent depiction of what Public Safety-officers see and deal with on a daily basis. A job well done. An excellent read.

Scott Reinacher
Retired Michigan State Trooper-2003
Thin Blue Line of Michigan-President 1999-present

TUEBOR

TUEBOR

I WILL DEFEND

AN ANATOMY OF A MICHIGAN STATE POLICE TROOPER

ROBERT MULADORE

PRINCIPIA
MEDIA

Tuebor is dedicated to the Michigan Department of State Police and to all of the past, present and future enlisted and civilian members who have and continue to give so much to protect the citizens and visitors of the State of Michigan, on the department's 100 anniversary, April 19, 1917–April 19, 2017.

Special thanks to the following who graciously contributed assistance in their own special way: Ralph Davis-R.E. Davis Motor Sales, LLC, Charlotte, Michigan; Margaret Kyser & James Pike and staff-Eaton Community Palliative Care, Charlotte, Michigan; Trooper Matt Lequia; Lisa McNeilley, PhD-The Writer's Alley of Grand Rapids, Michigan; Trooper Andrew Muladore; Benjamin Muladore; Trooper Brian Muladore; Dale Muladore; David Muladore; Erin Muladore; Jacob Muladore; Jean Muladore; Jennifer Muladore; Liam Muladore; Michael Muladore; Patti Muladore; Patty Muladore; Terry Whitten; Abby Whitten; and Trooper Lena Wileczek.

Principia Media, LLC
678 Front Avenue NW
Suite 256
Grand Rapids, MI 49504
www.principiamedia.com

Disclaimer

The views and opinions expressed herein are solely those of the author in his private capacity and do not in any way represent the views of the Michigan Department of State Police, or any other entity of the State of Michigan. The contents and photographs are not to be taken as any form of endorsement of the Michigan Department of State Police.

ISBN 978-1-61485-324-4

Photo credits: Robert Muladore
Cover and Interior Design: Frank Gutbrod
Cover photos: Robert Muladore
Photo of John Wayne on page 212 copyright 1972 Warner Brothers
Photos of Ronald Reagan, George Herbert Walker Bush, Bill Clinton and Barack Obama on page 312 are in the public domain
Photo of airplane on page 158 is in public domain
Photo of flea on page 62 is in public domain
Digital Imaging: Sherry Baribeau sherrydirk.com

21 20 19 18 17 16   7 6 5 4 3 2 1

Printed in the United States of America

TABLE OF CONTENTS

Part 5

PREFACE

Tuebor is intended, to the extent possible, to assist those contemplating a police career, to aid newly appointed officers, and to offer a helping hand to experienced officers who may need a gentle reminder to help move them along on the path of a truly professional, caring, and effective police officer. For those readers with no desire to pursue a police career, hopefully *Tuebor* will provide an insight into the world of policing to provide some level of understanding of the job and those who pursue it, or if nothing else, it may provide some valuable lessons wherever life has led you or maybe it will provide some level of entertainment.

The events depicted are as true as my recollection will permit with a few intentional changes for safety reasons. Many of the events depicted have been indelibly imprinted in my mind but with varying degrees of accuracy. I apologize in advance for any discrepancies that may have crept into *Tuebor* and I hope those readers whom I worked with as past partners or who were otherwise involved in the events shared, know that I tried to accurately depict all of the events to the best of my recollection. Please forgive any unintentional variances from the actual events.

The goal of this work is to attempt to capture the transition from civilian life to the working world of the police officer. It is also intended to depict the emotional side and the effect of police work on those who have chosen it as their career. Some chapters clearly point out some, but maybe not all, of the lessons that I took from my experiences. I encourage all who read it to learn from their own experiences rather than fail to see what lessons are being offered as we live our busy daily lives.

Tuebor is not intended to chronicle my career of big arrests, heroic actions, or other superhuman achievements, as many other officers have accomplished so much more. I only use my experiences as learning vehicles and offer the lessons that I have learned during my career. It is the human side of policing that I have tried to capture from the selected experiences during my career to share with the reader experiences that are common to many other officers as well.

I hope this work will find its way into the hearts and minds of officers and in some small way make a positive difference for them and their families. For the non-police reader, I ask you to learn from lessons presented to you in your daily activities that if recognized, will assist you in positive change for the benefit of you and your family as well. To all past, present and future professional and caring officers, I am proud to have shared the pledge of "Tuebor".

Woven throughout the following work are stories, fables and other writings that I gathered along the way in my police journey that helped me to develop into the police officer that I set out to be. Unfortunately, some of these did not credit the authors who first spoke their words of wisdom as the authors could not be located. The lack of credit to these authors is unintentional and I thank them for their words of inspiration.

INTRODUCTION

This is a collection of true stories drawn from my own experiences as a young boy growing up in mid-Michigan and my evolution into the mysterious world working as a police officer where I spent my career with several police agencies. A few events have been borrowed from other officers whom I have known who have experienced these events that I have had the opportunity to observe and sometimes share. Of the thousands of experiences that I have encountered, I have chosen the following which have had a profound impact on my criminal justice career as well as the positive changes in my personal and family life. This is the story of my transformation and journey from my life as a young man through my evolution into a new young police officer and on through my career as a professional, seasoned officer. Many of these experiences have shown me things I would have never imagined existed before entering my career in police work. These experiences will hopefully shed a little light on what it is like for those considering a career as a police officer and what that life might be like for them and their families. For those with no aspiration of entering the world of police work, I hope you find these life-lessons that I share enlightening and helpful in the endeavors you chose to pursue.

At the outset, I would like to honor the families of police officers who often quietly and unnoticed give as much, and often more, in their lonely sufferings and "taking up the slack" while their officer is on the job in harm's way. Unfortunately, too often the toll of police work is just too much for the family and the spousal bonds break. For those spouses and families who weather the many challenges of the job, I salute you and wish you Godspeed for your tenacity, understanding and unfaltering love in preserving the precious police family unit. It is the strong family unit from which police officers draw their strength to carry on each day and night performing the dangerous tasks that are thrown their way. Police work is very different from many other professions as it requires a dedication hard to understand for many and it can be very unforgiving in so many harsh and cruel ways. Conversely, there are many rewards along the way to be enjoyed as well. One thing that I learned early on in my transformation from civilian to police officer is that the only constant thing in police work is the sudden, unexpected and rapid change, for the better and oftentimes for the worse.

This is not a story of how one police department, whether large or small, or one officer is somehow better selected, better trained or somehow simply better than other police officers or police departments. Anyone who has worn a police uniform with any degree of dedication knows how it is to walk in those shoes. When times are difficult, we are all brothers and sisters working for the same goals. We are there to watch each other's back, offering praise for a job well done which comes far too seldom, to help with another officer's family in times of need-with labor or money when the officer is unable to do so for themselves due to injury, illness or worse, and to lend a humble listening ear to a fellow officer when times are just too difficult to get through it alone. We also comfort the family of a fallen officer who has given the ultimate sacrifice, on too many occasions. This is their story told from one perspective that hopefully speaks for many.

The average person's idea of law enforcement is as varied as those you might ask. Many people know very little of what goes on in the daily life of a police officer. For others, discussing police work is the stark reminder of the time they were arrested with long-lasting loathing of the police in general while others remain thankful that they received the jolt they needed to steer them away from a life of crime and onto a successful path in their lives. Others praise officers for saving them or their loved one from a perilous situation they found themselves in. More often, others are simply ambivalent regarding police officers and know little if anything about who they are or what they do, much less really care. I know not everyone I ever dealt with was happy with the outcome, but I always remembered my upbringing and training and I tried to do my very best for everyone involved in each situation and often in impossible circumstances.

Over time, police officers' attitudes become hardened from the endless investigations into thefts, carjackings, robberies, white collar financial thefts, rapes, and murders. Add to this the actions of government officials, legislators and judges who take their bribes (or political contributions) from those who want to buy laws to benefit the wealthy. Insurance companies, petroleum companies, the mining industry, chemical companies, the health care industry, large manufacturers, and others watch the laws very carefully and take every opportunity to buy even the slightest changes in the law that allow them to increase their profit margins and minimize the chance an injured party might win a lawsuit against the company for their wrongdoing causing them to have to part with some of their coveted money. Lawsuits equal lost profits and those lawsuits are squelched at all costs by an army of lobbying special interest experts. Millions of dollars are spent to ensure that the one sentence, that one word is changed to alter the case law following one court decision that hurts the industry financially. Tax exemptions mean millions in savings for the corporations and the politicians are influenced or bought with political contributions. Remember that old comment from one wealthy woman, "Only the little people pay taxes."

Experienced police officers cannot effectively function in police work for too long. They have seen too much and they know too much to quietly follow orders that ensure the status quo is maintained by those in power who have the money. The money ensures the status quo. The status quo ensures the money. The cycle is designed to perpetually repeat itself, and it does. It is all very neat, predictable and very orchestrated. Elections are won and lost on which of the power groups are able to fool voters the most, and of course who has the most money to buy influence to help convince the voters their candidate is going to do something beneficial for them. They rarely do. Police officers must learn to deal with all of this seemingly hopelessness to serve and help those they have sworn to protect.

In an effort to enhance my evolution into the kind of police officer I always wanted to become and to keep myself on the right path, I have collected stories, poems and, quotes, which I keep and reread frequently. In police work, as in many other professions, you can never afford to stop learning. The law is ever changing, new ways to break the law are concocted, and new ways to deal with various forms of human misbehavior need to be learned. Reading and re-reading this collection of stories along the way has helped me gain an introspection of myself and helped me learn how to achieve the best end result to the benefit of all parties involved. One small story was posted in the *Michigan State Police Trooper Magazine* which had been excerpted from "A Whispered Tale" by Siegfried Sassoon. I collected this many years ago as one of my first additions to my collection that helped me to remember the concept of humility and to not brag about myself or the things I was lucky enough to accomplish and survive. Little did I know that only too soon would I learn the harsh lessons suggested in this short but wise story. The story drove home the point that a good police officer, as well as a good person, needs humility both at work and at home. It goes like this:

I'd heard fool-heroes brag of where they'd been,
With stories of the glories that they'd seen.
But you, good simple trooper, seasoned well,
Endured experience in posts of hell,
Fatigue and vigils haunting nerve-strained eyes,
And your partner killed to make you wise;
You had no babbling phrases.

I invite you to immerse yourself into these experiences shared and try to really feel what it is like to transition from the private life into the world of police work. A line from the movie *American Sniper* sums up my view of policing: "There are three kinds of people in this world, sheep, wolves and sheep dogs". I believe police officers are sheep dogs, trying to keep the wolves away from the sheep. Given the current events involving ISIS/ISIL, police officers are now being called upon to provide a much greater level of protection for the citizens of America more similar to military duties, but in our own back yards. In providing this heightened level of protection, officers are becoming a target of choice for this vengeance.

PART

1

BEGINNINGS

I hate to admit, it but we were poor when my sister and brothers and I were growing up. It seemed that a lot of families were poor in Saginaw, Michigan. Although at times we did seem to be a bit better off, it was during those lean times, especially in the winter months when my dad did not have much work as a carpenter, that we realized things were tough for our family. How tough you might ask? I thought all houses had rats. Not little mice-like rats, but big rats that weighed a pound or so with large beady eyes that ruled our Michigan basement at night. Oh yes, for those folks who don't know what a Michigan basement is, it is a full basement under one half of the house with a concrete floor and a brick wall about four feet high which meets the crawl space under the other half of the house, which is dug out for only a few feet with a dirt floor. All sorts of vermin can simply burrow under the walls into your basement. I don't know if these basements are only in Michigan, but most houses here had them, hence the name, Michigan basements.

Skunks also found their way into our basement on occasion and for whatever reason they sometimes became startled. If you know anything about skunks, you know that when skunks are startled they spray their awful, nauseating stench that is so overpowering you gag and cough with every breath. Once on you, it also repels anyone that gets near you. One night a frightened skunk struck in our Michigan basement. The next day at school, my siblings and I smelled so bad that the other kids held their noses and demanded that we be sent home. Even though I slept three floors above the stinky creature! I guess we were so used to the smell during the night that we didn't even notice it when we left for school in the morning.

Mice, they were of little consequence and not worth mentioning. But yes, we also had them in our Michigan basement. I almost forgot that we also had an ermine living under our back porch. Ermine are somewhat rare and curious creatures. They are small weasels that are brown in the summer and a magnificent pure white in the winter with a black tip on their tails. These elusive and comical little creatures are a joy to watch as they cautiously dart about. They were once used to make magnificent ermine stoles for women to wear around their necks. I think our ermine only stayed for a year or two and was never seen after that.

I must have been seven years old when we moved into that old farmhouse in the early 1960s. That first year I remember my mother suddenly shrieking and running around the house hysterically yelling, "Bat! Bat!" Sure enough, a bat was flapping around the house in its frenzied flight, most likely looking for a safe place away from the flailing, screaming woman. Even at seven, I knew a bat shouldn't be out in daylight. They are nocturnal creatures foraging for food only at night. Nevertheless, it was the middle of the day and my dad was at work building houses and not available to save us from that swooping dreaded bat. I could see those beady eyes, leather-like wings, mouse-looking face and white fangs as it flittered around the house. And then I heard, "Pleazzzze send a police officer. No it can't wait, it's an emergency, there's a bat is in my house and I have little children. Please, I don't want them to get rabies from the bat, please hurry," my mother urged.

Amazingly, in what seemed like only a few minutes there was a knock on our front door. When my mother opened the door, I saw the most impeccably dressed police officer I had ever seen. This was no ordinary cop; this was a STATE TROOPER! In my young and innocent years I knew enough about authority figures and how they should look, how they should act, and how they had firm control of all situations. This officer was all of that and more. I instantly sensed that my mother felt safe when the officer took control of this large-scale emergency of epic proportions by his mere presence. I had to admit, I too was a little scared, partly because of the bat flapping around and partly due to the unnerving screeching of my mother's voice.

His voice was calm and in control, his gaze was steady. The look on his face showed he was treating this as a serious emergency, although he was most likely wondering secretly why he was even sent to such a minor call.

"Ma'am, what seems to be the problem?" he asked, smiling easily.

"There is a bat in our house and I am afraid it might bite one of my children and give them rabies," my mother tried to answer in as calm a voice as she was capable of under the stressful circumstances.

"Let's take a look," he replied in a firm voice.

I was intently studying the police officer. His uniform was not like those I was used to seeing in my neighborhood. I often saw the local officers responding to calls of car accidents, domestic violence at the neighbors, and other such common fare. This police officer was different. The medium-blue colored trousers had creases in the front and back of each leg so fine as though it could cut my finger if I were to run it along those sharp edges. The dark blue stripe down the outside of each leg stood out against the lighter blue of the pants as though standing at rigid attention. As I looked at his black shoes, polished like shiny glass, I could see my face reflected on the tops. The dark blue shirt was impeccably pressed and fit the police officer's body like a glove. The tall, slender officer's dark blue shirt was buttoned up to the neck and finished off with a gray tie. His hair was neatly trimmed and his hat was pressed on his head as though it was meant to stay there permanently.

The blue eyes instantly surveyed the inside of our house taking it all in with a scant few seconds, and as I would later learn as a police officer, looking for things that might have been hidden in anticipation of his arrival. As he held out his hand to shake my mother's hand, I saw that his fingernails were trimmed and clean, his handshake was gentle but firm. He instantly knew to be gentle with this woman in need. Then I saw the officer's badge. It was a bright and shiny silver shield pinned to the left side of his shirt over his heart, there to protect him while handling the world's problems. It said simply "TROOPER."

Of course my sister and brothers were all standing around waiting to see the demise of the dreaded bat. Would he shoot it? Maybe he would hit it with his hat. The Trooper started to enter our house. As he did, he had to bend down a bit so his tall frame did not hit the top of our doorway. He chatted politely to my mother, which seemed to instantly put her at ease. He also talked directly to us kids asking how we were as he patrolled our house looking for the bat. No one ever did that before, pay attention to the kids. Only grownups were involved in conversations with strangers back in those days. It made us instantly feel important. We asked him some questions. To be honest I don't remember what they were, but I'm sure they were pretty stupid. I mean, while looking for a dangerous creature like a bat, what questions could be important!

Too soon for this impressionable young boy, I heard the Trooper telling my mother that the bat most likely found an opening and left the house or it was hiding in some small place waiting until nightfall to make his escape. While he was leaving he told my mother that if the bat returned, she should call again for help. I could sense that this Trooper was sincere in handling this emergency for us, even though many years later I knew from personal experience these nuisance calls are avoided at all costs by many police officers, except the good, caring officers. The officers who truly cared took these calls seriously because the callers who had summoned the police took them seriously. Good officers learn this important lesson and for them, it is that simple.

As he walked down our steps to his waiting police car, I expected to see a dirty beat up old car with dents and dings like those I was used to seeing being driven by our local officers. Instead I saw an immaculate, polished, glimmering dark blue car, with a single red light on top. The black tires were like new with not a spot of mud on them. All of the glass was crystal clear, obviously recently cleaned. Two big spotlights were mounted on the car, one on each side of the windshield. On the driver's door was a blue and gold police shield bearing the words Michigan State Police with gold lightning bolts erupting from both sides of the shield. The shield had a moose and elk on it and the word "Tuebor." I wondered what the strange word meant, Tuebor.

As the Trooper folded himself into the car and started the engine, the power roared back at us. I was still staring as he drove out of sight and waved goodbye back at us. Never had a police officer left such a lasting impression on me. I was absolutely dumbfounded by the appearance, professionalism, patience, sincerity, and genuine caring of that officer during his handling of my mother's call for assistance. That was 55 years ago yet the images and words are so vividly etched into my mind that it seemed like only yesterday. Unbeknownst to me at that time, that single but impacting experience would ultimately lead me back to a career with the Michigan State Police where I would learn that *Tuebor* means *I will defend*, an oath I would live by.

Like I said, the winters were hard in Michigan. Lots of snow, very cold, and no global warming in those days. Our house was an old farmhouse built many years before modern building codes, but the rent must have been very low because we lived there. Single panes of glass were set in each window frame that only slightly slowed down the movement of icy cold air into our house. Holes from where putty had worked loose from between the glass and window frames in many places only added to the arctic blast into our house. At night when the temperatures dropped out of sight, cold winter wind easily found its way into the house and swirled around our little bodies as we curled up in bed trying to sleep under a mountain of blankets. On many occasions we awoke to a mosaic of patterns of ice almost an eighth of an inch thick on the inside of our bedroom windows. Beautiful designs commissioned by Jack Frost himself abounded on all windows without threat of any heat melting these magnificent works of art. We often lay in bed and marveled at the sheer beauty of the designs, no two ever being alike.

The really bad mornings happened when we got up for school and awoke to discover two inches of snow on the inside of our window ledges. At least the snow stopped some of the cold wind from blowing into our bedrooms. It reminded me of an igloo where we three boys slept together in the arctic room. Other mornings were even colder, if that was possible. When we poked our heads from under our covers, I could see my breath wafting across the room. This usually meant that we had run out of fuel oil for the furnace deep down in the recesses of our Michigan basement sometime during the quiet, dark hours of the night. We would hurriedly get dressed and run down the stairs to huddle around the open electric oven door my mom and dad had already turned on in anticipation of our collective presence. My older brother and I would go with my dad to buy a five-gallon bottle of fuel oil to start the furnace. We knew there was no money to ask for a fuel truck to come and fill the oil tank.

Those old oil furnaces had to be primed after running out of oil when the furnace, in an effort to draw in life-sustaining oil, found the tank empty and started to suck in air. This involved letting the air out of the fuel line so the oil could get to the burner. That always resulted in some oil dripping on the floor. I will never forget the smell of fuel oil in that basement. I don't like the smell of fuel oil to this day. When the oil stove sprang to life spewing hot air into the air ducts, we felt we had just experienced a miracle. Hallelujah! The icy cold of the sub-zero temperature in our old farmhouse would slowly begin to recede, pushed back by the hot air until it started to approach a tolerable temperature and I no longer could see my breath.

The upstairs did not have any heating ducts to channel warm air to our bedrooms. Back in those days I guess they were not deemed important enough to spend money to install heating ducts. A small square was cut in the floor and a metal grate placed into the opening that was supposed to allow hot air to rise up to heat the upstairs rooms. The term "hot air" is being used loosely here as it never reached the level of warm let alone hot in our bedroom. I always wanted to meet the genius who designed that heating system and explain a few things to him.

Yet, with all of these "hardships" we thought we had the world by the tail. We were surrounded by the best pheasant and rabbit hunting in Michigan. We supplemented the routine family food supply of elbow macaroni and butter using our little fiberglass bows and practice arrows that Santa brought one cold Christmas Eve to slay scores of rabbit and an occasional pheasant. Not too bad for seven- and eight-year-olds. When my older brother turned twelve, he was given a Remington Wingmaster 870 pump action shotgun by my dad. The pheasant and rabbits were in real trouble then. The next year I graduated to hunting with a shotgun. We ate fairly well in those days. The perch fishing in the Saginaw Bay and the smelt runs that blackened the streams of Lake Huron in the spring provided ample fish for the supper menu with the excess going into our freezer. "Save it for winter," my mother was often heard telling us, and so we did.

On one occasion after hunting ducks in the Saginaw Bay, we ran across a farmer selling "field run" potatoes. These were little potatoes about the size of golf balls unfit to sell in grocery stores. We filled the trunk of my older brother's Chevrolet Nova Super Sport with field run potatoes for a grand total of $5.00 for the load. My mom canned dozens of jars of those delicious, hardy spuds that seemed to last forever.

My next younger brother soon joined our shotgun expeditions, which we expanded into deer hunting by loading the shotguns with rifled slugs. Unlike birdshot which consists of many small pellets, a rifled slug was a single large lead projectile weighing one ounce. They

really did the job on a deer. Life clearly took an upturn in the cuisine category with three hungry teenagers on the loose with shotguns and our mother directing us to "go get something for dinner."

Like many others across America, we lived a hard life but a fun life. We saw the little things that existed all around us because we were inquisitive and were out there touching life on a daily basis. Video games were not even a thought in a computer programmer's head yet. A spider web covered with dew in the early morning sunlight was a wondrous sight to behold with all of the precision of each strand of the carefully laid webbing. An ice storm in the winter instantly built a crystal city in the woods and the sun shining through all of that glass created an image of a million twinkling lights. When the wind blew, the creaking noise in the woods from the ice-covered branches was deafening. If the wind blew too much, the crashing sound of a large icy tree branch scared the bejeebers out of us when it landed with a deafening crash. A true wonder to behold!

There are very few creatures cuter than a new batch of baby cottontail rabbits so small but so perfect in their rabbit fur nest plucked from their mother's own skin and tucked in a clump of weeds. They too sampled the new world around them with twitching noses and ever-moving ears to see what it had to offer, still untrained to the dangers lurking in this world. We would catch one, cuddle it, watch its tiny nose test the air for the smell of danger, and then we let it go back to its mother.

We valued all of nature because we had so little. My sisters and brothers were taught not to waste or steal and we helped those in need because they had even less then we had. That simply was the way we were raised by our parents. Our family didn't ask for handouts, we didn't take food stamps or other government

assistance, and we didn't want anything for free. We were taught to work hard to survive and when we had less, we used less, until more was obtained. My mother and father didn't use plastic cards to obtain instant loans that they would not have been able to repay, a lesson that was drilled into their children. We knew that the government didn't owe us free food, money or anything else and we didn't expect such things from it.

My story almost ended tragically when I was just sixteen years old. My brothers and I loved to be out in the fields and woods. One of our favorite pastimes was hunting ducks. On a cool October day, Dave and I decided to visit a pond near Bay City. Many ducks were flying that day and we took turns missing the fast birds. A lone hen mallard came in and I made a nice shot, folding the bird. I watched it splash on the water far from shore. No waves were present to wash the bird to shore and we had no boat. We wondered how we were going to get the duck.

I volunteered to swim out and retrieve it. Back then, I had a little swimming experience but not too much. As I stripped down to my underwear and stepped into the freezing water, I instantly developed goose bumps from my toes to the top of my head. With no experience of effects of cold water on one's ability to function, I started out toward the duck. All went well for a short distance until the cold water started to sap my strength. When I made it to the bird and turned toward shore, I realized I was a very long way from safety.

A sudden feeling of panic struck me and I began to realize I might not make it back to shore. I tried to swim but my muscles refused to work. I panicked. As soon as I did, my body went vertical and I went under the surface gulping in the cold, muddy water. I fought for the surface and flailed my arms screaming for help. Under the water I went again and again. At some point when I was about to simply let go of life, I heard a far-off voice telling me to hold on. I felt an arm around my neck and I heard my younger brother Dave screaming at me, "Kick, kick, kick!" I was next to worthless to assist my brother in helping me due to the cold, exhaustion, and fear.

After what seemed like an eternity, I felt my brother dragging me onto the grass. Cold or not, that solid ground felt like heaven. My brother Dave, on that remote pond, risked his life in that same cold water so far from shore to pull my heavy body to safety. Dave had saved a life, my life. On that day, I was spared to live and to help others in the years to come, thanks to my brave brother. Dave was and is a hero in every right, just like our grandfather Hugo who had also saved a drowning victim many years before. I owe him more than I will ever be able to repay. Rather than this story ending here, my story and my life went on. Life is strange like that. I later learned that things happen for a reason, often for reasons that we will never know.

I learned other important lessons that day. You can never, ever under any circumstances, give up or quit no matter how much pain or fear you may be experiencing. This lesson would serve me well in my future career as a police officer saving me from harm on countless occasions. Most often, you don't get to repay the person who helped you, but you can help others in need of your help. That is the way it has worked for me throughout the gift of my life that I received from my brother that day. In doing there is no room for less than your very best efforts and no room for failure, lest the consequences be severe and lives changed forever.

As we grew, we each sought out our own paths in life. My sister Patty, the oldest of the children, went to work at a hospital as a nurse's aide. My older brother Mike built American cars at an American auto plant and my next younger brother Dave became a top-notch welder, and later in life, a welding instructor at a local community college. My youngest brother Brian, well that is a story that will have to wait for a bit later. My sister Patty died at the young age of 43 to cancer. I still have images of her smiles in her last days trying to mask the pain and act brave for all of us as the cancer slowly and very painfully ate away her body. Her smile never dimmed, or at least she tried to make it seem that way for her family's benefit. She was a tough woman that had given so very much to her children through her own sacrifice. Unfortunately, she had made bad choices in husbands who all left her to fend for herself and to care for the children she had created with them. She lived a very difficult life, but that smile, it never waned up until her last day. She was a sister to be proud of to the end. I still see her face as though I am looking at it across the table at this very moment. In the dark hours of early morning when sleep just won't come, I see her smiling face, happy, comforting me. I will always be in her debt for the comfort that she provides me with her memories when I need it most.

And me, well I bounced around trying different things. I made hamburgers. I helped out as a draftsman drawing machines that would eventually turn out car parts. Later I tried feeding the machines that turned out car parts like my older brother did. That did not suit my need to use my ability to think and use my discretion to accomplish tasks. Fortunately for me, I was laid off. You see, the pay and benefits were just too good to leave that repetitious, mind numbing job on my own, so someone with a higher vision who had obviously been looking out for me helped by seeing to it that I was laid off. I tried the security business at an airport long before the words "airport" and "security" were used in the same sentence and it included searching luggage for dangerous items. Razor blades left lying loose in a suitcase gave me my first geyser of blood to punctuate my first day on that job. Those jobs were too confining for me and did not let me use my brain, which seemed to work overtime even while I was doing nothing.

Working at a construction site that was supposed to give birth to a nuclear power plant was interesting at first. The plant somehow didn't pan out and never produced a single kilowatt of energy from uranium, a symbol, perhaps, of my own career. I wasn't supporting my new wife who had been my high school sweetheart like I wanted to be able to do. I was frustrated and I felt ashamed for not having a better job that paid more. I started to attend the local community college. It was tough work to be the first in my family to attend college. My dad left high school in the 11th grade to fight the Germans in Europe during World War II. My mother finished high school and went to work in a commercial bakery while my dad was away in the war. My sister and brothers chose not to earn degrees and entered the working world. I initially studied engineering but soon lost interest. I then tried studying to become a teacher but lost my way pursuing that career as well.

As I sat through another engineering class, not sure where it would take me, a sudden flash of blue and the shine of a badge popped into my consciousness, as though someone was sending me a message. *Tuebor.* My mind struggled with those images replaying the event of the Trooper who was sent to protect my mother and her young children from the dreaded bat. I was just a young Irish-German kid from humble beginnings and I could not imagine that I could ever become a Michigan State Police Trooper. I felt that I was not remotely qualified to be a highly trained, physically fit, Michigan

State Police Trooper who on a daily basis saved the good citizens of the community. They were simply the best. How could I ever hope to be a Trooper with all of that confidence, conditioning, skill, and tenacity to confront danger from all sources and protect, preserve and defend the people and visitors of the great State of Michigan? After all, my qualifications included skills as a hamburger flipper, security guard, and a drawer of pictures of machine parts. Maybe, just maybe, I could become a local police officer requiring less demanding qualifications. I knew that they too did a good job in their community.

Criminal justice classes at the community college were difficult at first as I lacked good study habits. Many of the instructors were local police officers. At first, I found the instructors intimidating with all of their war stories of criminals arrested, fights with the bad guys, injuries suffered, and the sight and smell of death. As the classes came and went I realized my confidence in becoming a police officer and my study habits were steadily growing. Soon the instructors' stories of having to face dangerous suspects and physically arrest them even while sustaining injuries no longer seemed so scary. I read every police novel I could get my hands on and was fascinated by them. Titles such as *Serpico* (the story of Frank Serpico, the New York City detective who was shunned by his own brothers and sisters in blue for reporting graft in the police department), *The Onion Field* (about the Los Angles detective whose partner was murdered before his eyes and who narrowly escaped death by his partner's killers), *Choir Boys* (the hilarious adventures of Los Angeles police officers seemingly too bizarre to be true, but I suspect they were), and many other stories captured my interest in police work. In fact, I found that I wanted to encounter those same experiences with a passion. For sure, I was still apprehensive, but the intrigue of police work was slowly drawing me toward a career involving police work.

My dad and his two brothers fought in World War II. I had a high draft number and would not have been drafted but I felt that in 1970, at the heart of the Vietnam War, the Michigan National Guard seemed like the best way for me to show support for my country and at the same time pursue my career. Being a patriotic type, as many in my family had been, I joined the Army National Guard to answer the call of duty in some small fashion. I didn't know in those days the National Guard was never deployed into combat like they were in WWII and are again today in the Middle East. The part-time military pay wasn't great but it made the difference in my new family's meager monthly finances and paid for most of my college expenses.

Fort Leonard Wood, Missouri. We used to say, "Everywhere you go at Fort Leonard Wood, it's uphill." It did seem like it during those long months of training that tested my limits of endurance. Calisthenics, close order drill, hand-to-hand combat training, rifle marksmanship, grenade practice, land navigation, inoculations against everything evil in the world, and less than great food. I was in the best shape of my young life after that training. I was trim, fit, with a military bearing, and a deep sense of humility due to my parent's influence, which was honed to a fine edge by the army. I seemed to notice little things not everyone else saw. I was inquisitive and wanted to know the whys of things. I would later learn this is an essential trait of a good police officer.

PART

2

2

THE POLICE OFFICER

When I read the job opening for the police officer position, I knew almost nothing about Bridgeport Township located in Saginaw County. I thought that with an associate degree in criminal justice and my military training I just might have a chance at that job. The interview went well and considering there were only five applicants I figured that I might even get the job. A week after the interview, though Chief of Police, Louie Robinson contacted me to say he was going to offer the position to another candidate who had previous experience as a sheriff's deputy. I was simply devastated when I was turned down for that job. Three days later the chief called me again and offered me the job. I guess the $9,000 a year salary didn't excite the ex-deputy too much back in 1976. Needing my first police job, I excitedly accepted.

I was ready to be sent to a police academy when I was told by the chief that since the department consisted of only the chief and one part time officer, the law did not require that I attend a police academy for formal training. Only if the agency had three or more full-time officers were they required to send additional officers to a police academy. I was shocked and more than a bit apprehensive to start work as a police officer with no formal training. The first day I rode around with the chief and we handled a minor fender bender or PDA in police jargon or a property damage accident in official terms. Day two I worked the afternoon shift with the part-time officer who worked full-time at an auto plant making car parts like my older brother. Not much happened on my second night as a new police officer even in the poor, crime-ridden section of the township known as Genesee Gardens, which would normally generate many calls involving drugs, shootings and domestic violence calls. Looking back, I now know I was lucky I did not receive any serious calls for police assistance during my first few weeks with the township police department. Given my lack of training and experience the outcome may not have been conducive to my health!

My police uniform was a bit baggy and I thought that I looked somewhat like a circus clown. The pants were too long but the chief said they were supposed to be a little long. I did not like them too long as they bunched up by my ankles and looked sloppy. The shirts were not tailored for me; they were stock shirts generically made so to be "one size fits all." I certainly didn't look professional and because of that I didn't feel professional. But at that time in my young career, I wasn't overly concerned. After all, I was a police officer doing my duty to protect the public. I was proud of my job and myself, especially because I was now able to better support my wife.

My parents did not want me to be a police officer. They thought that most people did not appreciate the police and that I would just get hurt. They also thought the pay was way too low to risk my life for people that I didn't even know. That surprised me because I was making $4.33 per hour, the most money I had ever made per hour in my young life. My mother Jean worried and told me to be careful. My dad Dale said he was proud of me but I know he too was worried. When I told my dad that I had been hired for that police officer position he appeared to look right through me, which I didn't understand until I later learned about his experiences during World War II.

My dad and his older brother Milton had fought the Germans in Europe during World War II. It wasn't until years later I learned from dabbling in genealogy research that my dad and his brother Milton helped liberate Dachau Prison where he and my uncle saw train loads of rotting bodies of prisoners killed by the Nazi SS troopers in that concentration camp. He never talked about that, so until my research disclosed that information, I had never known what horrors he saw as a young soldier.

My dad told us a little about his experiences, but I didn't learn the whole story until after he was gone from this life. His division, the Army 20th Armored Division, had only eight days of credited combat because my dad joined toward the end of the war, but in that time, he saw enough horrors to be concerned about what I would encounter as a police officer. German artillery shelled his combat engineer company, killing 37 men, with many more wounded, in those eight short days of combat. My dad had been hit with shrapnel in his arms, and years later small bits worked their way out from time to time. He had seen death in combat and he had seen it at Dachau as they liberated the starving death-like Jewish prisoners, walking ghosts as they have been called. My dad shared that the American soldiers often were without sufficient food. To avoid starvation, fellow soldiers walked abreast of each other through small patches of trees to push the small deer hiding there into openings so he and other soldiers could shoot them. He said that the soldiers were so desperate that they used tracer

Dale

ammunition so they could see where their shots were hitting to ensure that they hit the running deer.

He shared with my brothers and me that when the war ended he was assigned to hunt down the German SS troops that had guarded the Dachau prison camp. The SS troops were fanatics and highly trained. To evade the searching American soldiers, they hid in haystacks, down wells, in attics, under manure piles and any other place they could think of. When the German SS troops were arrested, they weren't always treated kindly by American soldiers, so my dad told us. I guess the thought of these fanatical SS German troops and what they had done to other human beings was firmly imprinted on the young American soldiers' minds. It affected them greatly to see cruelty that was so foreign to their own morals and upbringing. My dad's stare was the result. He knew the dangers he had faced and he knew that I would ultimately face in my future career as a police officer. I was totally unaware of the upcoming dangers I would face.

I remember his photograph when he was in the army during World War II. He was a strong, lean soldier with a look of invincibility. I certainly didn't feel invincible. I had not been sent to the police academy and I had no other police training. My chief and the one part-time officer in my department had no police academy training. The only police training they had was from talking with State Police Officers, sheriff's deputies and local officers with whom they came into contact, along with what they learned on the job. No matter, I would just learn on my own. It couldn't be that difficult. At that time, I didn't know what I was in for working in that township.

I soon discovered a State Police Post was located in Bridgeport Township. I was too afraid to venture into that place. These were professional officers, Troopers, well trained, experienced and too busy to bother with me. While pulling over a car for speeding one summer evening on a busy main street in my township, I noticed a shiny blue State Police car pull in behind me and turn on the single overhead right light, the cherry as it is sometimes called. I wondered what the trooper wanted. He just sat in his car until I had finished my business and let the driver go on his way.

The trooper walked up to me and introduced himself, "Hi, I'm Trooper Bob."

I would later learn that many of the troopers at the Bridgeport Post openly shared their training and expertise with less experienced local officers. He was just like the trooper who came to our house to confront the bat so many years ago. He was thoughtful, impeccably dressed, and very polite. He treated me like an equal when he asked how things were going. We talked for a while and then he told me

I should stop in at the post to visit with some of the troopers when I had time. When I told him I was a bit nervous due to my lack of training, he immediately offered to ride with me to help me learn the ways of police work if I wanted. Did I ever! I couldn't believe my good fortune.

Trooper Bob gave his own off-duty time to ride with me and show me the ropes so that I would be safe when I patrolled my township. At that early point in my career, I did not know how important it was to call for backup on calls of domestic violence, a car parked by the door of a retail business at closing time (a possible armed robbery), or simply closely watching as I approached a driver stopped for a traffic violation who might be preparing to assault me. I was impressed by his generosity and willingness to help a brother police officer who was drowning in a sea of danger and who didn't even know it. Trooper Bob was the second influence in my life that helped guide me to a career in the Michigan State Police. Without the confidence that he instilled in me by his generous tutoring, I doubt that with my humble background I would have had the courage to apply to the Michigan State Police.

I later used the lesson learned from Trooper Bob to help other officers whenever the opportunity came my way. I learned to "pay it forward" and received a great deal of gratification watching other officers grow from what I was able to pass on to them. Hopefully the knowledge that I shared during my career with other officers helped return them safely to their families at the end of each of their shifts.

3

VOICES

ven this many years later, I vividly remember going to the old house with the chief in my first days on the job in that township to talk to the old timer who had been hearing voices. Though I no longer remember his name, I will simply call him Walt. His furnace had started to talk to him. It bothered him greatly, and he wanted us to help him out, to stop the voices that came out of his furnace to taunt him. My chief, who took the job after retiring as a mechanic from the Department of Natural Resources with no formal police training or experience, had an easy way of talking to people. He checked out the furnace, banged his hand on the side of it, and loudly announced that it seemed like the voice had stopped and it would probably not bother Walt again. The chief asked Walt if he owned any guns. He walked into his bedroom and opened the top dresser drawer. He proudly produced a nickel-plated .38 caliber revolver. The chief quietly told me that we had no authority to take the gun, so he told Walt to call again if he had further problems with his furnace. We left him alone with his gun. Even with my limited experience I knew Walt was not "right" in the head and we would likely be sent back there soon. It was about two weeks later in the heat of the summer when we received a call from a woman reporting that she had not seen Walt for nearly a week.

That was very unusual, she said. Plus his newspapers were stacked up on his front porch where the newsboy had thrown them. Odd indeed, as she told us he always took in the papers each day. Sweat ran down my back, caused no doubt by my dark blue uniform shirt with bullet resistant vest underneath in the hot searing sun. Maybe that strange feeling indicated something foreboding, something unknown and something bad about to happen, I thought. I came to learn that the feeling is known as a police officer's sixth sense, and it is to be taken seriously when it is felt. To ignore that feeling invited harm. The thought of a crazed, gun toting old man who was obviously irrational, no doubt added to my body temperature and the river of sweat coursing down my back. Something was not right and we were about to find out what that something was.

I had recently convinced the chief to have the township buy a bullet resistant vest for me. He had laughed when I asked for it, telling me that they were not necessary in our township; however the township board grudgingly voted the money from their meager budget and bought me one. When I walked into work that day, he laughingly threw it at me striking me in the chest with a thud and a look that said, "What a waste of money." So when we arrived at the old timer's house following a second call from the neighbor, I was surprised when the chief had me walk in front of him to act as a human shield as we walked up to the house to look in the windows and knock on the door.

No one answered the front door when I knocked. I tried the doorknob and found it was locked. I walked toward the side door of the old timer's house, my chief close behind me as I shielded his approach with my body. I slowly turned the knob on the side door and it opened. Knowing that Walt was old and was losing his mind,

I realized he might see us as a threat emanating from his furnace; I carefully peeked inside the house. Instinctively not wanting to fill the doorway with my body, I quickly slid through the door opening and stepped to one side, noting that there were no signs of movement inside the house. I called out to Walt, no answer. My voice echoed around the quiet house bouncing off of the walls with a series of eerie reverberations.

I started to move in my best deer hunting stalk, room to room, eyes constantly moving, ears attuned, listening for the slightest noise. My footsteps sounded like a herd of elephants despite my efforts at walking silently in the ghostly quiet house. The scuff of my shoe on the tile floor was deafening. The swish of my uniform pant legs rubbing together telegraphed my location to anyone listening to my slow methodical advance. My excited breathing sounded like a locomotive coming around the bend. The chief was directly behind me and seeing my questioning eyes said, "You're the one with the vest on." *Thanks a lot*, I thought. I stepped ahead toward the kitchen. Something crunched beneath my foot sounding like a deafening blast from a bullhorn in the dead still house. Chills ran up my spine.

"Damn, I have to be much quieter," I thought to myself as I eased forward. My central nervous system was on full alert. My fight or flight self-defense mechanism was at full alert, ready to launch me forward toward the danger or to turn and flee for my life depending on how my mind might perceive the nature of the threat and my chances of surviving it.

His bedroom was just around to the right as I remembered it from the last time we were there. I smelled *that* smell before I rounded the corner. It was that nauseating, vomit-inducing, rotting, stench that permeated all the air that I needed to breathe. I didn't know it at that time, but it was the smell of decaying, rotting, oozing, human flesh complete with maggots slinking their way around and through a decaying body. I did know that I wanted to get away from that awful smell, which I would come to recognize instantly in the years ahead. My first murder scene? Was the old timer hacked to death?

I slowly rounded the corner. I saw IT before I saw him. I was puzzled. It looked like dark reddish chocolate baked in the sun with cracks running through it on the linoleum floor, the way clay looks in a field when it is dried out from the sun. What was that? As I continued on, my gun in my hand, I saw a form on the floor that I recognized as Walt. His gaze fixed directly on me with his sunken, drying, lifeless eyes. I could see through his thinning hair the little round hole in the top of his head where the reddish chocolate had flowed to feed the large dried and cracked pool on the floor of his bedroom.

In his left hand, he gripped the shiny nickel-plated .38 we had seen only weeks before. Had he been right handed or left handed when we last saw him alive? I should have noticed and remembered that. Suicide? I holstered my gun. That's weird, I remember thinking, *the hole is in the top of his head, a very odd place for a person committing suicide and hard to reach for someone trying to do themselves in.* It would have been difficult to place the gun in a downward angle while holding the gun above his head to make that shot. Was this a murder with the killer placing the gun in the victim's hand to make it appear like a suicide? Did he have any enemies? Was anything missing from his house to indicate a robbery? What else had I learned in my criminal justice classes at the community college that would help me figure out what happened to Walt? With my almost total lack of police training and experience I tried as best as I could to work with the chief to preserve the scene, take photographs and measurements, and call the Medical Examiner. I had learned in my college classes that you treat all deaths as homicides until proven otherwise so as to not lose any possible evidence if the death turns out to be a murder.

As the EMS crew pulled the body off of the floor, the dried blood acted like glue between the Walt's face and the linoleum floor. An even stronger and nauseating stench overpowered the already revolting smell in the small bedroom as that putrid wetness on his head was exposed. Following his death, like many others, his muscles had relaxed and nature took its course, excreting bodily waste in his pants, which added to the stench in the small room. It took everything I had to not vomit all over the potential crime scene. Walt's face was flat, almost caricature-like, as though someone placed a hot iron on it. As nauseated as I was, I saw him as the person I had just talked to such a short time ago, and I felt sorry that he had to leave this world in this way, all alone. I wondered how I could have done more when I first talked to him. But what could I have done? Something, anything, and maybe he would not have met this lonely fate. Had I failed him? This would not be the last time I saw him. I would see his staring face looking at me again on many late nights when sleep just would not come.

My first autopsy was exciting, scary, and again filled with the stench of a rotting human body. It reminded me of field dressing a deer, but with a great deal more unpleasant smell as the deer were freshly deceased, unlike Walt's body. The medical examiner probed that hole on the top of Walt's head, slid in a pair of hemostats and pulled out a bloody lead bullet. When the autopsy was completed, the medical examiner asked, "What caliber was his pistol?"

"It was a .38," my chief said.

"Well this slug is a 9mm."

The chief and I looked at each other in the same instant, eyes wide open, jaws gaping. This was a murder! The old timer was trying to defend himself with the .38 that he had been gripping when we found him. From out of a fog we heard the medical examiner start a long series of deep belly laughs as he held the slug that he had just dug from Walt's head aloft. He was holding up the bullet in the light and he was examining it from every angle as though his eye was a crime lab comparison microscope. Tears of laughter appeared in his eyes and he exclaimed, "I had you two going on that one, didn't I?" *Welcome to the dark humor of police work,* I thought. The State Police Crime Lab later confirmed that the slug dug out of the old timer's head was in fact fired from his own pistol. He was the victim of a suicide after all.

This early experience quickly taught me that I must always look beyond the obvious facts of a situation. Had I realized the root problem that the old-timer was suffering from dementia or some other mental disorder, I might have requested the assistance of other resources and possibly prevented Walt's unfortunate demise. Had I had more experience or training, I would likely have searched for family members and brought other resources, possibly community mental health or his private physician, to assist Walt and the outcome may have been much for positive. The chief and I just did not have the training or experience to know any better at the time. I also learned that no matter how emotionally charged or revolting a situation might seem, I must put those emotions aside to fully focus all of my efforts on successfully resolving the matter at hand. Those who responders are called to assist deserve their very best efforts.

Knowingly entering that house with an armed person who was losing his mind and who might perceive us as a threat had been my first police-related encounter with the fight or flight defense mechanism genetically buried inside of me. But I made the decision to stay and find Walt, dead or alive. In police work, fleeing danger is seldom an option. Therefore, police officers must guard against the body's natural defenses that shut out any stimuli from the five senses that is not critical to immediate survival. Peripheral vision, for instance, is significantly narrowed to tunnel vision. Therefore, I constantly had to remind myself to keep my head moving beyond the immediate threat to see other potential threats lest they be missed (like other suspects, fire about to erupt, a hole I could fall into, downed electrical wires I might step on, other cars about to crash into the accident scene, and the list goes on). As an officer, I learned to redirect my brain's natural response to danger to protect those around me and myself.

4

THE BASEMENT

Months after I started with Bridgeport Township Police department, I was dispatched to back up Chief Chet who was the Chief of Police for Spaulding Township, the township adjacent and to the south of Bridgeport Township. He would later also apply for and be accepted into the State Police. He was the only officer in his township and I was the only full-time patrolman in our township, so we gave little notice to township boundaries. We were deputized by the County Sheriff, so we had full police authority in the whole county and we could help each other as needed.

"37-63, back-up Spaulding Township for a report of home-owners who just returned home and someone turned off their interior house lights as they drove into their driveway."

"37, what's the address?" I asked.

"37-63, 8814 Sheridan," added the MSP dispatcher.

"37, I'm only five minutes away, where is Chief Chet?" I asked.

"37-63, he is in sight of the house, he will meet you there," the dispatcher said.

It was a breaking and entering in progress, a B&E in police jargon (now known as a "home invasion"). In the darkness, we contacted the homeowners who were parked in their car just down the street from their home.

"What is the problem?" Chief Chet asked the homeowner.

"No one should be in our house and when we pulled into the driveway, our house lights were turned off, we backed down the block and called the police," replied the husband. His wife and three small children huddled together in obvious fear.

"Stay here while we check out your house. Give me the house key," the chief directed.

Well, I wasn't so sure about going into a dark house late at night with a high likelihood that one or more intruders might be inside. My classes at the college taught me if there was a person inside someone else's house, they more than likely had a gun. Even with my inexperience, I knew that darkness and guns make for a bad situation for a police officer. Neighbors, curious about the police cars parked in the neighborhood, watched as we readied to enter the house.

With simple nods of our heads, we each starting checking the exterior of the house in different directions. Just as we met in the back of the house, we noticed a basement window had been recently broken out. Fresh glass shards were lying on the ground with footprints in the dirt. I mentally reviewed the evidence we had: lights being turned off when the homeowners drove into their driveway, a broken window, fresh footprints in the dirt near the window. We now had a legitimate B&E with the very high probability that someone was inside, most likely with weapons. That sweat began to run down my back again.

The chief unlocked the front door and quietly open it. It's eerie to do something like open a door when all is dead quiet. All senses are heightened and on full alert due to impending danger. The body's survival instincts kick into high gear. Vision is tunneled to a pinpoint so as to immediately focus onto any potential threat. Any little sound is magnified. Breathing is heavy, but almost drowned out by the thudding of every heartbeat. Smells that are otherwise unnoticeable become overwhelming. My hunting experience told me the person or persons in the house could easily hear the sounds we made entering and walking about, and they knew exactly where we were, especially since they were standing still and making no noise. Unfortunately, we did not know where he or they were so the advantage was with the adversary. They could decide when to spring into action and we would only be able to react to whatever they decided to do. And they would get off the first shot or hammer blow.

Every upstairs room was methodically checked for intruders. Lights were switched on to reveal anyone that might be hiding in small dark corners or behind doors. Under the beds, in closets behind the clothes, behind the heavy curtains that covered windows, each of these places was carefully searched. We finished searching the main floor but we had found no one. We began to relax just a little, hoping that whoever broke the window may have fled the scene before our arrival.

The basement. Just a quick look around down there and we could grab a cup of coffee and chat for a while to discuss this latest caper. The light switch did not work. My first thought was that intruders unscrewed the light bulb to gain the advantage. It was dark down there that was for sure. Our flashlights revealed an endless sea of large cardboard boxes, shelves stacked high with typical basement stuff, and infinite hanging things of all sorts, meaning little chance of seeing any danger until it was too late. Our flashlights also gave away our position to the intruders lurking in the darkness even though we held them out to one side so we would not be hit by the bullets if the suspect shot at our lights. This was the perfect hiding place for a would-be killer.

The chief went first with his revolver drawn. He had been a police officer for a year now, although he had not gone to a police academy either. But he was the experienced one and the police chief in his township, so he led the way. I followed with my Remington model 870 12-gauge pump-action shotgun fully loaded with five rounds of 00 buckshot (pronounced "Double Ought Buckshot"), the same type of shotgun with which I had bagged so many pheasant, rabbit, ducks and deer. Each shell contained 9 pellets the size of peas intended to spread as they were expelled from the gun barrel so as to increase the odds of hitting the target in the darkness when gun sights could not be easily seen. They are also called scatterguns because the buckshot pellets scatter into a widening pattern the farther they travel from the barrel of the shotgun. Slowly, carefully, we peered around and into each box. We listened. We would be able to hear someone breathing heavily if they were scared because everything was very close and it was so very deadly quiet. Nothing. A spider web stuck to my face as I crept forward, shotgun at the ready. The dank smell of mildew was ever present in the basement as we searched for the intruder.

We looked behind the clothes hanging from pipes mounted to the ceiling. We listened again. No sounds to be heard but our own hearts pounding, and the sweat, dripping, no running, down our backs. My pants brushed against a cardboard box with a loud swishing sound. Crap! After what seemed like an hour we had checked every square inch in that basement or so we thought. An old couch was set diagonally across the back corner of the basement directly below the broken window. A white dingy blanket covered the couch. The probing flashlight beams revealed nothing unusual looking in that last corner. We started to relax. After a few deep breaths of mildew-laden air we started to turn off our bodies' defense mechanisms. We turned in unison to head back upstairs when the blanket covering the couch suddenly stood up. Every nerve ending sent an immediate danger signal back to my brain. I swung the shotgun, now only six feet from the standing, blanketed figure.

"Freeze," I screamed.

"Don't move," the chief yelled at the now motionless figure.

My finger had snapped off the safety of my scattergun and I squeezed the trigger two thirds of the way back to the firing position. Nine pea-sized lead pellets readied themselves to be blasted from my shotgun to maim and bloody anything in their path. To this day I don't know how that shotgun did not fire and cut that standing figure in half. Maybe it was the fact that the person under the blanket froze immediately upon standing up, maybe my eyes had quickly told my brain that I saw no weapon to justify firing at the figure, or maybe it was just dumb luck for him and for me.

I saw the chief with the hammer drawn back on his revolver. He too had almost shot the draped figure. The sweat ran like a torrent down my back and neck. I wasn't sure if I was scared of almost shooting the unarmed intruder or if I was afraid of being sued or sent to prison had I actually done it. The blanket shook like a tree in the wind. When he pulled the blanket off of his head, his eyes were wide and a look of sheer terror shone in them. His hands shot up into the air. His body was rigid and frozen. He had the look of impending death in his eyes as he stood before his would-be executioners.

"I'm sorry," was all the figure was able to manage, too scared to say anything further.

We handcuffed him and brought the burglar upstairs and out into the front lawn believing we had successfully made a serious felony arrest. The husband and wife with their little boy and girl stood huddled in a tight circle. Upon seeing the felon who had recently broken into their home, they seemed to relax, which confused me.

"Hi," the figure said to the husband.

"Jimmy, what are you doing here?" asked the husband.

"I forgot my key and when you weren't home, I kicked in the basement window and let myself in, I'm sorry," he sheepishly said.

"Do you know him?" the chief asked the husband.

"Yes, he is a family friend and we let him stay with us from time to time, but I didn't know he was coming over tonight."

"When I saw police officers pulling their cars up near the house I was scared and hid in the basement thinking the police would not come into the house to look for me," Jimmy offered.

"Do you want to press any charges against him?" the chief asked the husband.

"No, I am real sorry to bother you guys. Thanks for your help," the husband added.

We took off the suspect's handcuffs and the suspect and the family waved good-bye to us and entered their house. The chief and I got into our cars, drenched in our own sweat and a bit shaky, and we slowly drove away into the night.

Over coffee I was surprised to see my hands shaking so much. The chief and I both talked of just how close we had come to shooting the intruder, who we now knew as Jimmy. In that fraction of a second it took for us to train our weapons on him, with the aid of our combined experience, which was next to nothing at that time, we concluded that the shooting would have not been justified. The intruder did not have any weapons and hadn't made any threats directed at us. Our young careers would most likely have been over in the split-second it would have taken for the swarm of 00 buckshot and .357 slugs to cut the figure down. Welcome to police work. Damned if you do, damned if you don't. My back and chest were still soaked with sweat. The hot coffee felt good in my stomach. Sleep that night after ending my shift proved very elusive.

5

THE MISSING FARMER

It was a sunny day as I drove around Bridgeport Township. It was warm but not too hot and a gentle breeze was steadily blowing as I patrolled along the country road by the farm fields where farmers were just starting to harvest their crops. It was early fall. I now had six months or so under my belt and I was starting to adjust to my role as a police officer. I felt more comfortable around strangers whom I had stopped for traffic violations or those who had summoned me to handle their problems. A farmer working in his field waved at me and I waved back. Two little tikes on their tricycles stopped and waved as I drove by. It was a good feeling to have people treat me in a friendly manner. My mother may just have been wrong about police officers getting no respect.

"37-63, 37-63." It was the state police dispatcher who also dispatched for local police agencies back in those days.

I deftly picked up the microphone of the radio and answered "63-37."

"Respond to the area of 4573 Tower Road. We had a call from a woman who said her husband has not come home for lunch. He is supposed to be harvesting navy beans and he told his wife that he would be home for lunch at 12 noon."

"Roger 37." I checked my watch. It was 1:22 p.m. *The farmer probably just had a breakdown on his bean combine and was working on it*, I thought. I had uncles and cousins who owned a farm and from what I had seen there I guessed that is what had probably happened to this farmer. Recollections of the bat call my mother made so many years ago briefly fluttered through my mind, so I focused on treating this call for service as a serious matter even though it probably wasn't.

As I turned the corner and drove past the barn, I saw the bean combine running at full tilt. Dust was madly swirling like a miniature tornado surrounding the clanking monster. The smell of gasoline fumes filled my lungs. No one was around. That was odd. As I drove around the far side of the huge machine I could barely hear myself think due to the cacophony of noise. Looking up, I saw the limp figure of the farmer hanging from the overhead screw gear atop the bin that was used to unload the harvested beans. He must have gotten into the bin to make some adjustment or clear a jam. The powerful machine had caught his clothes in that overhead screw gear and twisted them tightly compressing his chest and forcing the air out of his lungs until he could no longer breathe.

I climbed up the huge roaring machine to where the farmer was suspended. The machine had unloaded the beans into the waiting farm truck, telling me the farmer had been hanging there for some time. His face had that telltale pale grayish-white of death with those blue lips, indicating his blood no longer flowed through his body. The eyes were opened wide and his pupils were dilated staring at me as if begging me for my help. I heard the siren and saw Chief Chet skidding up to the clanking monster. The dispatcher became concerned and sent him to help after I failed to answer the call checking up on my status. I did not hear the dispatcher calling me due to my preoccupation with trying to save the hapless farmer along with the ear shattering noise of the combine.

Chief Chet was on the radio evidently calling for medical assistance. He ran to the screaming machine and after what seemed like an eternity he found the off switch, suddenly stopping it. Eerie silence enveloped me. The total lack of noise was deafening. My ears rang and the clothes of the farmer's body hopelessly entwined in the overhead screw gear and its guard shroud confronted me. The farmer needed to be removed from the machinery immediately if we had any hope of saving him. The empty hopper that only recently held the beans loomed very large and deep. I climbed up to the hopper where the farmer remained trapped. I put one foot on the metal guard protecting the overhead screw gear and one foot on the side of the dust-covered grain bin. I tried to balance on the narrow metal edge of the hopper, which was very slippery from the dust of the harvest, some eight feet above the ground. I had started to carry an old knife on my first day as a police officer thinking I just might need it someday. The knife was deep in my pocket and I had difficulty getting it out because my hand was shaking. I nearly slipped and fell to the ground far below on several occasions. When I held the knife, I saw the blade was dull and loose.

I grasped the back of the shirt of the farmer and started to cut through the two shirts, leather belt and two pairs of trousers that had become entangled in the screw gear. The material cut away ever so slowly and I sawed and sawed with that dull cheap knife. My arms ached from the exertion. I would buy a good quality, sharp knife after this, I promised myself. (I did buy a good sharp knife after that struggle and I carry it always even though I have long since retired, as an officer never really ever, ever retires.) The dull wobbly blade tried to part the twisted mass of leather and cloth in an effort to free the lifeless farmer. My stance of straddling atop the machine some eight feet above the ground on slippery metal was tiring me quickly. One slip and I knew that I would regret it. That spark of life in that limp figure, I knew, was already gone. But he continued to stare into my eyes pleading for my help anyway. He had been trussed up for some time, the air forced out of his lungs, but I had to try. The sweat was pouring out of my body as I balanced, cut, and held the lifeless figure.

Suddenly he dropped like a heavy lead weight. I held on with all of my strength. One arm against 200 plus pounds! My boots slipping on the dust-covered grain bin edge threatened to fling me onto the ground below. I just couldn't let him drop; he deserved better than that. Finally I got my other arm around and grabbed his torn clothes. Slowly I was able to hoist him up onto the lip of the bin without falling and I slid his limp body over the edge of the bin. Nearly falling on the slippery narrow edge of the grain hopper for the Nth time, I balanced the slouched figure as I breathed heavily from the effort. Sweat was pouring out of me in rivers partly from exertion and partly from a very real fear of falling.

Chief Chet waited down below. I slid the farmer off of the edge of the machine again nearly falling to the ground as I strained with one arm to lower the body while using my other arm to keep from falling. Somehow I managed to maintain my footing as I eased the farmer down to the chief. He grabbed him and laid him on the soft cool green bed of grass. A trooper having heard the call for an ambulance suddenly arrived and Chief Chet and the trooper started CPR on the lifeless figure. I was so thankful for the two officers who responded to my call so they could perform CPR on the poor farmer because at that time, without the benefit of police academy training, I had no idea how to perform CPR.

I miraculously found my way down from the bean combine without falling. It seemed futile but they pressed on with the chest compressions and rescue breathing. Air had gotten into the farmer's stomach in the attempt to breathe life back into him causing the farmer's stomach contents to suddenly and violently spray all over us That acidic stench from the oozing stomach bile splattered over his chest and on to us. Then another smell, I would come to know quite well arose, the smell of emptying bowels when the muscles of a dead body relaxed. It was nauseating even in the open air in that field. The wailing siren of the racing ambulance was a welcome sound. The paramedics ran up and took over the medical efforts even though we all knew he was gone. The face, the endlessly staring eyes, the poor tired limp figure seemed to have simply given up. It was as though he was content to be in a better place without the worries, the hard work, and the hardships life had offered him. I thought my job was done once the ambulance drove away, siren blaring, red lights wildly flashing. All I needed to do was clean myself up, trade in my soiled uniform for a fresh clean one, and write the report. I was wrong.

The death message is one of the most difficult tasks a police officer is responsible for. It was my complaint, my township, my responsibility. I drove over to the house of the woman who had called to report that her husband had not returned from his farming chores for lunch. My uniform still had the stomach bile from her husband on it. I was terrified to get out of my police car. It was as if I were a rusty robot trying to make my legs move toward her door.

What could I possibly say to her? She was an older woman, some 40 years my senior, who had seen a long life of both happiness and sorrow. I was young and very short on experience.

As soon as she saw me, she burst into tears. At that moment I learned that the unexpected visit by a police officer with a serious face was never good news and the reaction by those visited was always swift and severe. There was little a police officer could do to comfort those confronted by irreversible news of the loss of a loved one, but I did everything I could for her to help ease her suffering. Both a neighbor and the family's pastor were summoned to tend to the poor grieving widow. I went home that day to my wife and I felt guilty in an odd way that I still had my spouse. That woman was left alone never again to see her husband of forty-some years. That was no way for her to have to part ways with her husband. It was no way for the farmer to part ways with his wife. Life can be so unforgiving, and I was reminded once again that a life can be snatched away in a moment.

Those memories and those lessons were indelibly etched into my young brain, which helped to shape my attitude and to guide me in the coming years. I remembered the trooper who responded to my mother's bat call. He had been there for her and her family, not for himself. I also learned that some things are just beyond human control and I needed to put aside those experiences to be able to effectively handle the future calls for service that were sure to come. I learned valuable lessons that day, unfortunately at the expense of the farmer and his wife.

6

A GLIMPSE OF ROUTINE CALLS

There were many other experiences that helped to shape my character and attitude as a police officer with that township police department. Even many years later, I still recall a few that significantly impacted me and helped lay a foundation for me in police work. These events remain forever locked in my memory and are often revived by some random occurrence that suddenly replays the videotape in my mind.

Bank alarms-real or not? I had entered the bank to cash my paycheck, as meager as it was, wearing my uniform since I just started on duty. I smiled warmly to the bank tellers whom I knew casually. The closest teller commented that I arrived to the bank alarm very quickly, within one minute, she proudly announced. Even with my minimal police experience my body suddenly went on full alert. I quickly did a 360-degree scan with my head to see if anyone was lurking in the bank, maybe hiding behind the counter or a back office.

"What bank alarm?" I nervously asked.

"I accidently set off the bank alarm and you walked into the bank less than a minute later," the teller said.

"You are not being robbed?" I quickly asked as I continued to look for anything out of the ordinary.

"Oh heavens no," she answered sweetly.

I walked into the bank before dispatch could even put out the call for the bank alarm. Had the alarm been in response to an actual bank robbery, I most likely would have walked into my own death as the robbers would have immediately identified me given my police uniform, and I would not have known what they were up to unless I had seen their guns before they could react. On a different day, it may well have been a seriously different result. I learned an important lesson that day, always, always be aware of your surroundings, working or not working, responding to a call or not.

B&E, suspect or homeowner? It was dispatched as a B&E in progress. It was dark. Of course it was night, as most B&E's occur in the darkness when it is the most dangerous for the police officer. I responded and arrived within two minutes having been close to the location. A trooper was pulling up at the same time that I did. He deftly produced his long-gun (a rifle or shotgun rather than his pistol). We immediately saw in the darkness an adult male carrying a long-gun himself. The trooper and I lay on the grass below the small rise in the lawn with weapons trained on the person.

The trooper instantly took control of our response and loudly ordered the man to stop and put his gun on the ground.

"Drop the gun," the trooper commanded.

The man continued to hold the shotgun and then he slowly turned toward us, his gun aimed at the ground. The tension skyrocketed as this was rapidly nearing a justified shooting situation out of self-defense. In my time as a police officer, I had never actually shot anyone, and certainly never killed a man. The very real possibility that his would be the first ran through my mind. My mouth went dry and my heart seemed to expand into my throat, pounding full force against my windpipe and chest. I made myself take a breath and then another, as my body pulsed with apprehension.

"Drop the gun now or I will open fire on you! Drop the gun now!" the trooper again ordered, his voice channeling his own feelings into the authority I knew I would also have to assume.

The figure hesitated. I could hear the seconds tick away with each thump of my heart, second after second mounting to what seemed like five minutes but was really only a brief moment. The man slowly laid the gun on the grass.

"I live here, I'm the one that called you guys. Thank you for responding so quickly. I heard someone trying to kick in my door but I never saw him," he said.

We checked the yard and found no one. My tension, high blood pressure, and sweat all returned to normal only a minute after it had all started. The trooper and I said our goodbyes and went in our own directions, to feel relief or annoyance or indifference about the call. This was a routine call that could have turned out so much worse, but which had fortunately been just an emotional roller coaster ride. Every time officers face a person with a gun, they must choose between taking the risk of waiting to assess the threat or shooting to protect themselves and others. There are times when waiting before shooting first could cost the ultimate price by giving the person an opportunity to shoot first. Those options weigh heavily on every officer's mind in the balancing act of the moment-and linger as a flutter of doubt each time such calls come in. The fact that the decision worked in my favor this time didn't mean that the outcome would be as benign the next time. Every officer has one goal in mind as they go to work each day, they too want to go home to their families at the end of their shift.

Evictions, dangers big and small. I was dispatched to a house where an eviction was pending in court to check the house to see if the woman continued to live there so I could serve her with eviction papers. When I knocked on the door, no one answered, so I tried the doorknob. Since it was unlocked, and the door opened, I walked through the house. Not a single stick of furniture. The woman had moved out without a trace of where she had gone. The carpet was covered with animal feces and countless urine stains that appeared to have been from both dogs and cats. A gut-retching smell permeated the house. I went downstairs. There was not one square foot of space on the concrete basement floor that didn't have animal feces on it. I tried to avoid stepping into the droppings but that proved impossible.

I returned to my patrol car and wrote some notes while the wafting stench of animal crap on my boots surrounded me and just would not leave through the car's open windows. As I started back to the police station, I began feeling itching on my legs. When it started to affect both legs, I stopped my car and stepped out. I pulled up my pant leg and saw hundreds of fleas on my right leg alone! The left leg proved to be as infested as the right leg. I felt fleas crawling on my back and chest as well. I drove to the township fire station that had showers and stripped off my flea-ridden uniform. I couldn't believe my eyes. There were hundreds of fleas being washed onto to the shower floor and down the drain. I had fleabites all over my body. I put my uniform into a plastic bag and sent it off to the cleaners.

It was difficult to imagine how a woman could have lived like that. Human beings are, of course, a form of animal, but most dogs and cats wouldn't defecate in the place where they lived. I alternated between despair and disgust as I contemplated humanity, our weaknesses, our cruelties and our banality. My fundamental belief was that in the time we have on earth, we should strive for lives of beauty and service. There was no way to reconcile those living conditions with that belief.

Family fights, winners or losers? They now call these domestic violence calls. Back then, they were family fights. The call was in Genesee Gardens on California Street, a place known for crime in Bridgeport Township. As part-time officer Dave and I pulled into the driveway, loud shouts and screams of obscenities filled the air. We wondered if they were armed with a gun or another type of weapon as we ran to the door. How many people were inside? Were there children present who likely needed protection while we tried not to get ourselves injured or killed? Any barking indicating dogs that might pose a serious threat? Some serious possibilities to consider in the 3-4 seconds it took to sprint from the car to the front door of the shabby house.

As we entered the rundown house, we saw that the husband had been drinking (of course) and the wife was crying with a black eye and swollen cheek. A scared little girl about three years old stood behind her mother gripping her pant leg. Tears ran down the little girl's cheeks. Behind the three year old, and barely peeking around her sister, was an adorable one-year-old who appeared petrified by her parent's screaming. After surveying the interior of the house as best as I could in those first 2-3 seconds, I stepped inside. I was immediately greeted by the husband.

"What the fuck are you doing coming into my house? Get the fuck out of here, now!" He shoved his face into mine and his spittle splattered my face.

"We were dispatched here for a family fight," I said evenly without taking my eyes off of him. The hair on the back of my neck immediately went rigid as I tensed for a physical attack. His nose stopped only two inches from my nose. His breath stank of a mixture of stale beer and poor dental hygiene. His eyes were afire with rage. He sported a few days of facial hair growth. He wore a dirty tee shirt with the straps on the shoulders, the kind often referred to as a wife beater. *How appropriate in this case*, I thought.

I noted his hands were clenched into fists. His shoulders were hunched forward as if he would lunge at me any second. I steadied for the punch I was sure was forthcoming. He stopped very carefully just short of making contact with me and continued to scream and berate me for being there. Trying my hardest to maintain an air of calmness, I simply told him I had been dispatched to a disturbance.

"I don't give a fuck why you were sent here, get the fuck out of my house," his response was quick and as sharp as a knife.

"We need to make sure no crimes were committed before we leave," I offered back to him.

"Go ahead and ask her, no crimes here," he slurred. I left him with my partner.

I walked over to his wife who had obvious recent injuries and disheveled clothes. Her two young children shook with fear as they watched their father.

"Please tell me what happened," I coaxed.

"Nothing happened, I should not have called you," she lied.

"It's okay, we can't help unless you tell us what happened. We can take him with us tonight if you tell me what he did," I prompted.

"I accidently ran into the closet door and gave myself a black eye, honest," she lied again.

"You're not going to tell me, are you?" I asked.

"No, I have to live with him. It will only make it worse for me and the kids. Thank you, but you need to leave now," she pleaded.

While I tried to get her to tell me what had really happened, the husband was suddenly at my side screaming, "What do you want, a date with my wife? Leave my wife alone."

His rage never subsided. The wife would not press charges. Back then, few laws existed to deal with these types of situations, so there was nothing we could do. With the laws now in place officers are not only allowed to make arrests for domestic violence, they are mandated to do so when there is evidence that a domestic assault has occurred, even if the officer did not witness the attack.

I turned back to the husband knowing we would not be able to arrest him without the wife's testimony. I looked at the battered woman and her vulnerable daughters. My anger rose to a near explosion.

"Why don't you take a swing at me? I'll give you the first shot." I quietly said to him in an even and polite voice. He didn't move. I said, "Come on, why don't you hit someone who can fight back? Come on, take a shot at me!" As I leaned over him, my nose and his nose were again only an inch apart. My steely eyes met his with a look of stone determination transmitting the message that to take a swing at me would result in some severe pain to him. He just wasn't that brave. At this point, my confidence was building along with my experience.

He had it in him to beat a defenseless woman, but he was not going to chance getting his ass kicked by a police officer who he perceived had the ability to hurt him. Doing so would also subject him to arrest for assaulting a police officer. Back then, that was my only chance to arrest him, but he opted for the coward's way out and did not move. I longed to have him make the first move on me, but as an officer, especially one who strove to be good, I couldn't just punch him. Cops actually do play by the rules most of the time, at least the good ones do. After what seemed like an eternity I turned, and my partner and I walked out of their house since the wife would not press charges. I left the two to deal with their problems on their own with their scared children cowering nearby. I felt so helpless getting into my patrol car and driving away, forced to admit that I couldn't fix every situation and that some lives did not have a happily ever after in them. Everyone who serves the public has that realization, and we have to decide if it will break us or compel us forward to keep trying. I drove forward to my next call, and the next after that, stoking optimism with every small victory.

These calls, and many more like them, provided on-the-job training to substitute for my lack of formal police academy training. I had the good fortune to have many other experiences with the township police department, some good, some not so good. Each one taught me important things that helped me later in my career, both on the job and off. After I was on the job for nine months, my chief sent me to a police academy for training. There were 23 different academies scattered across Michigan and most were run by community colleges. My chief had waited for an opening at the Michigan State Police Academy in Lansing, Michigan so I could be the best trained officer I could be. Fate has a way of interjecting itself into one's life. I now know I was meant to enter the State Police Academy as a local officer to mentally prepare me and boost my confidence for a future career with the state police. I just did not know it at that time.

The State Police ran basic police academies for local police officers back then when they didn't have a trooper academy going. They have since stopped running basic police academies. I completed the twelve-week police academy, which seemed much longer than that. It was hard, and in many ways much tougher than my Army basic training had been. I was grateful to have been able to attend a premier police-training academy, which provided me with an excellent base of knowledge and experience with which to start my police career.

I was honored to have been selected by my classmates to receive the "Team Builder" award for helping other recruits when they needed help. I was also selected as the Class Orator to give the graduation speech on behalf of our 4th Basic Police Academy Class. The instructors, all State Police Officers except for two local officers, had been tough on us. I learned that was because they sincerely cared about us and wanted to prepare us to the best of their ability to do a professional job and to be able to handle the suspects we were sure to encounter as police officers. One day during a driving exercise the troopers in the front seat, Troopers Bill and Lenny, told me I should apply to the State Police. Those excellent troopers made me promise that I would indeed apply. I told them I would, never expecting to be accepted even if I did apply. I forgot about that promise and went back to work in my township now trained by the State Police and with an added level of confidence and an excellent background of professional academy training.

PART

3

7

THE DECISION

I'd thought about it on many occasions. I could apply with the State Police to be a trooper. I always put it out of my mind unconvinced I would ever qualify. The stories of the Trooper Training Academy were legendary. Thousands would apply for the few academy seats offered to the few successful applicants. Fifty percent of those fortunate enough to even start in the academy were either washed out, injured or quit on their own. Fifty percent! To even obtain an invitation to start the academy was a feat in and of itself. Back in those days applicants had to be at least 5'-9". My 5'-10 1/2" frame allowed me to continue in the hiring process. Minimum height requirements for applicants were standard hiring criteria among police departments in the 1970s based on job requirement studies. To ensure that height requirement, applicants had to take off their shoes and a sheet of paper was placed under their heels. Any lifting of the heels to attempt to gain a little height would disqualify the applicant!

Stories circulated about the boxing training. If you didn't bleed in the boxing ring you would be put in with another recruit until you were either bleeding or knocked unconscious. Push-ups, sit-ups, and chin-ups were said to be the bread and butter of the physical fitness regime. Stories were told of torturous sessions of hundreds of each exercise until arms nearly fell off. Running was an exercise that the academy was said to hold near and dear. Rumors had it that within the first few weeks, recruits were running five miles each morning-after the inside workout regime. Five miles!

Then there was the death swim. The death swim was a name given by the recruits themselves and it was the capstone of the water safety program. As the rumors went, all of the swimming instructors plus other instructors who wanted to get in on the fun lined the sides of the Olympic sized "training tank" and the recruit had to swim one length of the pool to rescue a simulated drowning person. Explicit instructions to make sure their nails were closely trimmed to minimize scratches and bleeding had been handed down to the recruits who were all huddled in the shower room awaiting their turns. Those in the know heard that the drowning person never wanted to be saved and fought like a wildcat, emitting blood curdling screams to taunt the waiting recruits. Stories told of gallons of water being sucked in by the hapless recruit while trying to "save" the drowning person.

Recruits who survived the rescue of the drowning person (who was actually an instructor who could swim like a fish) then swam back to the other end of the pool. During that swim, the other instructors lining the pool dove in and wrestled the exhausted recruit to the bottom of the tank. The recruit had to fight off each instructor in succession until finally reaching the end of the tank to struggle out of the pool. Breathing water, bloodied noses, black eyes, cut lips and scratches were the order of the day. Those that made it continued on in the academy, at least that's what the rumors said.

My two year college degree in criminal justice, army basic training, and a year and a half as a local police officer in no way qualified me to even submit an application with the Michigan State Police.

Yet my mind flashed back to the dreaded bat, to the professional demeanor of the trooper who had responded to my mother's "emergency." I was taken aback by Trooper Bob James and his kindness, openness and willingness to help me learn police work. I remembered promising Trooper Bill and Trooper Lenny that I would apply to the state police. My memories were consistent with my views of policing and I was impressed with what I saw in these fine, confident, professionals. They obviously were extensively trained and finely honed for the job they were sent to handle. I wanted to be like them. Plus I had promised that I would apply. My dad always told my brothers and me that you have little in life that really mattered; your word was everything, and you never gave it lightly. That meant that you carried through with your promise to the very best of your ability. I knew that I had to keep my promise.

The application was very long and asked every conceivable question. It took weeks to locate all of the information I was asked to put on those long pages. I didn't remember every job I ever held, not all of the part-time ones. How much had I been paid? What was my boss's name? Loans, every detail of every loan, were you behind on any payment? Any family member ever been arrested? Was I ever given a traffic ticket or involved in a traffic accident? Where, when, by whom? Did I pay the ticket? I had to provide the names of my neighbors and the names of three references with their contact information. Health history questions of every conceivable ailment, injury, disease and surgical procedure undergone were asked. When it was done, I dropped it into the mailbox and forgot about it. I had fulfilled my promise to apply to the state police.

I was in shock the day I grabbed the mail out of the mailbox and saw the letter inviting me to participate in the civil service examination which proved to be another interesting process. I showed up at the Michigan Department of Civil Service building in Lansing to take the exam. The exam consisted of many written questions, some of which seemed quite odd. Many questions were restated several times in different phraseology. Some questions seemed to force me into taking a position on some issue I didn't want to take. The recollection portion consisted of looking at a drawing of an intersection with buildings, people, cars, dogs, a clock tower, a cloudy sky, and other things. After viewing the picture for several minutes we flipped the page and answered a series of questions regarding what we had just seen. Was the man wearing a hat? Was he wearing a wristwatch? If so, which hand was it on? Was there a car behind the man? What color was the car? Did the man have on tie shoes or loafers? Was anyone standing in front of the bank? Was there even a bank in the picture? On and on the questions probed. I must have remembered enough from the picture and answered most questions correctly because I soon received another letter.

The letter directed me to, "Report to the Bay City Post for an initial pre-employment physical assessment." Standing broad jump in the garage of the post. Push-ups. Chin-ups on the post radio tower support bar. Sit-ups. Some of the applicants could not pound out the minimum number of repetitions for the various physical tests and were sent home with a look of dejection on their long faces. I survived! I mean, I passed!

The rumors had it that thousands of applicants applied but few were ultimately selected to even start in the Academy. Even fewer graduated. I was committed and I would not quit, I would see this process through until I was accepted by the state police.

I received another letter advising me that a background investigator would be conducting my background investigation. Trooper Al was assigned to the Bay City Post. Every detail revealed in my application would be verified, checked and rechecked, and information not found in the application was ferreted out and put in the background investigative report, including things I had not remembered. I didn't think that a short-term summer job long ago was important, but they did. I forgot about the minor fender-bender accident I had years before. It all came out during the investigation. I received calls from acquaintances that I had not talked to for years who told me of being contacted by the trooper with all of the probing questions about me. What was he like? Do you think he would be a good Michigan State Police Trooper? My parents and wife were interviewed. My wife answered that she knew the job was dangerous but that she supported my becoming a trooper. Little did she or I know at that time what this would mean once I actually started working as a trooper.

The MCOLES pre-employment agility test was next. This was the Michigan Commission on Law Enforcement Standards physical agility test that was put together after a job study of the physical things police officers do on a regular basis, or at least that is what it was supposed to be. All police academies in the state were required to give this physical agility test to all police applicants. The tests consisted of push-ups with a staff member making a fist under your chest so the assessor knew if you have gone down far enough with each push-up. Another screening test included performing as many sit-ups within a minute the applicant could do. Right and left hand grip strength was recorded and scored. A timed shuttle run was included and scored. The tests were not too hard for those applicants in decent shape. Applicants that were not in good physical shape had difficulties that often resulted failing scores, and were sent home with crushed and deflated looks on their faces. Of course, I would not do a single push-up as a police officer, but I would pull myself up on objects a few times while I worked the road. I did, however, chase after fleeing suspects often, and I can say I never lost a foot chase. One time I even chased and caught two suspects during the same chase, so all of that running in the academy paid off.

Passing the test meant moving to the next phase of the hiring process courtesy of another letter inviting me for the employment interview.

There were three people sitting at the long table when I walked into the interview. That was the first time I had been in the old brick State Police Headquarters in East Lansing across the street from Michigan State University, which has since been replaced by a new one built in the City of Lansing, and most recently yet another move to space near the training academy in the old General Office Building. It was as imposing as I thought it would be. It was very clean and very organized. I was directed to have a seat until I was summonsed. It had not been a request, even from the receptionist. The door opened and a confused looking applicant walked past me as though in a daze, causing my confidence to waiver right before my name was called. One of the interviewers was from the Michigan Department of Civil Service. The other was a lieutenant from the state police who was wearing his uniform, which was neat and perfectly fitted to his frame. Every detail was flawless, from his erect posture to his precisely trimmed hair. His eyes watched my every move as he rose to introduce himself with a friendly but official manner. The third member of the interview panel was a woman in civilian clothes who introduced herself as a sergeant with the state police.

The light chitchat slowly evolved into probing questions. These morphed into more difficult decisional questions.

"If you were sent to a robbery in progress and saw a man generally matching the description of the robber would you shoot him?"

"Of course not," I said.

"If you told the man to stop and he did not stop would you shoot him?"

"No," I said.

"If he suddenly reached behind his back would you shoot him?"

"No."

"If he quickly brought his hand around toward you would you shoot him now?"

"No," I answered, less sure of my answer.

"Are you sure, do you want to get shot? Would you be able to shoot someone if necessary?"

"Well, maybe I might have shot."

"Well he only had a handkerchief in his hand!"

Damned if you do, damned if you don't. These questions were designed to make you think, make a quick and correct decision, and modify your answers as they changed the facts, but stick to your decision if you felt you were right. I was sweating when I left the interview as they shook hands and told me I would be receiving a letter soon regarding the results of my interview. I too walked away with that confused, dazed, applicant look.

I came home from work on a Friday after my shift with the township police department had ended. It had been quiet in the township. A few traffic tickets written, some warnings and little else had happened. That was the policing model they wanted there. Keep the peace, don't stir up trouble, and don't make waves. My wife told me the state police recruiter had called asking if I would be able to start the academy a week from Sunday. I wildly looked at the clock, 5:03 p.m. They were closed for the day. I stewed over the weekend arriving at the decision that since they had given me so little time to make such a career changing decision, which included a huge risk of not graduating from the academy, there was no way I was going to start the academy next Sunday. I needed to give my current job two weeks' notice. Would my chief be mad? No, I wasn't going. Ok, these chances only come once in a lifetime, I'll go. How rude of them to give me such short notice, so I'm not going. But this could be the start of my ideal career. Yes, no, yes, no, well maybe.

My wife and I sat at the kitchen table to discuss the choice we had to make. I knew it would be difficult for my wife. I also knew that once we started our family, I wanted my children to look at me the way I had looked at the trooper so many years ago.

I called at 8:02 a.m. on Monday morning giving the recruiter a chance to get to his desk somewhere in Lansing. The recruiter asked, "Are you interested in starting the state police academy the next Sunday?"

I barely gave the recruiter time to finish the sentence before I said, "Yes."

No hesitation, no time to think it over. It was done. I was told to report to the academy in Lansing on Thursday for my medical examination, and if I passed it I would start the academy three days later. I told my chief of my decision. I asked him if for some reason (highly likely) I didn't make it through the academy if I could have my job back. He looked intently into my eyes for a few seconds and simply said, "If they don't want you, neither do I." To this day I don't know if he was giving me tough love encouragement as an incentive to complete the academy or simply being truthful. I knew that he greatly respected the state police. His stern statement did motivate me as I needed the job with the increased pay and benefits. My wife deserved that much from me. I had just been given a chance to become a trooper! I was not going to blow the chance I had waited on for so long, especially now with no job to return to.

Thursday came and I reported to the academy. The doctor took my blood pressure, checked my ears and eyes, felt my neck, and had me perform an eye test. The hearing test resulted in me being told my hearing had a deficit in the higher frequency ranges. I knew I should not have gone to that Harry Chapin concert Wednesday night! Dental records were recorded. I've been told in the event you were killed on the job it would make identification easier and positive. That was disconcerting. I was worried about the hearing issue. The doctor looked me in the eyes and told me I had passed, barely, due to my hearing deficit. He asked me if this was what I really wanted. I told him yes without hesitation. He signed off on my medical exam papers and I was in the next trooper recruit school only three days away.

I came to realize that often the biggest impediments to a person seeking to move forward in life come from within. My initial self-doubt had almost cost me the opportunity that lay before me to fulfill the dreams I had since childhood. I wondered how many times I had stifled my own aspirations and if this was the norm for most people.

What was it that kept a person from grabbing something better, an impulse that should be natural and instinctive? I felt that I had to take the first step of believing in myself before I could run forward into the future. From that point forward, I vowed to never undermine myself or set artificial roadblocks in the way of my life's goals.

MICHIGAN STATE POLICE

TRAINING ACADEMY

8

THE ACADEMY

Sunday, only three days later, came way too soon. I barely remember driving to Lansing and arriving at the new state police academy located by the General Office Building Complex near the Lansing State Police Post. I pulled into the parking lot where we had been directed to park, farthest from the academy building. I just sat in my yellow Ford Bronco, not wanting to leave the safety of my vehicle. After some time I looked around and saw other bald headed recruits (instructions were clear to report with a recruit style haircut (bald), a white shirt and tie, black trousers and black leather shoes) sitting in their cars staring at nothing. Each of the other trooper hopefuls had that faraway look in their eyes. The smell of fear permeated the parking lot.

Eventually recruits started to leave their cars and we all approached the front steps of the seven-story academy building. The letters we had received instructed us to report to the state police academy at 5:00 p.m. It was only 4:57 p.m. We were three minutes early. An ominous foreboding ran through the long line of would-be troopers, which included ex-military types, marines, navy, air force, and army. Some National Guard and reservists were mixed in. The others were a mixed bag of former gas station attendants, department store stockroom employees, prior police officers, EMTs, teachers, and other hopefuls.

The transition was quick. I thought that my army basic training at Fort Leonard Wood, Missouri, seven short years ago would have prepared me for what was about to come. In some ways it did, in many others, not so. I quickly found that the physical training was more intense. An obvious goal was to build strength and endurance and along with that came an uncompromising focus on never, ever quitting until the goal was accomplished. We were taught to look beyond the blood, the emotional issues, the screams, the broken bodies, and to focus on what we could do to resolve the emergency at hand. Whether it was one more push-up, one more mile to run, or physically subduing a suspect in the numerous patrol scenarios, a trooper never, under any circumstances, gives up, ever. Mental toughness was demanded in every activity, large or small.

Academics were another story. There was so much information coming at me from many different courses it was mind numbing. Legal classes were very complex and detailed. Use of Fatal Force, Search and Seizure, Law of Arrests, Admissions and Confessions, Domestic Relations, Criminal Law, Juvenile Law, and Evidence Collection, to name just a few. Then there were Patrols, Defensive Tactics, Precision Driving, Firearms, First Aid-course work and practical exercises, History of the State Police (this was taught to develop a deep sense of pride, ownership, and to build esprit de corps, and the course accomplished it's goal), Crime Scene Investigation, Accident Investigation, and many other courses all converged on each recruit. The transition from civilian to trooper had begun. My confidence rose as I absorbed the material from each of these classes. I knew that I could conduct an investigation, render first aid, and know when I had sufficient evidence to make an arrest. There were so many different classes they all seemed to blend together. These were intense courses that had to be mastered. The state police tested each topic requiring a score of 70% along with a requirement that each recruit achieve a cumulative overall academic score of 70% for all courses combined. Certain courses, the legal courses, were considered "core" courses. If a recruit failed any course examination, they were provided remedial instruction and given a second examination. Failing any core course twice resulted in dismissal from the academy. Then at the end of the academy the Michigan Commission on Law Enforcement Standards gave a certification test that was cumulative of all topics covering the entire academy curriculum. To fail this test meant you would not be allowed to function as a police officer in Michigan and all of the hard training would be for naught.

Up at 5:00 a.m. Morning physical conditioning (or P.T. for physical training) at 5:30 a.m. always brought knots to my stomach. Not a minute early or a minute late at the gymnasium door was the directive. A severe price was paid for the class commander (a rotating position that each recruit endured) as the recruit in that position was held responsible for the sins of any and all other wayward recruits who did not enter at exactly 5:30 a.m. The ways of exacting pain were limitless. The usual suspects of push-ups, sit-ups, squat-thrusts, chin-ups and running were included. Another exercise routine included circuit training. Circuit training consisted of doing ten push-ups, followed by running up the seven flights of stairs to the top of the dormitory, running back down, doing ten sit-ups, running up seven flights of stairs and back down, doing another ten pull-ups, running back up seven flights of stairs and back down. This order was repeated until I was sure that I would simply die during one phase or another of the circuit training.

Other mornings included a variety of various strengthening exercises on top of the regular itinerary, and each day after the gymnasium routine it was outdoors for a trot around the countryside, and I do use the term trot loosely. After eighteen weeks of morning physical training, I think the recruits were morphed into deer with all of the miles run culminating in the ten-mile graduation run. The physical training never slacked off as the school wore on; it only increased. Completing the ten-mile graduation run instilled great confidence. That training paid off handsomely and prepared the new troopers for what was to come. The roadwork of a trooper is demanding, dangerous and if a mistake is made, it can be deadly. Potentially deadly results awaited the trooper that became complacent or out of shape. This lesson was reinforced in every topic covered in the trooper recruit school.

Water Safety. Water safety focused on perfecting swimming strokes because in Michigan you are never more than six miles from a body of water. Drowning victims could be anticipated during my career. Surprisingly, arrests in the water were common enough to be taught by the instructional staff. And as always, a trooper could end up in the water from a variety of mishaps and need to draw upon the ability to save oneself or a family member. I thought of my brother saving me and knew I had to master this skill. To make sure the lesson of never giving up worked its way into the Water Safety classes, wind sprints were common and were repeated with each blow of that dreaded whistle until the recruits could barely pull themselves from the pool (I mean training tank. When the plans for the new State Police Academy were first submitted to the Legislature for approval, they were denied as it was thought that a "swimming pool" was an unnecessary luxury. The name was changed to "training tank" and the Legislature promptly approved the new academy plans).

Then there was the treading water exercise (while holding heavy bricks above our heads) to help recruits learn to save themselves if they found themselves in the water. Lap swimming perfected strokes used to save drowning victims and the troopers themselves. Recruits swam under water for distances that seemed like an eternity. Surface dives were taught, along with other water skills, which were practiced until they became second nature. We were taught to "throw, row and go" in that order. The first, and preferred, water rescue technique to employ was to throw some type of floating item (life ring, rope, anti-freeze bottle, or spare tire, anything that might support the drowning person). If that didn't work, then we were instructed to obtain a boat and row out to the person. If all else failed, then and only then, were we instructed to "go" and attempt a swimming rescue.

As all those past rumors predicted, the culminating exercise in the water was saving a training staff member who was "drowning" but fought like a wildcat. I was both surprised and grateful that the death swim had met its Waterloo before my academy class and I did not have to experience that much-talked of event. The lessons in holds and releases were invaluable and all of that physical conditioning made the difference in subduing the drowning, frantic, fighting victim. Thankfully we did not have to endure the additional swim staff jumping in to join the fray, as we rescued the drowning victim, like so many past schools had to do. The huge lesson learned here was that to panic in the water is to die in the water. Remaining calm and using the skills at the academy would ensure the best chance of a successful outcome.

I was practicing treading water one day when I suddenly felt that awful dread of impending harm (the police officer's sixth sense) just before I was hit by an instructor, Trooper Marshall, jumping off of the diving board. He dropped onto my back with his 200 plus pound frame, wrapped his arms and legs around my arms and legs, and we went down thirteen feet to the bottom of the training tank. Panic engulfed me from suddenly being driven to the bottom of the pool without any warning. When I panicked, any conscious thought about how to get the "drowning victim" off of my back was lost somewhere in my memory banks. With no available air and a great deal of water between me and the surface of the pool, I pushed my panic aside, and the training I had been given took over. I used the release techniques to pry his fingers, hands, and legs off of me, take control of him and I towed him to the edge of the tank "saving" him.

His smile was barely discernable on my job well done. I had not seen any other recruits given this impromptu test. I later surmised that he must have felt that he needed to know if I could do what was necessary and I had responded as trained to his satisfaction. He has now passed on from his peaceful retirement to a better life far from this world, but I'm still grateful to him for the tough lesson he taught me that day in the pool. From him I learned to overcome my fear, dig deep inside myself to find that mental toughness, and to use my skills to prevail. I never had to use these water safety skills as a trooper, although many other troopers did. I did use them off-duty to save more than one drowning victim, my nephew in a swimming pool, my son Andrew from our pond, as well as myself once in a canoe/fishing mishap. The lessons learned (once again) were to stay calm, think, do whatever is necessary to resolve the emergency and survive.

Firearms. We shot thousands of rounds of ammunition. We didn't just shoot. We were given excellent instruction on *how* to shoot. Firearms instructors repeatedly reminded us to watch the sight alignment on our weapons, use proper breathing techniques, use proper finger control on the trigger, and follow-through until the shot broke. These were all essential lessons in being able to put bullets where they were intended to go. We shot with our strong hand and we shot with our weak hand (in case we were wounded in our dominant arms). We shot standing, lying down, from cover, and out in the open. We shot after we were forced to run to make us tired which mimicked how we might find ourselves on the road. We shot from the draw from our holsters. We shot rifles and shotguns.

The instructors cared deeply for each recruit and gave their very hearts and souls to help us become the best shots we could. Shooting was one of those skills that when you needed it, you needed it desperately, because at that point, lives were in danger of being lost. However, it was one of the skills that police officers rarely used on the road, so quarterly practice was essential to maintain those skills. Our instructors Lieutenant Bernie, Sergeant Les, and Sergeant Tom, excelled in bringing out the very best in each recruit.

Defensive Tactics. Defensive tactics involved many skills including both defensive as well as offensive maneuvers. We learned to parry a knife thrust aside to avoid being stabbed, then quickly follow up to subdue the suspect and how to handle guns in a similar fashion. We practiced removing a driver who refused to come out upon command. Boxing lessons were helpful but to be used as a last resort because the bones in a fist smashed up against a suspect's bony face can break fingers and knuckles, disabling an officer. Skills like suspect takedowns, handcuffing, the use of collapsible batons, and impromptu weapon use (a chair, bottle, anything) were drilled into our heads. Though we never had them, today's Troopers are outfitted with Tasers reducing the need for physically subduing suspects. Controversial in some circles, they do stop dangerous suspects without the need to use firearms or to inflict physical injuries, thereby benefiting both the officers and the suspects.

Extra-Curricular Activities. Prior to being accepted into the academy, I had already reenlisted with the Michigan National Guard, and I had applied for and been selected to attend the Officer Candidate School (OCS) to become a commissioned officer in the National Guard. This training consisted of a two-week session, which I had completed, one weekend per month, and then a final two-week session all of which involved grueling physical and academic training, similar to the training at the State Police Academy. Rather than rest on the weekend as were instructed by the state police instructors, I endured this additional training. It was intense, difficult and I was subjected to much of the same training we were experiencing in the state police academy. I guess I was just too dumb to quit the National Guard or maybe just too patriotic.

As a result, I was away from my family a great deal of the time. Each weekend when I returned home from the academy, I embraced my wife for what seemed like an eternity. My wife and I would talk during the weekend about what she had done that week, and I would tell her about my training, trying to make it less brutal, so she wouldn't worry too much. Sometimes she would quiz me on the concepts I was trying to learn, other times, we would fall asleep, exhausted but excited at the prospect of my graduation.

Graduation. Graduation Day was magical. Graduation from recruit school was an emotional, exciting family event. Grandparents,

parents, spouses, and children filled the academy gymnasium. The highlight of this event occurred when the Governor of Michigan gave the commencement speech thanking each recruit for their dedication and decision to serve the citizens of Michigan. My wife was proud of me, as were all of the spouses of the other recruits. My mother Jean, and my father Dale, proudly watched me throughout the graduation ceremony. I saw the pride they were feeling for their son, as they could not stop smiling as they watched me. They had raised me well, instilling manners, a strong sense of honesty, and the drive to overcome all obstacles to succeed. In turn, I was proud of them, but I knew I would never be able to repay them for their sacrifices and all that they had done for me. Their presence was my biggest reward that day.

The morning before graduation was the ten-mile graduation run, which is the culmination of a series of tests that examined every aspect of each recruit. There had been over 3,000 applicants seeking to be troopers in the 92nd Michigan State Police Trooper Recruit School. Of the class of 86 who started the academy, 52 graduated. I was one of them. After all of those years of trying to be selected to attend the state police academy, after each grueling day in the academy, of wanting to quit to make it all stop, I had survived it all and I had made it. I was a MICHIGAN STATE POLICE TROOPER.

At the graduation ceremony 52 recruits swore to uphold the laws of the State of Michigan and of the United States. Each was handed a badge and sworn in as a probationary trooper. When the Colonel placed my badge in my hand, I instantly saw the word TROOPER and 248, my badge number. On my badge I also saw a familiar word that I had first seen as a young man on the trooper's car who responded to handle my mother's bat call, "TUEBOR." And as we learned in the State Police academy, that Latin word means "I WILL DEFEND." It was beyond my ability to comprehend at that moment, at that time that I had finally made it. As a final confidence builder, a song entitled "Blue Diamonds," written by Michigan native Sean Ryan and set to a video that overviews the mission of the Michigan State Police, was played for the recruits and their guests.

The State Police Academy had reiterated what my parents had instilled in all of their children, and which was honed by the U.S. Army training. Nothing valuable in life is free or easy. Achieving something really important and worthwhile requires hard work and perseverance. The transformative lesson to learn is that each of us has much more mental and bodily strength than we know. As my parents told me, and I told my children, it is life's difficult challenges that reveal to you just how much you actually possess if you never quit trying.

Within two or three days, I realized that the protective environment of the academy was now behind me. As a new trooper, I started down that path travelled by so many before me since the establishment of Michigan State Police on April 19, 1917. I would no longer participate in scenarios, but I would now participate in real life situations calling on all of my skills, physical ability, judgment, knowledge and training. There are no do-overs on the road like there were in the police academy training scenarios. Mistakes can become deadly. As of 2014 there have been 52 Michigan State Police Troopers who have lost their lives in the line of duty. One of those would prove to be my future partner. Life under these circumstances became very real, very fast. The transformation from civilian to trooper symbolized by graduation day was truly underway.

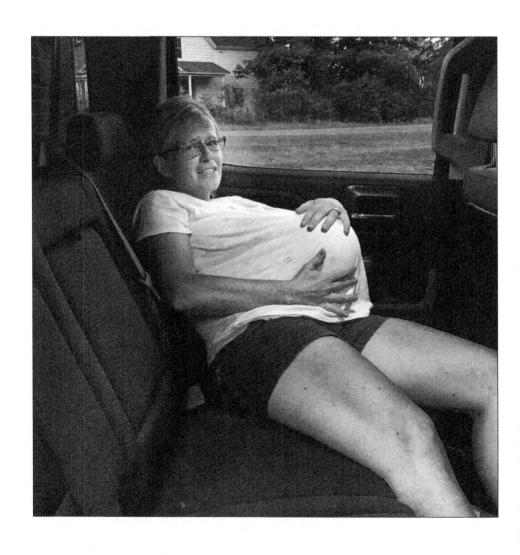

9

PROBATION

New troopers were fully vested with police authority, but were on probation for their first year from their date of hire (now new trooper probation extends for 18 months). We had a laundry list of experiences that we had to participate in as part of our probation: attend an autopsy, make a felony arrest, work with the detectives, use the post camera on a real crime scene, make a plaster cast of a tire print, lift latent fingerprints from a crime scene, roll a set of inked fingerprints from a suspect (they now use a live-scan imaging machine), watch the crime lab personnel analyze the evidence we had collected and submitted so we knew what they could do for us and our investigations, and on and on and on. The real life of a trooper was just beginning for me.

Oh Baby! It was my first week at the Northville Post, also called Post 21, on 7 Mile Road in Northville Township, which was located in the Detroit Metropolitan area. (Post 21 has since been relocated to Oak Park). I was told to drive the powerful police car, a Plymouth Fury 440, so my training officer, Trooper Mike, could see if I had what it took to make it off of probation. It was evening and it was starting to get dark. As we drove through the city of Livonia, a car was stopped on the side of the road with its emergency flashers blinking. Had they hit a deer (yes there were deer in the city) or did they have a flat tire or some other calamity? I was already thinking like a police officer, anticipating what I was about to get into before it exploded in my face. As I stopped behind the car and activated the emergency lights, a middle-aged woman burst out of the driver's door shrieking at us something that sounded like, "Baaaaaaaby. Or did she say, "Maaaaaaaaybe?" My partner was already out of the car running up to the back seat of the woman's car.

His eyes were trained into the back seat when the woman grabbed me by the shirt sleeve and screamed into my ear, "My daughter's having a BABY!"

I too ran and looked to the back seat of the woman's car. Yep, her daughter was obviously very pregnant and in a great deal of pain.

My mind quickly replayed the first aid training we had received using training dolls. There was also that very graphic movie of an actual childbirth on wide-screen showing every detail an officer would ever need to know about childbirth. My mind was replaying all that could go wrong, a breach presentation, a prolapsed umbilical cord, fetal distress, and other scary and bad things that can happen during childbirth threatening the life of the baby and the mother. I was suddenly snapped back to reality as I heard my training officer screaming at me to open the back door of our patrol car. The mother's back seat looked like someone had just dumped a bucket of water all over it. Oh, the mother's water had broken. Birth was imminent.

Were we going to deliver the baby on the side of the road, right here, right now? One look at my partner answered that question without a doubt. He told me to drive as he had already loaded the mother into our back seat and he was sliding into the front passenger's seat shouting for me to hightail it to St. Mary's Hospital in Livonia. I drove like a banshee asking him for directions, as I was new to this strange city. Directions came back erratically as he shared his attention between the soon-to-be-mother and my panic driving at speeds that made the hair stand up on the back of my neck. It took less than five minutes to reach the emergency room. They were ready for the mother as my training officer had enough sense to radio the Post and have them call the hospital to alert them of our (and the baby's) impending arrival.

It was less than five minutes after our skidding arrival at the hospital emergency room that the beautiful new baby arrived to greet the world. We left and went on with our business as though these things were a regular occurrence. The next day we received a call from the mother thanking us for helping her in her time of need. We stopped at the hospital just before she was discharged and saw her smiling with her newborn in her arms. The feeling was hard to describe. I knew we did a good job and I felt reinforcement in my decision to become a trooper. I wonder to this day if my high-speed driving helped hasten the arrival of that young man.

Single officer patrol was assigned when I was deemed ready by my Senior Officer (now called an FTO, or Field Training Officer), who closely monitored my every move. My senior officer documented such things as whether I selected the proper location and patrol car positioning on violator car stops, how effective my interview techniques with suspects were, if I handled evidence properly, and a whole host of other activities. After that, there were still hurdles to jump. The first was an interview by the District Commander who held the rank of Captain. Probing questions were asked with correct answers required promptly and succinctly. I also had to complete continuing education involving readings and answering many questions on all topics of study. Finally at the end of that year of probation I was a full-fledged Michigan State Police Trooper. My dream had been realized. As the U.S. Marines say, "Always earned, never given." The Michigan State Police subscribe to that same philosophy. That is why it is such a great honor for every academy graduate to be handed a state trooper badge as a mark of achieving the position of Trooper, with its mark of pride and competence.

I was now working single officer patrol. I made my own decisions and I lived with my own mistakes trying to learn something new each day. I helped many in the process, and my enforcement efforts hurt others who chose to do wrong. Sometimes I wanted a do-over but there is no such thing in real life working as a police officer. But the next time I encountered a similar situation I used what I had previously learned to arrive at a better resolution which made me a better police officer.

On a personal note, I learned that a successful day was going home safely to my family at the end of my shift. Some of my fellow troopers were deprived of that simple privilege having given the ultimate sacrifice for those they had sworn to protect. Their families paid a similar price for the rest of their lives when their trooper failed to return to them for the last time. Living with the constant knowledge that life is precarious compelled me to think seriously about my priorities and values. I like to believe that the sacrifices I made and those I was prepared to make led me to a deeper appreciation of all humanity and to insights about human behavior and motivations. I share some of those experiences in hopes the reader may benefit from what I learned to help in their life's journey, whether working as a police officer or in an entirely unrelated line of work.

PART

4

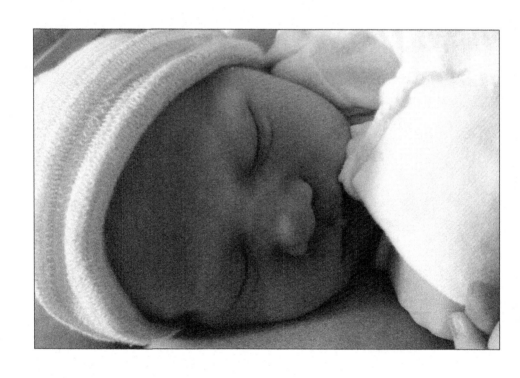

10

THE DELIVERY ROOM

It's interesting how fate plays into many things in life. I was fortunate to be present for the birth of my first two children, Erin and Ben. That experience was one no father should miss. The memory of seeing my own children enter this world is something I will always treasure. Those are events burned into my brain that always bring a smile to me when I think of them. Both of my first two children were born by cesarean section and I knew my third would be born the same way. My third child, Andrew, almost had to do it without me at my wife's side to welcome him into this world because my duties as a state trooper nearly precluded me being present.

I had been dispatched to a barricaded gunman call. It started as a domestic violence call where the suspect assaulted his wife and fortunately she was lucky enough to get out of the house with only minor injuries. Her husband had holed up in their house with a rifle. During these calls, it was difficult to fathom how someone could hurt the people he loved, but I had seen enough to feel this was all too common. This man had decided to extend his violence beyond his family, again for reasons that most people couldn't comprehend. He of course threatened to shoot any police officer on sight. We had surrounded the house with officers from various police agencies trying to coax the husband out before he or a police officer was shot or killed. I was crouched behind my patrol car trying very hard not to expose myself to the potential shooter when I received a radio call from the post advising me that my wife thought she might be going into labor and I should call her when I was able to do so. (There were no cell phones in those days so getting to a telephone was a bit problematic!)

Under the stress of the standoff, my defense mechanisms had caused my brain, eyes, ears and nose to focus narrowly on the threat at hand. I could not fully contemplate lesser issues (I know my wife didn't think this was a less important issue in her time of pain and impending childbirth!), but when it was all over, I would have been disappointed to miss the birth of my child. My mind worked double time to find a solution to both problems, assist the other officers in disarming the gunman and find a way out safely to attend to my family. After my wife had made her third frantic call to the state police post, I was advised by the desk sergeant that he was trying to locate another officer to replace me. Finally, another back-up officer arrived to take my place. I was able to jump into my patrol car and back out of the suspect's driveway as my new probationary trooper partner, fresh from the academy, hopped into the passenger seat without either of us getting shot as we exposed ourselves to the suspect's view in making our getaway.

As I raced toward my waiting wife, I was advised that she had called again, and in a bit of a raised voice (which is a gross understatement), the desk sergeant notified me that I needed to get my wife to the hospital immediately as she was going into labor. With cesarean section births, going into labor can be very dangerous for the mother and baby and presented a true medical emergency. The drive was typical of an emergency run, red light and siren with white knuckles gripping the steering wheel. As I slid into my driveway, my wife was waiting not too patiently. As it was July 4th around 11:30 pm, I wondered if my son would be born on the 4th of July.

"I'm going to give birth now, get me to the hospital," my wife commanded.

"Just hold on, we will be there in three minutes," I almost pleaded.

"I've got your kids in the patrol car, let's go," my excited probationary partner managed to say.

Erin and Ben had their footie pajamas on. They looked nervous from the excitement but fresh-from-the-bath cute. I helped my very pregnant wife into the front seat. We left my driveway the same way we had entered it, fast and loud. St. Mary's Hospital was only a few miles away but the pressure to get us all there safely and quickly dominated all my thoughts. I constantly looked from side to side, checking my rearview and side mirrors, changing lanes, making sure traffic was clear.

"I'll be right behind you, as soon as I park the car," I told my wife as I dropped her off at the hospital emergency entrance.

"Hurry up," she managed between contractions.

By the time my partner and I parked the car and grabbed my two young children to follow my wife into the ER, I was told by the operating room nurse, "If you want to see your newest son born, you need to get into the operating room STAT!" My adrenaline was high, and I was overtaken with concern for my wife and with excitement at finally seeing the baby we had been waiting for.

At close to midnight, the usually busy hallways were quiet and empty. As I ran down the darkened hallway I dropped my gun belt, shirt, and bullet-resistant vest for my partner to secure as he followed behind, knowing those items would not be allowed into the operating room. I took one look back and saw my new partner picking up my equipment and leading my two children down the hall, their little feet pumping trying to keep up, and my partner grabbing everything I was dropping as I ran to the changing room and pulled on my hospital gown and mask.

Once I was ushered into the operating room to take up my usual position shoulder-to-shoulder with the physician, I saw that he had already made the first incision. With my police mind fully engaged, I couldn't resist seeing the similarities of a cesarean section to that of an autopsy. With the former the outcome was much happier. After a few minutes my son was taking his first gasp of air and looking at the new world before him.

"Waaaaaaaaaaaaaaaaaah," my new son proclaimed as I proudly looked on seeing another miracle of birth.

My son was born just after midnight so he was not a 4th of July baby after all. No doubt my fault as I was delayed by the barricaded gunman in getting my wife to the hospital. I was a very proud dad indeed. Mom was excited with her newest healthy baby. As fate would have it, this young man would grow up to be a trooper like his dad. I still suspect the siren, lights, fast driving and excitement in getting him to the hospital as he was contemplating his impending birth instilled into his blood a desire to follow a career as a trooper.

The birth of my youngest son as I came off of a dangerous barricaded gunman call reinforced my need to look for the lessons in everyday activities and calls for assistance as I was seeing similar themes over and over again. I once again realized that I needed to examine and incorporate these lessons into my daily life to allow me to continue to grow as not just as a trooper, but as a person. I continued to make better decisions by noticing and then using what I had learned. Patti and I celebrated this new life and the love of our family knowing that the only way I could enjoy them was to constantly learn, pay attention to what was around me, and respond-either with caution and compassion as a trooper or with love as a person.

11

THE DRUNK DRIVER

He hit our car without any notice. I was working with Trooper Valerie, the new trooper at our post. It felt like a Howitzer round had hit us and exploded. At 3:00 a.m. we had only seen one other car on the road in the last two hours. In the backseat we had the drunk driver we had just arrested on the Michigan Avenue bypass in the Ypsilanti Post area.

Earlier, we had followed him out of the Northville Post area as he weaved his way to some unknown destination. While he sat in the back of the patrol car and I sat in the driver's seat next to Trooper Valerie, I filled in the usual forms with the drunken driver's answers to the first few questions. I asked him if he would take the Breathalyzer test. He stared at me as if in a fog, his red eyes blood-shot and watery and told me in no uncertain terms where I could shove my test. His clothes were disheveled and he sported a small stain from vomiting onto himself before we had stopped him, matched by a small spot of urine in the crotch of his pants. These were typical indicators of a very drunk driver. His responses had been slow as if he was trying to understand a foreign language. He was tired and he needed sleep badly. He started to mumble something I could not understand. BAM! Brilliant, intense, searing, blinding white light, with an ear shattering crash of metal exploding around us, then nothing.

Was I dead? When I realized that I was conscious and not dead, a strange sight engulfed me. Small squares of glass were moving in slow motion with some seemingly hanging mid-air and others covering every flat surface as though a sudden snowstorm had deposited a blanket of glassy snow inside of our patrol car. The patrol car driver's door was now only inches from me and it looked like a twisted mosaic of metal. I could not hear anything and I felt like someone had stuffed a pound of cotton in each of my ears. My mind was having difficulty grasping what my eyes saw. I fought to understand how I was just talking with someone in our backseat and now this police car had suddenly been transformed into a broken, twisted mass of steel.

I saw a car with a smashed right front fender slowing to a stop a quarter of a mile ahead of us illuminated by our flashing overhead emergency lights. Debris from the car littered the road between our patrol car and the suspect's now disabled car. It seemed like I was trying to run but the fog was so thick I just could not break through it. My partner's soft female voice came slowly, peacefully, to me as if floating in a foggy meadow pulling me from that tranquil place back to reality.

"Are you okay?" she asked.

"I think so, what happened" I asked, groggy from the impact.

"A drunk just smashed into our patrol car," my partner said.

Slowly I started to regain my senses. Rage engulfed me as I realized that another drunk driver, the only other car on the road in the last two hours, had just crashed into us and then kept driving without stopping. The drunk driver was drawn to our emergency lights like the proverbial moth to the flame and had headed straight for our car crossing three traffic lanes. He had to have been traveling

55 mph when he slammed into the back of our patrol car. The impact was tremendous.

"I'll get him," I told my partner.

I heaved on my door to get at the second drunk driver of the night, but it was welded shut by the devastating collapse of the patrol car when the other car had slammed into us. My mind just could not connect the damage to the car and my inability to open the door.

The drunk in the back seat let out a series of blood-curdling screams and wailed, "My neck is broken, it's broken."

His screams continued while my partner and I tried to do many things before more bad things happened to us. Protect the back seat drunk driver, check the drunk driver who hit us, put out flares so we wouldn't get hit by any other cars, check to see if gasoline that would explode if we lit a flare was leaking from our car. Are we injured? Too much too fast! Get moving, get things done, does the radio work? Why does my neck and back hurt so badly? Is my partner okay? She said she was all right, but I wondered if she was really aware of her condition given the impact that we had survived. Anybody have blood running from any injuries? Call for an ambulance for the back seat drunk. Wreckers, other troopers, what other help do we need? That all reeled through my fog-clouded mind in the first 2-3 seconds after I regained consciousness.

"I'll get him, check on the drunk in the back seat," she said.

My partner jumped out of our car and ran off after the other drunk driver immediately sensing that if I had gotten to him he may not have fared too well during the arrest.

I also knew I might not have been able to keep my emotions in check like we were taught in the academy. She was the one who took the low-key approach to most situations when we worked together so I was secretly pleased she was the one to arrest that other drunk driver. I grabbed an emergency blanket and fashioned a cervical collar to immobilize the back seat drunk's neck to protect him against spinal cord injury. I heard the welcome sirens approaching and saw an ambulance and back-up troopers arriving. I helped load the first drunk into the ambulance. He was heavy and still screaming about his broken neck and I saw blood flowing from his head. The smell of intoxicants was in the air. Yes, you can smell alcohol in the flowing blood from a drunk driver at an accident scene.

It was very dark and the emergency lights from all of the vehicles wavered eerily off of the bridge overpass near where we were parked. Photographs and measurements were being handled by other responding troopers. My partner and I answered questions directed to us from our sergeant who had rushed to the scene to make sure his troopers were okay.

He asked the usual questions like, "How did this happen?" and "Are you two okay?" The rest of the questions were just a blur of words.

Looking at the patrol car I saw that from the middle of the trunk to the left front fender, the car was crushed in to form a near straight line. Luckily, the drunk in our back seat had been sitting on the passenger side of our patrol car. Patrol car 21-16, a Chevrolet Malibu, had suffered K injuries (fatal) and was slowly towed away to the scrap yard.

Our sergeant ordered us to get checked out at the emergency department at St. Joseph Hospital in Ypsilanti. We drove ourselves there and waited as neck pain, back pain, arm pain and other strange tingling feelings in our arms and legs continued. My mind was still fuzzy. A cursory check from the E.R. physician concluded we probably had minor concussions, bumps and bruises, but nothing worth further treatment.

The sun was coming up and we were off shift. My body had not stopped aching, my eyes were tired from the night shift, so I changed into my civilian clothes at the post and drove home.

"How was work?" my wife having just gotten up for work routinely asked

"Ok, we had our car totaled out from under us by a drunk driver."

"Are you ok?" she asked.

"Sure," I said.

"How is Trooper Valerie?"

"She's ok too. We both got checked out at St. Joe Hospital in Ypsilanti and the doctor said we will be sore, but we should be okay"

I drifted off to sleep while she was still quizzing me. My wife took the information in, too used to such news without being afforded all of the minor details. She wondered how close to not having me return home for good it really was. She shrugged her shoulders, quietly closed the door and left for work. No need for her to worry, I was safely home once again. Little else mattered at this time and in this place.

Many months later when we appeared for court on the drunk driver we had arrested and placed in the back seat of the patrol car, he was sitting there all dressed up in a sport coat and tie. His hair was neatly trimmed and he was clean shaven. Obviously he had not been drinking this time. He certainly had not been so well groomed when we had arrested him. No vomit on the front of his shirt or urine spot on his trousers from peeing his pants. His shirt was now tucked in. He was coherent, alert and polite. No hint of, "No I'm not taking your fucking breath test!" It was all, "Yes, your Honor," and "Yes, Sir Judge." Because the second drunk driver had hit us at a most fortunate time for him, before the drunk driver in our back seat had a chance to change his mind and submit to our breath test, the defense attorney demanded the case be dropped.

The question to me from the defense attorney was, "Trooper, have you ever allowed a person arrested for drunk driving to change their mind after initially refusing to take the breath test and then allow them to do so?"

"Yes," I answered truthfully.

"Was my client given that same opportunity in this case?"

"No, because another drunk driver hit us before we had a chance to do so."

The judge looked down at all of us, ever so slightly shook his head sadly, and simply uttered, "Case dismissed." But for the circumstances of the accident, the drunk in the back seat could have been the one to hit us or some other family and cause their untimely destruction. "Don't take your cases too seriously" was the wisdom handed out at the academy. Tell that to my wife had I been seriously injured or killed by the drunk driver. Or tell it to some other family member unfortunate enough to have gotten in the drunk driver's way requiring me or some other unlucky police officer to deliver yet another death message. The drunk driver shook the hand of his defense attorney and slipped him his attorney fee with a thick wad of $100 dollar bills and they parted ways. The attorney smiled slightly, folded and then stuffed the cash into his pants pocket. The attorney had already forgotten this case and mentally switched to the next one.

I never learned what happened to the second drunk driver that hit our car. I was never called to court so I simply assumed that he pled to some offense, or his case may have been dismissed as well.

The cycle keeps repeating itself and life goes on, for everyone but the victims who are left in the carnage caused by these drunk drivers. I left the courtroom and drove to the Post. I put on my uniform. After loading my patrol car, I decided to turn left out of the Post parking lot not knowing what might be awaiting me in that direction. What might I have encountered during my shift had I had decided to turn right out of the Post driveway? I would never know the answer to that question. Back on the road again and into harm's way. I shifted in my seat to ease the lower back pain from the accident. The pain would crop up from time to time, and it would never fully go away. I suspected not many people out there even noticed or cared that I was back out there on the road trying my best to protect them from dangers they didn't even know existed which was a good thing. They should not have to worry about unknown and unseen danger every day. They had their lives to live without such worries.

I was learning to recognize those things I had the ability to change and to realize there are things that I had no control over and could not change, and I was gaining the wisdom to know the difference.

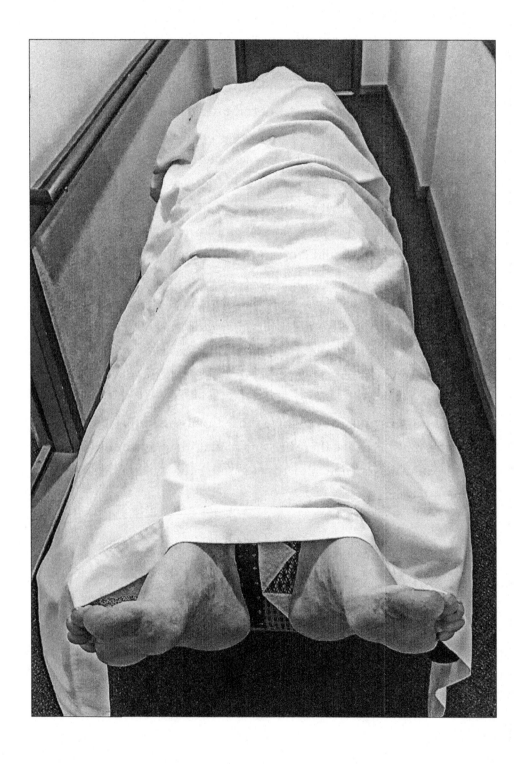

12

THE AUTOPSY

As part of new trooper training in the first year after graduating from the training academy, we needed to attend an autopsy to learn what evidence could be gained by the medical examiner carving up a human body and analyzing the little bits and pieces. The fatal motor vehicle accident that created the need for the autopsy I was assigned to observe was initially investigated by a trooper from our post. This fatal accident involved an AMC Gremlin that was struck in the rear by a Cadillac, caught fire, and burned the front seat passenger to death.

Before the autopsy began I walked into a side room deep within the Wayne County Morgue located in the City of Detroit. I was startled to see so many bodies on stainless steel gurneys. My attention was drawn to a gurney where I saw a young man staring at me with his one remaining eye. At first I thought someone was playing a joke on me. The face did not have that pale, gazeless look most dead bodies had. This face was alive, the eye looking at me as though from a living human being with deep dark skin vibrant and full colored instead of death-induced dullness. As I looked closer I could see that a shotgun blast had carefully and with some exacting precision removed a grapefruit-sized portion from the front of his face directly to the back of his head as cleanly cut as if it had been done with all the skill a seasoned surgeon could muster. He and his friend were playing with a shotgun when it accidently went off while pointed at his face, the medical examiner explained to me when I asked him about the demise of this young man.

My mind took a very vivid photograph of that face at that moment and permanently stored it in my brain to be reviewed over and over again thousands of times over the years. Each time that photograph is taken out of storage and viewed by my mind it is as if I were looking at that young man all over again, staring at me and asking for help. I wanted to help but there was nothing I could do for him. Many other gurneys contained once living, breathing, happy people with family members who loved them. Now they were gone forever, lying there, waiting to be disposed of in due time.

"Come on, we don't have all day." The medical examiner ushered all five of us into the examination room. The dark, shapeless form on the stainless table was about a third less in size than an average human body. The appearance was that of a marshmallow that had been set ablaze over a campfire until it was thoroughly charred, I thought morbidly. The main form was accompanied by two small twigs protruding from where arms should have been. No hands, no arms, no skin, just twigs, and the smell. The smell was not unlike a pork roast on a grill that had been left a little too long and been charred. That smell permeated the room and clung to my clothes. The bottom of the shape also contained two stumps that also resembled charred marshmallow. No feet, no legs, no knees, no skin, just stumps. The small bulb-like protrusion that had once been a neck, head and face was crumbly and now consisted of black ash. No hair, no ears, no lips, no face. It was very difficult to recognize the figure as that of a former human being.

When the coroner rolled the form to one side, a crunching sound could be heard as the black marshmallow crumbled off in small pieces. Only a small patch of actual flesh-tone skin on the right buttock area of the body remained.

"What does that mean?" he asked.

"Well, um, I, not sure," I offered.

"It indicates she was sitting on the seat with her seat belt on so she stayed in her seat following the rear-end collision. The seat protected her skin on her one buttock during the fire," he instructed.

The coroner then cut away some of the black around the bulb-like protrusion that had once been a head. The scalpel cleanly cut through the black ash to the skull bone from under the chin area up and around the skull. Next he took his small circular saw and cut a small "V" shape in the top of the skull bone. It was explained that the top of the skull would be replaced after the autopsy and the "V" would help hold the skullcap in place, not unlike the top of a Halloween jack-o-lantern. The skullcap was removed and we were asked what the brownish material between the front of the skull and the Dura (membrane between the skull bone and brain) was.

"Um, well, I dunno," one of the other troopers said.

"It's cooked blood" the coroner said. "Cooked blood turns from red to the brownish color with the application of heat from the car fire. It tells me that she struck her head on the dashboard when the car was struck from behind because the blood is in the front of the skull. The blood pooled there so she was alive for some time after the car struck the rear of the car she was sitting in. If she didn't have her seat belt on, she would have gone through the windshield and not remained in the car." He removed and weighed the brain, cutting slices to be subjected to further microscopic analysis.

The coroner used a large bolt cutter-like device to cut the ribs at the sternum to expose the lungs, heart and other organs. A nauseating stench emanated from inside of the shapeless form as the open chest cavity released the stored putrefied gasses. One new trooper rushed from the room vomiting as he ran. Strangely that smell of fresh, burnt pork engulfed us.

"See the color of the lungs? What does that tell us?" the coroner asked. We all stood gasping for air, but no one offered a response. "Ok, I can't wait all day for an answer. The bright red color of the lungs indicates they contain carbon monoxide. It tells me that she was alive and breathing in carbon monoxide from the car fire for some time before the fire killed her. Due to her head striking the dashboard, she may or may not have been conscious but she was alive for some time period during the fire. If she was conscious she experienced tremendous pain from the fire that burned her body while she was alive."

When the autopsy was completed, we jumped in the patrol car and drove from Detroit to Farmington Hills where we had a favorite restaurant. The lunch special was Charburgers. We were starving as it was already past noon and we began eating the burgers and chips with gusto, discussing the autopsy and all that we had learned when it suddenly hit all of us at once. We all stopped, looked at each other, and burst into uncontrollable laughter. Tears ran from our eyes and we nearly choked on our Charburgers. Other patrons stared at us. We realized that the Charburgers looked and smelled just like the marshmallow we had just watched being dissected during the autopsy. That sick police humor! Later I would learn this is a normal defensive mechanism that kicks in to protect and allow emergency responders to deal with the depravity seen on the job.

While such reactions may seem utterly offensive to others, I learned that they are completely human and natural. Black humor acts as a defense mechanism to allow responders to deal with things the average person would not be able to deal with and to put aside what is seen in order to accomplish the unsavory and often disgusting tasks we were confronted with on a regular basis. We intend no ill will toward the unfortunate victim of the fatal car crash. In fact, we all felt terrible for laughing after we thought about it. A strange mix of emotions engulfed us as we all struggled with what we had seen and how we had reacted. This was to be only the beginning of the hard lessons we would later learn.

We would see such ghastly scenes too many times again. It is not normal for most people to have to deal with such horrors involving other human beings, but as troopers we had to take control and perform our duties in spite of what we had to deal with. I recalled the rotting bodies my dad and uncle saw at Dachau during World War II and understood the impact of what they had seen and how it must have altered them. I only hope those not having to deal with such things in some small way understand when they see responders acting in a manner that may initially seem inappropriate. I am willing to bet that most of these responders will have to relive what they have seen, the unimaginable, in their dreams over and over again wishing they could have changed the outcome and saved the victims. I know that I am visited regularly by this woman on more nights that I care to remember.

Later while attending the criminal law class at the Detroit College of Law, I was discussing class material with a woman seated next to me in preparation for questions from the professor that were sure to come. As an example regarding some point in our readings for the class, I related my experience regarding the crash of the AMC Gremlin and the Cadillac. The talk turned to the autopsy of the woman burned up in the crash with some of the gory details. Suddenly, my classmate drew in a deep breath, her face went stone cold, and tears started running down her cheeks in torrents. I thought she must be a very sensitive woman and I immediately felt bad sharing this gruesome story with her.

After a short time when she regained her composure somewhat, she tried to tell me something but her voice came out all garbled and I had difficulty understanding. She again tried to regain her composure. I leaned in closer and tried again to understand what she was saying. Finally, she said a very quiet voice staring into my eyes, "I was driving that Gremlin when it was struck in the back by that Cadillac. The woman whose autopsy you just described was my aunt." The air left my lungs in a sudden gush, my face turned bright red, and I didn't know what to say to this poor woman to relieve the suffering I had just caused her. I felt so sorry for making her relive such a tragic event. I had just been trying to share an experience to make a point with a topic for class. I kicked myself over and over during class thinking, "What are the chances of such a random encounter and in my causing so much pain to this woman?"

We are all interconnected, not only in our human condition, but in the webs we weave and interweave with others around us. At a deep level, I knew every person I encountered had a past and a story and connections to other people. The coping mechanism of dark humor was a result of this sense of humanity and it never obliterated that fact. The discussion with my classmate drove this to my core, reinforcing the need to treat everyone with care and understanding.

13

THE DEATH MESSAGE

It was Sunday morning around 7:30 a.m. as I neared the end of my shift. By the looks of the quiet houses, most of the inhabitants were still asleep this early and peaceful Sunday morning. It was very still out and the sun was just peeking over the horizon providing the first rays of light and promising a warm, sunny spring day full of life. The flowers had started to bloom as spring was transitioning into early summer and they flashed their brilliance in every yard in the upscale subdivision. Birds could be heard providing their wake-up calls in the early morning hour announcing the new day. The warm breeze felt good as I drove along slowly after working the midnight shift and the refreshing wind flowed in through my open window. It had not been very busy during my shift and as usual I enjoyed the quiet time experienced when the lonely, dark midnight shift gave way to the dawn of another promising day. Life abounded everywhere, almost.

As I contemplated the end of my shift and a warm bed, the radio call shattered that serene innocence of that morning. I was informed by the police radio that a young college student had been killed only hours before while riding in a car with her friends. She was a first-year student at Central Michigan University, a college about three hours north of the Northville Post. She and some friends had been out on the town drinking and one of the others in the group had been driving while intoxicated and crashed the car into a tree, killing the girl instantly. The only additional information that I was provided was her name and home address, which was just a short distance away. I was then told to deliver that death message to the parents and directed to have the parents call the Mount Pleasant Police Department, who had handled the fatal car accident.

Why me on this beautiful Sunday morning, I wondered. A sick feeling began gnawing in the pit of my stomach. What could I possibly say to the girl's parents when I went to their home? The student wasn't much younger than I was. This was one of the most dreaded calls for service that face police officers, telling a family their loved one has been taken from them, never to be seen again. Although it is a horrible duty to have to perform and humbling for the officer, it can be somewhat rewarding if done with the utmost compassion, helping out wherever possible in a family's time of need to lessen their burden.

The moment I received that call I knew I was about to destroy a family's life. As I drove near the front door of the home with the well-manicured lawn, it was a surreal experience. This was not my first death message and it wouldn't be my last, but they never get easier. If anything, each death message delivered weighs heavier on the mind. It was as if I was driving in a dense, sticky, fog that enveloped me and would not let me pass so I could do my job. My mind reeled. What would I say to the mother and father? Should I just tell them what I knew? Experience told me to break the news somewhat slowly. Then as the reality sank in, provide what few additional details I knew. The rest depended on the family's reaction. I had my plan formulated. I parked my marked blue state police car in their driveway and stepped out. I placed my hat on my head, straightened my tie, and noticed in my rearview mirror that I had a very solemn look on my face. It seemed to be a very long walk to their door, but in reality the door was only some twenty feet away. I could only imagine what it would be like for them when I told them what I had come to their house for so early this Sunday morning.

Even before I could knock on the door, I saw the mother staring at me. She was standing at her doorway evidently having seen me pull into her driveway. She must have watched me putting on my hat and straightening my tie. It was very obvious to me that she immediately knew why I was at her door and dreaded my presence. Her face crumbled before me as I started to raise my hand to ring the doorbell. Clearly she knew the worst nightmare of her entire life had come true. I wasn't entirely prepared for the scream that erupted from this poor mother who spun around and fled from the door before she even had time to open it, possibly hoping if she didn't answer the door this nightmare wouldn't come true.

"No, no, noooooooooooooooooooooooooo," the woman hysterically wailed as she ran away from me standing solemnly at her door. With my heart aching, I wondered how I could help ease her pain but I knew there was very little I could do to help her in her time of unthinkable sorrow.

I stood stock still not sure what I should do. My carefully contemplated plan to break the news to the dead girl's mother and father was irreversibly shattered. The minute or so since I first entered their driveway seemed like hours. Finally a very solemn-faced father painstakingly looked through the glass door straight into my eyes as if to say, "Tell me it's not true." He opened the door in a gesture of duty and respect, all rolled into one. "Please come in." I knew that he really meant it. He knew, but he was valiantly trying to be polite until I could do what I had been sent to do and leave him in peace. He saw that I was not much older than his own daughter with limited experience with such things. I now know he was trying also to help me, the very young trooper at his front door so early on a Sunday morning, who he intuitively knew was not having an easy time delivering the message.

I managed to provide the few scarce details I had been given over the radio so he could make his telephone calls to obtain more information regarding his daughter and to start the unimaginable task of planning her funeral. He so politely thanked me that I could hardly understand how he could be so calm. But I saw it in his eyes, a father's duty. A duty rising out of love for his daughter, and a husband's duty to care for his wife at an unbearable and tragic time. I have never met a finer gentleman in all of my years, before or since. I could never thank him enough for the life lesson that I have carried with me all of these years. He showed me humility, compassion, and steadfastness in the face of the unthinkable, as he cared for others in his own time of need.

"Can I contact anyone for you or assist you in any way?" I asked.

"Thank you Trooper for asking, but I think we can handle it from here." I knew he wanted me to be done with this difficult task. I sensed he wanted to help make my job of delivering this death message easier on me. He simply wanted to close the door so they could start their grieving. I turned and walked out the door pulling it shut behind me on parents who just learned that their daughter had been forever taken from them, wondering how they could possibly "handle it from here."

14

DON'T DO IT!

A favorite Aesop's fable I read early on in my career as a new trooper helped me grow a little quicker than I might otherwise have. It taught me that there are different ways to accomplish any goal. It helped me convince many suspects to admit to their crimes. My past partner, Trooper Valerie, who I later lost in a car crash, also tried to teach me this lesson long before I read this fable, but I failed to realize it at that time. Sometimes I had to learn the same lesson over and over until I finally realized I was being taught something of value to make myself better. It's called "The North Wind and the Sun."

The North Wind boasted of great strength. The Sun argued that there was great power in gentleness.

"We shall have a contest," said the Sun.

Far below, a man traveled a winding road. He was wearing a warm winter coat.

"As a test of strength," said the Sun, "Let us see which of us can take the coat off of that man."

"It will be quite simple for me to force him to remove his coat," bragged the Wind.

The Wind blew so hard, the birds clung to the trees. The world was filled with dust and leaves. But the harder the wind blew down the road, the tighter the shivering man clung to his coat.

Then, the Sun came out from behind a cloud. Sun warmed the air and the frosty ground. The man on the road unbuttoned his coat.

The sun grew slowly brighter and brighter.

Soon the man felt so hot, he took off his coat and sat down in a shady spot.

"How did you do that?" said the Wind.

"It was easy," said the Sun, "I lit the day. Through gentleness I got my way."

I learned from working the road that many more confessions were obtained by treating even the most hardened criminal with a level of respect. Informants are developed by entering their world and simply talking to them. There were times I needed to use my position and authority in my job, but not very often. Most of the time I did my best work by simply being human and treating people with respect. The lesson I had learned proved its worth in a sensitive criminal sexual conduct case.

I had been on the road for five years or so when I received the radio call to contact a family at a trailer park regarding an unknown assault-type problem. When I arrived, I immediately sensed that this situation was worse than usual. The look on the faces of the father and mother was a combination of fear, hatred, and despair. I was politely led into their trailer home. Their words were jumbled and garbled with emotions. Tears flowed from their eyes.

"That old man hurt my daughter," the father said.

"What did he do to her?" I asked as gently as possible.

"He took my daughter and four other girls from this trailer park and molested them," he spoke now with a total lack of emotion, like a man on a mission.

"Our doctor told us that our daughter had reddening of her vagina from some sort of contact," the mother added, barely able to discuss the topic.

I learned that their five-year-old daughter had been sexually molested by a neighbor in the trailer park. It was difficult to listen to what they knew about the sexual assault they had been told by their little girl and the family physician. My heart sank thinking of my own daughter who was nearly the same age. It was unimaginable to think someone could do such things to a young innocent little girl, undoubtedly scarring her for life.

"I will take care of this, Trooper," he said while staring out of his window, motionless.

"Sir, please don't do that. For the sake of your daughter and family, let me handle it," I said trying to reason with his mind that was beyond reason.

The father's face took on a zombie-like demeanor when we sat down at his kitchen table. He looked at me with pained eyes that spoke volumes.

"I'm going to take my shotgun down there and molest him, permanently," the father calmly announced.

At first I thought he was simply trying to let out his emotions or show his protective instincts toward his daughter. As he continued to tell me of his plans I knew he was deadly serious and was mentally preparing himself to kill the man. I knew if I didn't get this case investigated professionally and quickly, the suspect would be dead, the father would be in prison for murder of the suspect, the young daughter would be even more deeply emotionally ravaged, and this family would be destroyed forever.

"I know I cannot fully understand your pain, but this won't solve anything and it will just end up with you going to prison. Your family will have to live their lives without you. Let me handle this for you." I more firmly told him.

"Okay," he muttered.

"Promise me right here and right now, that you will not go anywhere near that man. Promise," I said.

It was as if something snapped in him. He went limp, then looked up at me and said, "Okay, please hurry with your investigation."

"I will get back with you very soon and let you know how my investigation is progressing. If you have any questions or just need to talk, call me any time," I told them and handed each of them my business card.

The little girl's mother walked me out to my patrol car. She told me that she was worried that her husband would try to kill the suspect. I knew there was a strong possibility the father might just do so.

"Promise me that you will call if you think that your husband might go to the suspect's trailer and we will get a car over here right away," I told her.

"I promise that I will, but please hurry. I know my husband will try to, but this is destroying him," she pleaded.

"I will investigate this as quickly as I possibly can," I promised. I knew I had to bring this investigation to a conclusion very soon or there would be multiple suspects and multiple victims to deal with.

I drove directly down to the suspect's trailer. Mark was an old man in his mid-70's who had lost his wife a year before. After he let me in to talk, he told me that he only let little girls from the trailer park into his trailer since boys were troublemakers. I immediately noticed a 24-hour reel-to-reel audio recorder.

"What do you use that recorder for?" I asked him.

"When I have the little girls dance naked for me, I record them and tell them that they are movie stars," he said nervously, his false teeth chattering as he spoke. This explanation was consistent with what I had been told by the young girl and what I would also learn from several of the other victims later.

He told me that the four or five little girls he let into his trailer regularly performed stripteases for him as he let them use his deceased wife's cosmetics to play make-up. As he talked about specifics his false teeth again began to chatter. The computer check revealed that he had never been arrested before in his long life as a bricklayer.

He agreed to submit to a polygraph (commonly known as a lie detector, but in reality the instrument does not detect lies, rather it detects deception). Although the suspect was generally cooperative, he would not admit to penetrating the little girl's vagina to the polygraph examiner. That evidence of a penetration of the little girl's body was needed for a first-degree sexual assault charge; otherwise, only a lesser charge could be proven. A few days after the polygraph examination I went back to his trailer and talked to him about the polygraph results. At first he would not admit to the necessary element of penetration of the little girl, only to touching her in a sexual manner, which would constitute a lesser crime of second-degree sexual assault. My gut emotions wanted me to interrogate him and force him into a confession, but I knew better. That would not work so I decided to use the simple interview approach.

I saw that he had tomatoes growing in his garden behind his trailer. I grew tomatoes so I knew about growing and canning them.

"Mark, how long have you been growing tomatoes?" I asked.

"My whole life. I can them too," he offered.

"Do you use the hot pack or cold pack method for canning them?" I asked using my knowledge and experience with tomatoes.

"Sometimes I hot pack 'em, sometimes I just freeze 'em," he said, somewhat proudly.

We continued to talk about canning tomatoes and he told me stories about the long history with tomatoes and then told me that he really enjoyed doing so. While we talked about the benefits of using the hot pack versus cold pack method of canning tomatoes, I suddenly asked him why he had penetrated the little girl then lied about it to the polygraph operator.

"Mark, the doctors have said that the little girl was penetrated. I can prove that."

"Uh uh," he said.

"What I don't understand is why you did it and then lied about it. It makes you look like you wanted to hurt her," I offered.

"No, no I never wanted to hurt her, but I didn't put it in her," he muttered, looking down at the floor, water welling up in his eyes.

"Then why are you not being truthful? I know you did it. I just need to know what you did." I told him.

His eyes looked straight into mine, his false teeth began to chatter and he suddenly blurted babbling.

"I didn't mean to hurt her, I love those little girls. When they danced naked, I let them use my wife's makeup. I didn't want them to get into trouble with their parents so before they left, I washed up that little girl's groin area, my finger accidently slipped into her vagina, maybe more than once. I didn't mean to hurt her, honest."

"Okay, Mark, I understand," a wave of relief washed over me. I was shocked by his sudden revelation after the very experienced polygraph operator had been unable to find the right button in this suspect to elicit such an admission. I had the evidence to prove the penetration element of this CSC.

Up to this point, the medical examination of the young girl could only establish a reddening of her vagina not necessarily from a sexual assault. The suspect had only used his finger therefore no semen was present for collection and comparison. The victim being so young and totally inexperienced with sexual activity could not articulate exactly what had been done to her by the suspect and she was unable to testify to penetration of her vagina. The other victims were so young and immature that they were unable to provide any statements that could help the case. The recordings of the girls dancing were void of any incriminating evidence and were therefore of no evidentiary value. The results of the polygraph, and even the fact that he took the test, were inadmissible in court. My only chance to prove the element of penetration was the suspect's confession. A wave of relief swept over me at obtaining that admission on the issue of penetration, confirming the results of the earlier medical examination and the victim's vague account of the assault.

I submitted a warrant request and the judge issued the arrest warrant for criminal sexual conduct, first degree. The maximum was imprisonment for life, but with no previous criminal record he would not get that. However at 70 some years old, even a short sentence would in effect be a life sentence for the old man. Within a few days the suspect was arraigned. A week later he pled guilty and was sent to prison for 1-20 years. I later heard that the defendant had been treated very well by the other prisoners and they had given him the name of "Grandpa" in prison. The father was spared of having to take matters in his own hand to protect his little daughter. The mother was relieved knowing the suspect was locked up and could not hurt their daughter any more, and thankful that her husband would remain with her. Unfortunately their grief would remain for many years to come.

I had conducted a meticulous and speedy investigation to obtain the admission of penetration and saw a guilty plea in record time. What I could not do was undo the pain and suffering the innocent girl and her father and mother had endured and would certainly endure well into the future. I learned that the little girl underwent counseling for her emotional trauma. I never found out how she dealt with all that happened to her.

I worked on that case 12 hours a day, 7 days a week, for four straight weeks. My own five-year-old daughter gave me inspiration to solve this case, but that was hardly needed after looking into the eyes of the mother and father, and yes the little girl who knew something was wrong but did not comprehend the full gist of what had happened to her. But this case had another casualty. Following this intensive investigation, it occurred to me that anyone is capable of almost anything, even those with no previous criminal past.

So many years after this terribly painful investigation I realized that I had been a bit too distant from my own daughter. I had been a little too hesitant to hug her, and hold her, and to just be a normal dad. After investigating too many sexual crimes, often perpetrated by relatives, I must have been subconsciously too scared to express my love. There seemed to be such a fragile line between love and transgression, one that was difficult for so many to manage. I knew I would never cross that line. But I defensively put up an emotional barrier between my daughter and myself. Out of a defensive posture, I now know that I have kept my own daughter at arm's length and deprived her of a normal father's love. I regret the distance between us and I only hope that in some way she understands. Investigations and experiences such as these take a heavy toll on police families. I know they have with my family.

15

TENNIS ANYONE?

Trooper Dale and I liked to play tennis at the courts in the City of Northville. The tennis courts were located in a city park that was meticulously manicured. Families frequented the park with their small children and pets, and enjoyed the swings, slides, trails, and other park equipment, usually in the evenings and weekends.

We were off-duty that day so we played tennis for some time tiring ourselves out with some good exercise. When we decided to call it quits for the day in the early afternoon, we saw that a car with the engine running had pulled in next to us so close that I had to walk sideways to get into Dale's car on the passenger side. I noticed that it was around 3:30 so I thought that they might be high school students who had just gotten out of school. As I walked up behind their car, I saw the driver handing something to the front seat passenger. I then saw the passenger place his right hand to his mouth area. Smoke rose from the passenger's face area. Experience told me that people don't usually share cigarettes, but they do share marijuana cigarettes. I closely focused my attention on them and saw the front seat passenger hand something to the back seat passenger who also placed his hand to his face. Blue smoke rose from his face as well. My mind categorized what I was seeing and I was suspicious. As I was opening the passenger door of Dale's car, I smelled the unmistakable odor of burning marijuana. I now knew all three of those young men were committing a crime. I looked into the car next to me from only a few feet away and saw three teenagers all with red bloodshot eyes, a reliable indicator of marijuana use, staring guiltily at me. The back seat passenger had a hand-rolled cigarette that my experience told me contained marijuana. The telltale pungent odor and the accompanying blue haze of marijuana smoke was clearly visible in the car.

Without much thought, I pulled my state police badge out of my pocket and identified myself as a trooper.

"State Police, turn off your car and step out," I commanded.

The driver's eyes bugged out as he looked into my eyes. He gulped, and then he suddenly dropped the gearshift lever into drive and punched the gas. The back end of his car swung toward me as the tires of his car threw the loose gravel of the parking lot in all directions. I thought I was about to lose my legs between his rapidly accelerating car and my partner's vehicle. The only option was for me to jump onto the hood of Dale's car to avoid having my legs crushed. The teenagers sped away narrowly missing crashing into us and raced off around a curbed boulevard toward the park exit and ultimately downtown Northville, which was to be their road to freedom.

I ran across the boulevard with the speed of an antelope from the adrenaline now surging through my body screaming repeatedly for them to stop. I was furious that I nearly suffered serious injuries from these three offenders.

"Stop, stop the car, now!" I yelled at the fleeing car.

For some strange reason the driver stopped the car. As I raced up to the car I reached in the passenger's window which they had thankfully rolled down and grabbed the front seat passenger by the front of his shirt. I had seen him with the marijuana cigarette before they had tried to run me down and escape. Possession of marijuana was a misdemeanor punishable by up to one year in the county jail. I had probable cause to arrest him. Since he had not had his seatbelt on, I was able to yank him out of the car through the open window. I was surprised that I had been able to pull the passenger out so quickly and with only one arm.

Dale arrived just behind me and we removed the other two men from the car. Upon searching them (following their arrests), we recovered more marijuana from each of them. When we searched the car, more marijuana and amphetamine pills were found on the occupants of the car and additional arrests were made. They were all lodged in the city jail.

When we interviewed them, we learned that they had just gotten out of school and decided to go to the park to smoke marijuana. They all lived in Northville with affluent families. The driver was not the least bit remorseful for nearly hitting me, rather he was mad at himself for stopping and getting arrested. I explained to him that had he run, he would have faced additional charges and I would have called dispatch who would have had every police officer in the area looking for them. I told him their escape would not have been successful in any event.

When we finished booking the three, we went home. The rest of the paperwork would be completed the next day when we would be back on duty. We could have simply ignored the violations and gone our separate way, but we had sworn an oath to fully and fairly enforce the law. Maybe the arrests made a difference for those young men and they changed their ways, maybe it didn't. We never found out if they pled guilty, pled to a deferred dismissal, or some other disposition. That had been just another relaxing off-duty day as a police officer.

16

NEW TROOPER AT THE POST

Trooper Gary had just transferred into the Northville Post from a post south of us. I was assigned to drive him around on his first day to acquaint him with the area. As soon as we got onto the road, a call came from an undercover narcotics officer requesting we stop a car to identify the driver, who was the subject of one of their drug investigations. We were on 7 Mile road approaching I-275 in Livonia.

"I-176 to any marked unit on southbound I-275 in Livonia," the narcotics officer queried.

"21-16, I-176, go ahead," I answered.

"21-16, can you stop a silver 1980 Chevelle driven by a single white male southbound I-275 at 8 Mile road?"

"I-176, we just saw your car southbound, I am trying to catch up to it now."

"21-16, when you stop it, just identify the driver and let him go, unless you find any violations," the officer further requested.

"I-176, roger, will do," I replied, as I slammed the accelerator to the floor and I heard the engine screaming to reach top speed of 130 mph on southbound I-275. Traffic was heavy but negotiable.

I was quickly approaching a car in the fourth lane of the southbound freeway trying to pass it when I observed the woman looking in her rear view mirror at me. I knew that she saw me, and she started to move over into the third lane as I rapidly approached her car. I was easing around her partly in her lane and partly on the left shoulder of the freeway. As I was partially alongside of her, for some unknown reason, she jerked her car back into the left lane. In that split second the high-speed driver training I had received at the state police academy kicked in and I snapped the steering wheel to the left to pull fully onto the shoulder of the freeway at 130 mph. As she was traveling about 75 mph, a traffic crash would have been very serious, most likely fatal for some, if not all, of us.

As I shot past her car I saw a wooden pallet lying on the shoulder directly in front of me. I quickly realized that it was a new and strongly built, not a broken down old pallet. I had nowhere to go. Traffic was very heavy on both sides of the freeway. I could not strike the woman next to me and I certainly could not steer on the grassy median strip. To do that would cause me to go head-on with oncoming northbound traffic, resulting in certain death for the occupants of the car I would undoubtedly hit, as well as my new partner and myself. I knew in that microsecond I had to hit the wooden pallet and hope for the best. It was my responsibility and my danger to accept. I saw that the pallet was turned in my oncoming path to make it the widest it could be. I instinctively knew if one of my tires hit that sharp, hard wooden corner of the pallet, one or both of the front tires would blow causing our patrol car to flip over, likely killing both my partner and me and very possibly others around us. You can pray in a nano-second. I know, because I did.

The front axle universal joint struck the hard wooden pallet at 130 mph. The explosion was deafening and for a moment I could not determine if we were still alive or if we had gone to another place far above that freeway. When I realized that we were still alive I looked in my rearview mirror for the pallet. It was nowhere to be seen. Then I saw the splintered pieces coming down from above and behind the patrol car. I realized that I had hit the pallet exactly centered because the tires didn't blow. Luckily we continued on without further incident as I watched pieces of splintered wood land all over the freeway in my rearview mirror. The whole event did not take much more than three or four seconds and it was over.

We caught up to the suspect's car and stopped it well out of our post area due to the speed of his vehicle and heavy traffic. His car was near the Detroit Metro Airport and the noise of the airplanes passing overhead as they landed and took off one after the other, made conversations with the suspect difficult to hear.

"Sir, may I see your driver's license, registration and proof of insurance?" I asked him.

"You want what?" he asked as a large commercial plane with engines at full throttle clawed for altitude just over our heads.

"Sir, I need your driver's license, registration and insurance papers," I repeated.

"I know I was speeding a little, trooper. Can I have a break? Can you just give me a warning?" he asked, showing no emotion.

With a quick look at my partner and with confirming nods, I concluded neither of us saw any contraband or other reasons to look further into his car. After documenting the driver's name, birthdate, address, and vehicle information, I let the driver go on his way with a warning for speeding.

"I-176, 21-16, copy your information," I radioed to the undercover narcotics officer.

"21-16, go with the information," he replied.

After I gave the narcotics officer the information, we exited the freeway and headed back to our post area. The rest of the day proved routine and somewhat uneventful. Trooper Gary (now retired Captain Gary) mentions that incident to me every time I see him, even though it was many years ago. It was just life in the fast lane as they say.

We never heard what the requesting officer did with our information. We never learned if the suspect was arrested on drug charges or if the case was somehow resolved. As human beings, it is natural to look for closure, to expect to find the reasons behind events and to understand outcomes. As a trooper, I learned to live with ambiguity and not learning the resolution of everything I was required to become involved with. I learned to live with knowing that there was always going to be a disconnect between the certainty of the order of the laws, and the chaos of the world in which I had to apply those laws.

But I did learn something that day. The lesson I relearned was that it is imperative to stay alert even during routine assignments. Unusual events have a way of popping up when they are least expected. I had allowed myself to relax during this routine request for assistance to perform a vehicle stop, and I drove too fast without considering all of the possible dangers that could arise. Incidents such as this one added to my experience and I knew that the better trained and more experienced I was becoming, the better the outcome will likely be in future assignments.

17

ANOTHER DRUNK DRIVING ARREST

Complacency in police work can be very dangerous and it has resulted in the death of many police officers. Officers relax because many calls for service turn out to be false alarms, or not the violent suspect they first thought they might be. After hundreds or thousands of such calls, officers start to assume that all of these monotonous and routine activities will also be simple. One such call I assumed would be simple involved a drunk driving arrest, where the suspects appeared to be law abiding and well-educated.

The middle-aged woman was obviously drunk. Even before I asked her to step out of her car I knew that I would arrest her in these early morning hours. Just another routine drunk driving arrest, this one following the hundreds I had previously made. The only thing different in this arrest would be the name, date and location. She was well dressed and obviously from an affluent family. Her expensive jewelry, diamond-studded necklace, large wedding ring, and ruby earrings spoke of significant wealth, causing me to relax. Wealthy people are almost never prone to violence. Obviously she was the one to drive because her husband, also wearing expensive clothing, was even more intoxicated than she was. He was slouched in his wrinkled tuxedo, his tie askew. She told me that she was only trying to help him out by driving them home because he had too much to drink that evening. After administering sobriety tests (counting on her fingers, reciting the alphabet, walking heel to toe, closing her eyes and trying to touch her nose with her extended fore-finger, noting the smell of alcohol on her breath and blood-shot watery eyes), I advised her she was under arrest for drunken driving.

I heard the husband yelling something unintelligible about his wife and that she should not be arrested as my partner talked with him. I had heard that all before. I took out my handcuffs, turned her around and was putting on the handcuffs, when my partner yelled, "Look out!" At the same time I heard my partner yell, I felt something slam into me from behind, knocking the wind out of my lungs as we crashed onto the hard ground in the darkness. It takes a brief moment to realize what is happening to you when you don't see it coming. As I started to grab onto to the husband, I heard my holster unsnap. It was not me trying to grab my service weapon from its holster! The initial routine drunk driving arrest was now a fight for my life. What would he do if he got possession of my gun? Would he in his drunken effort to protect his wife's honor simply order us to let them go without an arrest? Would he unthinkingly pull the trigger and accidently or intentionally kill me or maybe both my partner and me? I had read of the many other police officers that had met that same fate in similar situations. I could not afford to take any chances. My actions were swift, instinctive, and severe.

One hand went to the husband's hand that had grabbed my gun to prevent him from gaining control. My other hand formed a V between my thumb and forefinger, which I slammed with tremendous force into his windpipe. I clenched my fingers tightly together so that my fingertips nearly touched around his windpipe with all of the force I could muster and I kept squeezing. A few seconds later his hand on my gun went limp, his body once thrashing violently on top of me lay still and his gasping sounds could barely be heard as his lungs vainly fought for life-giving air. He had started "doing the chicken," which is the phrase we used to describe that reflexive flopping of a body as it passed out from lack of air.

I rolled him off of me and as he gasped for air, I handcuffed him. While doing so, I slowly realized that his wife who was handcuffed with her hands behind her back was kicking me in the ribs as my partner tried to restrain her. In the heat of battle with her husband, I never felt her kicks. Finally they were handcuffed, formally placed under arrest and secured in the back seat of our patrol car. What a sad pair, two very affluent mature adults, forced into stupidity by overconsumption of alcohol. Same story, different day, different people. As my brother, also a trooper says, "Anybody, anytime." Anyone, no matter who they are or what their background is, is capable of anything, given the right circumstances, at any time. Another lesson learned (or more accurately re-learned), never, ever assume that anyone is beyond being dangerous, no matter how they initially behave or how they are dressed.

After the dust settled and the pair realized the wrongness of their actions, they explained that they had been at a lavish party and he had too many alcoholic beverages to drink. That had been obvious to everyone but them, apparently. Knowing he could not safely drive, his wife felt that she was in good enough condition to drive. They now realized their mistakes and explained just how sorry they were.

"Trooper, I am very sorry, I don't know why I did that, I am sorry," the husband lamented.

"Me too, Trooper, I am sorry for kicking you," the woman added.

"I'm just happy no one was seriously hurt," I said.

"I am an executive for an automotive manufacturer in Detroit. I have never done anything like this before. I don't know what came over me. I am so sorry," he explained.

"We have never been in trouble with the law before, not once, Trooper," the wife said meekly.

"I understand. We will have your car towed to a safe impoundment where you can pick it up in the morning after you are released," I told them.

The pair were driven back to the post and the wife took a breathalyzer test, blowing well above the presumptive level for drunk driving. They were fingerprinted and were lodged in the Livonia City Jail for the night, her for drunk driving and him for assaulting a police officer.

The pair agreed to plead nolo contendere (not contesting the charges but not admitting them either to avoid possible civil liability if I had decided to bring a lawsuit for assault and battery) on the condition that I signed a release of liability absolving them of all potential liability and that I agreed not to sue them for assaulting me. When the husband slammed into me he had committed a criminal assault and battery as well as a civil assault and battery. The former could have resulted in a criminal conviction. The latter could have allowed me to file a civil suit for monetary damages had I not signed the release. As the prosecutor later told me, police officers get paid to get assaulted once in a while. In my mind, I questioned the wisdom of that prosecutor's statement recalling when I was fighting the drunk for my weapon and I did not know how that fight would end.

Much later I learned police officers can, and in many cases should, sue the offenders when they are injured on the job. Money damages may be available for the officer and his family. In Michigan, however, some injuries officers receive in the line of duty may not be pursued in civil court due to a change in statute known as the Firefighter's Rule. The bottom line is that if injured on duty, the officer should check with an attorney if injuries are severe enough to warrant possible civil action. Like most officers, I considered the assault part of my job and put it out of my mind. Since that time the legislature has made disarming or attempting to disarm a police officer of a weapon a felony. I went home to my family as the sun signaled the dawning of a new day full of possibilities. I fell fast asleep pushing aside the events of the previous shift and what could have been.

18

THE WINGLESS AIRPLANE

As I jammed on the brakes of my patrol car, it took some time to stop from traveling at 120 mph to a safe stop. Even though the crash was in the City of Northville, which had its own police department, I thought that I just might be able to pull a survivor from the plane wreckage if I hurried since I was the closest car when the call went out. As I was slowing down, I saw a grove of maple trees. An odd swath had just been cut down the middle of the grove with fresh white wood exposed at the treetops at one end. The swath angled down near the ground at the other end of the grove of trees. It was far too narrow for the wings of the small single engine plane to have negotiated. Odd, I thought, as my brain once again started to gather bits and pieces of evidence to try to make sense of what had just happened.

As I bailed from my car and ran toward the trees I instantly realized why the trees were as they were. The wings of the single engine plane had sheared off upon striking the first trees. Only the wingless body of the small aircraft had cut that narrow swath in the woods, leaving pieces of the wings scattered haplessly around the crash site. Upon impact, the fuselage carrying two passengers had created a crater several feet deep. While running towards the remains of the airplane I looked skyward toward a dark, low-hanging bank of clouds. The plane must have tried to get below the clouds in a futile effort to gain visibility revealing the high school only 40 or 50 feet below them. With their downward angle of flight they must have tried to avoid slamming into the school knowing it was filled with all of those children. Had that airplane crashed into that school, the death and destruction would have been much more tragic, and the victims would have numbered into the hundreds. From what I saw that day, I suspected that the pilot had pulled off a small miracle by flying that airplane just beyond the school building before crashing.

The strong smell of aviation fuel permeated the air. The crumpled and dissected fuselage failed to provide any protection to the two people who only moments before had surely prayed for a miracle that might have saved their lives. In an odd and twisted way they did get a miracle. Death for them had been quick with no suffering, although the fear they felt moments before the crash when they realized there was no hope must have been horrendous. I quickly realized there was no chance to help save a life in this accident, so my mind focused in a different direction. Protect the scene and contact the Post who would then contact the FAA as they will want investigators on the scene.

"21, 21-16, I'm at the scene, no survivors, need fire equipment, ambulances, and call the FAA so they can get their investigators started this way," I directed.

"21-16, 21, will do, Northville City officers should be there any moment. I will contact the FAA," replied the post dispatcher.

"21, 21-16, we need officers for crowd control," I added.

"21-16, 21, will do," the dispatcher answered.

It was mayhem as police cars, fire trucks and ambulances stopped all around the crash site, each responder hoping to help those involved in the crash. Their faces quickly reflected that this would not be the case for this accident on this day.

I stood and surveyed the thousands of small pieces of red and white lying around the point of impact. It looked as though the trunks of the trees and the ground around the plane had recently been spray painted a bright red. When the plane angled into the ground, the force of the collision threw everything forward and to the sides. I quickly realized that the white and red pieces I saw were thousands of pieces of human flesh, skin and bone scattered in a fifty yard semi-circle forward of that ill-fated plane. Amazed at how a human body could explode into a thousand pieces, I acted quickly to move the growing crowd of gawkers back as they unknowingly stepped on bits of the airplane's passengers that covered the road adjacent to the woods.

"People, please step back," I shouted as the crowd of gawkers started to walk onto the small body pieces scattered under their feet.

"I wanna see, the plane, what is that, oh that's gross, move over I can't see, look at all of that blood, I see a piece of a body in the plane," the crowd of onlookers jumbled voices shouted.

"Move back," I again shouted as I tried in vain to move the now large crowd. Other officers were trying to keep the crowd at bay with minimal success.

I stared in amazement as one guy who walked quickly up to me and who was barefoot suddenly shook his foot to dislodge something wet and slippery from the sole of his foot, never noticing it had recently been part of one of the occupants of the plane. In their zeal to see this latest blood and gore, gawkers just did not see the human flesh scattered below their feet, or if they did, they simply did not care.

It took quite some time to recover all of those small bits of the two passengers. At least most of the noticeable pieces of the unfortunate victims were collected while some of the smaller pieces fell under leaves and sticks, hidden from the searcher's sight and nestled into their final resting place.

Why do people become so enthralled with the sight of others' misery, what is the fascination? I asked myself. I slowly shook my head and wondered what they would think if they had realized that they had been walking on the remains of the poor victims of the plane crash. Hours after arriving at this horrendous scene I drove slowly away as the local police continued with their photographs, reports, interviews, and other routine tasks. My role assisting the city police department was over, so I could now forget that incident and move on to my next call for assistance or my next traffic ticket to be written. But the truth was that cases like this were never over. The image of the crumpled and wingless airplane with the scattered flesh, muscle and bone fragments contrasted against the red bloody backdrop was painted indelibly in my brain. I knew from experience it would forever be replayed when all was quiet or when some familiar incident caused this one to be relived.

19

JURY VERDICTS

Concealed weapon — The stop was a routine stop for speeding just like the hundreds before this one. It was night and very dark out on M-14 in Plymouth Township. As I shone my flashlight beam into the car I immediately saw the butt of the handgun protruding from under the front seat of the car. This was a straight forward and very legal, plain view search, one of the 10 exceptions to the search warrant rule emanating from the Fourth Amendment to the U.S. Constitution.

"Sir, do you have a concealed weapon permit for the gun under your driver's seat?" I asked him.

"What gun?" he said playing dumb.

"The one between your legs under your seat. I can see it," I said.

"Um, well no," he finally admitted and started to reach for the pistol.

"Stop, don't reach for the gun," I commanded as I started to draw my own weapon.

"Okay, I only carry it for my protection," he said.

"Put your hands outside of your window and open your door from the outside, slowly and step out of your vehicle," I directed.

Once he was outside I placed him under arrest, handcuffed his hands behind his back and searched him. Finding no evidence on him, I placed him in my patrol car.

I seized the handgun from under the driver's seat and saw that it was a .22 caliber, six shot revolver. Upon opening the cylinder and removing the ammunition, I saw that it had been loaded with three hollow-point bullets and three birdshot cartridges. *Strange*, I thought, knowing that hollow-point bullets were very lethal but the birdshot pellets in a .22 caliber cartridge are the size of ground pepper, suited only for rodents at very close range.

I ran his criminal history and saw that he had a number of previous felony convictions with several stints in prison for weapons and drug charges. He was processed, which consisted of taking his booking photographs and fingerprints, and then I submitted the gun to the crime lab for open shoots (cross checking unsolved shootings where this gun may have been used), and I wrote up the investigative report. He was lodged in jail pending his arraignment the following morning. This was just another routine felony arrest for CCW (carrying a concealed weapon) and it was soon forgotten.

Months later I was subpoenaed to attend a motion hearing on the legality of the search. After my testimony, the judge, defense attorney and prosecutor went to the judge's chamber. When they returned the judge granted the defense attorney's motion.

"Your honor, the defense moves to strike the pistol from the evidence that the trooper allegedly seized from my client, having been seized in violation of my client's rights," the defense attorney addressed the judge.

"In reviewing the trooper's report and testimony, I find that the seizure of the weapon was in violation of the defendant's rights to be free from illegal searches and seizures and I am excluding the gun from evidence. As the gun is the only evidence of the charge, I am dismissing the case. Case dismissed," the judge dryly announced.

In other words, the judge decided that I had conducted an illegal search when I found that gun. I was pissed. After the judge left the bench and the defense attorney hurriedly left the courtroom, I told the prosecutor that I wanted to talk to him. The prosecutor hesitated and looked at me with apprehension.

"What just happened?" I asked him.

"You heard the judge, bad search," he said.

"What? That was a plain view search, textbook and clearly legal," I said.

"Well the judge has ruled and the case has been thrown out," the prosecutor said.

"That is bologna and you know it. The guy has many felony convictions and has been in prison a number of times. The search was clearly good. What happened in the judge's chambers?" I asked.

"Hold on, cool down, let me talk to the judge," the prosecutor said, obviously because I had raised such a fuss that he told me to wait while he went in to talk to the judge.

When the prosecutor returned, he told me that the judge knew of the previous criminal history of the suspect and his previous prison sentences. The judge also said that if he found the search to be valid, which he admitted it was, he would have to send the suspect back to prison, which would cause the suspect to lose the job he currently had. When he got out of prison, he would be back on welfare because no one would hire him with yet another felony conviction on his already lengthy rap sheet. I was flabbergasted.

At times, the best solution is uncertain. It's possible that the suspect was rehabilitated and the judge's decision would allow him to make a life for himself outside of the prison system, which would have been unlikely had he gone to jail. I had my doubts. If he had a gun, it was likely that he would use it. Then the victim of his crime would pay the price for decisions made that day, though nobody would realize that was the case. Besides, being a convicted felon, he was guilty of carrying a concealed pistol and of being a felon in possession of a firearm. In my mind, the suspect had not, and would not, learn from being treated gently in this case.

I never knew if the judge actually believed what he had told the prosecutor, or if the judge and the defense attorney were golfing buddies with the judge doing his friend a favor. I just knew that I had done my job, but the other parts of the criminal justice system had failed. If that suspect was carrying a gun, there was a reason behind it, a reason which I will never know. I hated the bizarre outcome, but that was outside of my control and I needed to learn how to put that kind of thing behind me to focus on my job; otherwise, it would give me ulcers.

Bad checks — The jury foreman stood and announced to the judge, "Not guilty, Judge." That smug look, a crooked smile, he had fooled the jury. Those 12 average citizens had bought a concocted defense theory. The suspect had stolen the victim's checkbook and written hundreds of dollars' worth of checks against the victim's account. The handwriting expert stated the writing was consistent with handwriting samples obtained from the suspect, although he could not say the suspect was definitely the person who wrote the checks and signed the victim's name. I had learned that most handwriting opinions never positively identify handwriting samples from a suspect with the written evidence, but result in an opinion similar to that provided in this case, something the jury probably did not know. The latent fingerprint expert testified that he found no identifiable fingerprints from the suspect on any of the checks that were cashed, but he did find some on the unwritten checks I found on the suspect when I had arrested him. The lone witness, a store clerk who accepted one of the checks, testified she could not positively identify the suspect as the person who handed her the check, but he look similar to the person she remembered at her store.

The defense attorney looked pleased. The family looked violated. I tried to shrug it off, but I knew he wrote the checks and he was guilty. The family thanked me for all of my efforts and compassion during my investigation and I knew they really meant it. They huddled together then slowly disappeared from the courtroom wondering what had just happened.

Juries often struck me as strange, made up of people that, in some cases, believe any story spun for their purposes by artful defense attorneys and suspects. Watching defense attorneys over the years reminded me of a line I heard many times that defense attorneys are merely frustrated actors. What a show some of them put on for naïve juries. I spoke to one motherly looking juror after the trial where the youthful suspect who had been charged with breaking into a residence was found not guilty. She said that the reason she voted for a not guilty verdict was that the suspect looked just like her son and she just could not convict her own son. The evidence was much more than needed to prove guilt beyond a reasonable doubt as the law required in criminal cases

Jury members are just people from the area in which the court is located. They often try to do what is right and follow the law as the judge explains it to them. Sometimes they bring prejudices with them that affect their decisions. Other times the testimony of a suspect, witness, an attorney or police officer sways them. Jury members might reach a verdict because the trial hits them the wrong way, in spite of the evidence presented at trial. In one of my cases where a juror fell asleep shortly after the trial started, he went on to become the foreperson of that jury, which convicted the suspect as charged. When I talked to that person after the trial, he told me that as soon as he saw the suspect and watched him for a few minutes he knew the suspect was guilty, even though no evidence had been introduced yet.

The vast majority of the criminal cases that I investigated ended in guilty verdicts. I have come to realize that it was not my job to convict anyone. My job was to fully and fairly investigate every incident, whether it was consumption of alcohol in a motor vehicle, a B & E, or a rape. If I did my job, the judge, prosecutor, defense attorney and jury would do theirs. It is sometimes very difficult to stay neutral, but the best results usually happen if officers do just that. What are the best results you might ask? I have learned over the years after many trials that the best results are what the system produces. The best results are based on what evidence and effort is put into the system by all parties involved, and depending of course, on who ends up being selected to sit on the jury.

As the saying goes in the law, "Better that a thousand guilty people go free than convict one innocent person." I can't argue with that logic.

20

A NO-BRAINER

I t was a sleepy night with not much happening to keep us awake, the kind of night that let my partner and me recharge our batteries after other nights when we ran from one investigation to another. It was a welcome night but a boring one.

The radio crackled and I heard the state police dispatcher, "21-16, 21. Copy a report of a P.I."

A P.I. in police jargon means a personal injury motor vehicle accident. This means that one or more persons have sustained bodily injuries. With these injury calls, officers waste no time getting to the scene most often with emergency lights and siren activated as the injuries are assumed to be potentially life-threatening. If no injuries were reported, the terminology would be PDA, or property damage accident.

"Go ahead 21," my partner answered back.

"We have a report of a two car P.I. on Eight Mile Road near Beck," the dispatcher advised. "I have sent an ambulance and wrecker to that location as well."

We were only 5 minutes away and we roared up to the accident scene with red lights flashing but no siren. No need, there was no other traffic at 3 a.m. on this lonely country road. We spotted the two cars. A Ford was partially across the road at an angle with the front end pushed in almost to the windshield. The other car was an Oldsmobile, also sporting a smashed front end. A woman in her late twenties was standing in the road holding her hand on her forehead with bright red blood streaming between her fingers and running down her arm. Her blouse was spotted with large dots of blood.

She had a distant stare and didn't respond when I asked, "Are you alright?" *Shock, maybe a concussion,* I thought. I sat her down on the hood of our patrol car and opened the first aid kit. A small split in the skin on her forehead emitted a slow but steady flow of hot red blood. Facial wounds bleed easily with all of the veins and capillaries located there. A gauze compress with a wrap stemmed the red flow quickly. She told me by the time she saw the Oldsmobile stopped in the road as she approached, it was too late to stop and she slammed into it. She brought her car to a stop on the grassy shoulder of the road. She had been able to stop before she plunged into a deep ditch less than a foot from the passenger side of her car. Had she steered a bit more to her right, she would have ended up in the deep ditch common on these lonely and remote country roads.

My partner was tending to the other driver, a male in his late forties. The driver who was obviously dazed from the collision, stated he didn't remember what had happened and he had just awakened as the woman's car had struck his car. He was very sorry for stopping in the road. He had been drinking but we quickly determined that he was not drunk. I suspected he had just fallen asleep. I was on the radio calling for a wrecker for both cars as neither car was drivable. It appeared to me that neither driver needed to be transported to a hospital as their injuries were minor and they had refused further medical treatment. When only minor injuries are discovered and the victims refuse further medical attention, dispatched ambulances are often called off by the investigation officers. The safer course of action is to let the ambulance arrive so the ambulance crew can examine the victims and make the medical determination regarding further treatment. But in this instance, both drivers had refused further medical attention so I relayed that message to the post dispatcher to cancel the ambulance.

I relayed telephone numbers to the post dispatcher to have family members called so they could pick up the injured drivers after we dropped them off at the Post. I picked up the traffic accident pad and started to fill out the accident report. Name of driver number 1, address, insurance company, injury type –"B." The injury codes included O, for no obvious injuries; C, no visible injury but complaints of pain; B, observable but non-incapacitating injuries; A, incapacitating injuries; and K, fatal injuries.

I then asked the woman to describe in detail how the accident happened so that I could write the information on the accident report. She looked at me strangely for a few moments and quickly blinked her eyes as if her mind suddenly cleared away the fog. It appeared to me that her memory had snapped back to full consciousness. She matter-of-factly asked me if I was going to check on the "other car."

"What other car?" I asked.

"The one way down the road that way," she said pointing her finger.

I realized that this was not a single two-car accident, but rather two separate, two-car accidents. I looked down the lonely road and saw nothing but darkness.

"How far down the road is the other car?" I asked her.

"A small Honda was hit by this Oldsmobile here, way down the road," she impatiently said to me.

"Okay," I managed.

"The driver here, hit the Honda with his Oldsmobile and bounced off of the Honda stopping in the road. That is when I didn't see him in time and I hit his car. He didn't have any lights on, so when I did see it, I could not stop in time to avoid hitting it," she said.

A very strong and instant feeling of dread came over me. We had been at this accident for over five minutes and nothing had been said of this third vehicle. Was someone bleeding to death? Maybe they had stopped breathing and needed CPR. I dropped the accident report pad, yelled to my partner that there was a third vehicle involved in this accident and I needed to check on it right away. I had decided to leave our patrol car where it was to warn any approaching cars of this accident and to protect the victims from being struck by any other cars that might happen along.

I started running toward the location the woman told me the Honda was stopped. Out of breath, I finally saw the small compact car over a quarter of a mile down the road partially on the shoulder. The front end of the vehicle was pushed all of the way up to the windshield with the most damage toward the driver's side. Again I felt the tingling sensation of the hair on the back of my neck standing up. As I neared the Honda, I did not see the driver behind the wheel of the car.

When I came up to the passenger's side of the vehicle, I saw the driver. Due to the terrific collapse of the vehicle, the driver's feet were on the floor beneath the steering wheel, but his upper body had been pushed across the passenger's front seat and he was leaning up against the passenger door. His eyes were closed and I could not see his chest rise or fall, so I instantly sensed the fate of this driver. I yanked on the door handle again and again. It was jammed from the damage sustained in the crash or maybe it was just locked, I couldn't check from where I was standing because the glass was still in the window. I ran around the front of the vehicle as my huffing and puffing partner ran up to the passenger side of the car. The driver's door opened easily. I leaned over the body and unlocked the passenger door.

As it happens in traumatic situations like these, my mind slowed down to a crawl noticing the minutest detail. A palpable, still, death-like feeling hung in the air inside of that small car. My eyes scanned the driver. No breathing could be seen or heard. No blood flowed from any obvious wounds and no sign of a heartbeat from his chest or carotid artery could be detected when I placed my fingers on his neck.

"Can you hear me?" I asked the man, but I received no response. Shaking him slightly failed to get any response either.

I then saw a strange white mosaic pattern on the passenger door. It looked as if someone had taken a pint of cottage cheese and randomly slung it across the inside of the passenger front door. My mind struggled to grasp this odd sight. I saw no cottage cheese containers, no lunch bag, no signs this driver had been eating anything white at the time of the accident. With my flashlight in my left hand, I leaned toward the driver so my face was less than six inches from his head.

My partner was now feeling for a pulse on the victim's carotid artery in his neck. It was then that I saw the depression on my side of his head in his dark, wet hair. Looking a little closer, I saw it was a hole in his skull about the size of a half dollar. I urged my mind to work faster, but it took its time in comprehending what it was seeing. Raising my flashlight, I shined the bright beam of light and pulled back the damp wet hair with my bare fingers so I could look into the hole in his skull. I blinked again to make sure I was seeing what I thought I was seeing. Where the driver's brain was supposed to be was an empty dark void. No brain. Nothing. It was very clean and sanitary looking inside of that skull. *Mmm, a no-brainer*, I thought. As I placed my hand on his shoulder checking for signs of life, I felt, then saw a small amount of cottage cheese, or what my mind told me was cottage cheese, on his shoulder. Some object in the car had punched a hole in his skull and the pressure of the impact had literally blown out the driver's brain sending it to scatter across the passenger side door. Death for this hapless driver had almost certainly been instantaneous and painless. Our boring evening was no longer and suddenly we had many things to do.

"Help me get him onto the ground so I can start CPR," my partner yelled to me.

"Forget it, I checked his pulse and he has none. He's not breathing, and his brain is scattered on that door that you are holding open," I told him.

I relayed to him that the white matter on the door was the driver's brain and that I saw no remains of brain matter inside of the driver's skull. My partner stopped, looked at me then at the door and wiped the wet white matter that had gotten on his hand on his trouser leg. He looked at me and said nonchalantly, "I'll let dispatch know we will still need that ambulance."

The ambulance arrived shortly after that.

"What do we have troopers?" the ambulance driver asked me.

"Two minor injuries up the road at the second accident and both refused treatment. This guy has no brain. He lost it upon impact. See it on the passenger door?" I asked him.

"Yep, but we have to try. Help us get him out," he stated in a non-hurried, routine manner.

Once the driver was on the road surface, the EMT's went to work with a mechanical CPR pump, and put their oxygen mask on him. They quickly loaded the man onto their gurney and put him into the ambulance. I watched the ambulance crew performing their perfunctory efforts at CPR. No brain, but I guess they were following their protocol. Maybe we should have done so as well. The ambulance roared off with lights and siren announcing to the world an emergency transport was coming through.

I would go to the hospital to follow-up on the disposition of the body as soon as we finished with the accident scene. The hospital would contact the family and have them come to the hospital. I went back to the living and attended to them and continued to fill out the accident reports. Fatal traffic accidents create a huge amount of work. We were kept busy long after our shift was supposed to end with photographs, measurements, witness statements, evidence to be collected and sent to the crime lab, and reports to be typed.

We were dog-tired when we arrived at the hospital, the sun having come up hours ago reminding our bodies that sleep was badly needed. It is always exhausting to have worked in the hours of darkness and see the sun come up. As we secured the information from the nurses station and prepared to go home for some much needed sleep, we were told the doctor wanted to talk to us. The doctor probably just had a few encouraging words on a job well done, we assumed. We just wanted to go home and to bed and put these sights, sounds, smells and memories in some small recess of our brains, hopefully to be forgotten forever. From experience, I knew that was likely wishful thinking.

We weren't prepared for the tirade that started as soon as the doctor came around the corner. Her starched white lab coat was flapping around her, which I swear was making a strange hissing sound as she approached us. She had fire in her eyes, and she was yelling at us at the top of her lungs. The spit spraying from her lips reminded me of images I had once seen of an evil serpent in a horror movie. All eyes in the area, patients, visitors, nurses and the janitor, were focused on the doctor, my partner and me.

"Why didn't you perform CPR on that man?" It was clearly an accusation fired at us. We didn't know what to say, was she being serious? Obviously she was as she was delivering her verbal attack on us within earshot of everyone working in that emergency department.

I finally overcame my shock and confusion and said, "Doctor, the man had no brain. I saw the empty skull and his brain matter all over the car door. He had no pulse and he wasn't breathing." She just stood there, hands on her hips, glaring at me, fire bellowing out of her nostrils.

She shouted, "We have case histories of people living on their brain stems alone. You should have started CPR immediately!" My partner and I glanced at each other. We weren't sure which one of us was more tired and craved sleep the most. We just stared at each other, then at the doctor, and back at each other. Living on a brain-stem alone?

It was as if we were communicating telepathically. Neither of us had to say a word. We both made eye contact with the doctor and her fire-red face one last time and then we turned in unison, putting our backs to the doctor and walked down the hallway toward our waiting patrol car. She didn't like that one bit. She hurled another tirade at us. "Don't you two turn your backs and walk away from ME! Get back here right this minute!" The fire and brimstone faded as the distance between the doctor and us grew. We kept on walking, our boots clacking on the waxed tile floor in unison drowning out the continuing tirade launched at us by the doctor. The pneumatic doors joined the fray instantly taking sides with the doctor and emitted a menacing hiss at us as we walked carefully past them and out of the hospital.

We stepped into the now sunny morning, tasted the fresh air and climbed into our waiting patrol car. Feeling safe once again, we settled into the sanctuary of our Blue Goose (State Patrol Car) and drove away, our minds trying to grasp what had just occurred. Maybe we had been right and maybe we had been wrong in not performing CPR on the No-Brainer. Clearly the doctor thought we were wrong in not trying to save the man. But my partner and I knew that it wouldn't have made any difference for that driver. By now, we were totally exhausted, physically and emotionally. Sleep that morning was a welcome friend.

21

MY HUSBAND DIDN'T COME HOME LAST NIGHT

I t was a very cold, dark early Sunday morning with a healthy blanket of fresh fluffy snow on the ground. January in Michigan is usually like that. My partner and I were in Northville Township less than two miles from the Northville State Police Post nearing the end of our shift. With any luck we would be home asleep in our beds before the sun started to turn up the lights on this new day. Sleep always came easiest before it got light outside.

"21-16, 21."

"Now what?" we both thought in unison. "Go ahead 21."

"Check with the woman at 1234 Sumpter Lane. She reports that her husband did not come home last night."

"Roger, 21."

We were not far from the call and the location was not far from our post and our personal cars, waiting to carry each of us home and into our warm beds. Hopefully this call would involve a simple few checks, so we could find the husband, relay the information to the woman, and end our shift. When we were just pulling onto the narrow dirt road where the caller lived, the post informed us that the woman had called back. She reported that her neighbors told her that they had seen a car similar to her husband's stuck in a ditch down the lane past the woman's home. We decided to pass the woman's house and go directly to the car reported by the neighbor. The husband had apparently driven past his house and his waiting wife onto a narrow two-track dirt road. When he tried to turn around, the spinning tires had caused the car to sink into the frozen road. The car was at an angle to the road. We got out and looked at the car. No accident damage was apparent. No one was present in the car, though the doors were unlocked. Inside the car were several empty beer cans. Two more empty beer cans of the same brand lay in the snow nearby. We ran the license plate to confirm that the car was registered to the woman's husband. The picture of what had happened crystalized in our tired brains.

The wind had blown most of the snow off of that frozen muddy road surface, but a few very small red dots could be seen on the hard frozen mud just outside of the door and on the edge of the driver's door. Getting down on our hands and knees we saw that the line of red dots continued up the lane toward the house of the missing husband. This evidence confirmed our initial suspicions.

Clearly the husband had been out drinking that Saturday evening. He had consumed too much alcohol but decided to attempt to drive home anyway. Due to his intoxication he drove past his own house. At some point he realized he had missed his driveway and had gotten his car partially turned around in the narrow lane, only to become stuck in the mud that had melted from the friction of the spinning tires. Once he realized that he could not get his car unstuck, he walked those 500 yards to his house. Evidently he had fallen on the frozen muddy road as he was getting out of his car and cut himself, dripping his blood on the car door and the roadway.

Based on what we had seen, we suspected that we would find the husband sleeping somewhere in the house unseen by his wife, and we would be headed home and to warm beds very soon.

We called the post and asked that they call the woman back and have her check her house for her husband who we were sure had gotten back home and was likely sleeping it off somewhere in the house. The post called us back very quickly and told us the woman had checked her house and did not find her husband. That was odd. Our visions of a warm bed slowly began to cool.

The blood trail was not difficult to follow in the beam of my flashlight, even though the amount of blood was meager, indicating the wound was not very serious and causing us to hope for the best as we continued to follow his blood trail. Those years of tracking deer blood trails was really paying off now on this cold dark morning. As with deer, the amount of blood and the blood pattern left on the road provided clues as to the seriousness of the wound as well as the direction of travel for the prey. I kept looking for that telltale shine of the frozen blood given off when the bright beam of my flashlight focused on the continuing trail. Many deer that I had shot with my bow had been much harder to follow than this. In trailing deer, I hoped to ultimately find the prey that I had humanely killed for food. On this morning, I was hoping to find the prey alive, healthy, and back in his warm home with his wife who was worried about her wayward husband.

The edges of the muddy lane were choked with dense brush and bushes. As we followed the blood trail, we could see the woman's house just down the road. An old coat or rug of some type appeared through the brush in the driveway. The husband must have dropped his coat as he was nearing his house. We would check on that coat for possible clues and then look for the husband in the house; obviously the woman had missed finding him when she had checked earlier.

As we rounded the last of the thick brush on the edge of the road we turned into the driveway. The coat in the driveway was now apparently trying in vain to protect its wearer. We immediately saw his legs, shoes and unprotected hands with that telltale pale bluish coloration of a body no longer sending blood and oxygen to the extremities. We knew instantly that this poor man was dead. There was no need to check for a pulse as his body was now frozen and rock hard. The fact that he was frozen stiff signified that he had been dead for some time.

We approached him and saw that this man was only 10 feet from his front door just out of sight of his waiting wife. His eyes were open looking at his front door, where the warmth of his house awaited him. He had not been able to go those last few feet where safety, warmth and a possibly irate wife awaited his arrival. His right hand was outstretched toward the door as if he had been reaching for the doorknob. In his drunkenness, he had fallen, passed out, and met his fate only a few feet from the safety of his house. *Life comes and goes in the blink of an eye*, I thought. I could not help feeling sorry for him and for his wife. They deserved better than this sad fate.

Instead of getting off of our shift on time, we realized that we would not be getting into our warm beds anytime soon, as we had another death message to deliver. Another family would be notified of an unfathomable loss too difficult to cope with. How would that woman support herself? How would she be able to carry on with her life after losing her husband of many years? Unfortunately, there was scant little we could do to lessen this woman's burden. We knocked at the door and saw the immediate reaction of this poor woman to our somber faces staring at her. It is always the same; they always immediately know and the reaction is very predictable and very violent.

We had more to do now. We had photographs to take, measurements to record, other evidence to locate and seize. Every death is treated as a homicide until proven otherwise, lest evidence be lost or destroyed. The ambulance we had summoned pulled into the driveway. The paramedic driving the ambulance approached us as his partner started to unload medical gear.

"Good morning, Troopers, what do we have?" the EMT asked.

"The man missed his driveway last evening, got his car stuck, and due to his intoxication, crawled to where he froze to death," I quickly replied.

"It looks like we are going to have to pry him off of the concrete. It looks like he is really stuck," the second EMT, who acted like she had seen this a thousand times, announced.

The man's face and hands had been frozen to the concrete of the driveway for some time judging by the tight bond between his exposed skin, the urine soaked pants and the pavement. His post-death face had that typical flatness from lying against a hard surface for a long period of time. The EMT's, my partner and I peeled his exposed flesh off of the concrete as gently as we could. At least he was fresh and his body had not reached the stage of rotting, stinking, oozing flesh as was often the case with dead human bodies we encountered. We placed the body with limbs frozen in odd angles onto the gurney. Frozen bodies were difficult to keep on the ambulance gurney because they tended to twist into odd shapes until they thawed out. I was glad to see them drive away with the body so the woman would no longer see the ambulance crew working on her departed husband. That had to be some very minor relief for her.

We said our good-byes to the widow and drove to the post to write our reports. When I finally dropped my head down on my warm pillow much later that morning I was exhausted. No matter how hard I clenched my eyes shut, I just could not get him to go away and to stop staring at me with those sorrowful eyes asking for my help so he could make it those last few feet to his front door and the warmth of his house. I would have helped him with all of my ability to crawl those last few precious feet if I had had that opportunity, but I hadn't. I felt a deep sense of guilt that I was warm and safe in my bed, but the man we had found so close to safety would never again feel the comfort of a warm safe bed. I can only hope he is now eternally safe and warm in another and hopefully better place.

22

A FIRST

Female troopers in the Michigan State Police were relatively new with only a handful in the ranks when I joined. I had worked for four years at the Northville Post with no female troopers assigned. Opinions were mixed in those days regarding women in police work. At one of our regular squad meetings before the start of our shift, the sergeant announced that we were getting a female trooper who was transferring in from another post. She had six years of experience and she would be placed in our squad. The meeting went abuzz with opinions.

A few days later, rumors were rampant that most of the troopers would not work with her because their wives were upset that their husbands might be assigned to work with the female trooper at all hours of the day and night. Concerns ranged from potential broken marriages to fears that the trooper would not be able to hold her own in tough situations. My shift sergeant asked me if I would work with her. My wife had no major concerns, at least that she shared with me. I knew Trooper Valerie had more time in the department than I had so she would be the senior trooper. When push came to shove, out on the road, her decision would be the final word. That was department policy, and I felt that I could accept that and work with her.

We got along well right from the start. As with all pairs of officers, we had our own styles, quirks, and preferences on how to handle any given situation. Like all pairs of officers, we became close, in spite of any minor differences. Police officers experience so many life-threatening situations that draw them together with their partners. They become very protective of each other, by choice and by necessity. Often, no words need to be spoken between partners; only quick looks, a motion of the head, words silently mouthed so as not to tip off the suspects are all that is necessary to fully communicate between partners. I knew Trooper Valerie's hobbies, fears, favorite quotes, marriage status, family problems, and she knew mine. We became each other's sounding boards for work and personal issues. I would step unhesitatingly in harm's way for her and she would do the same for me, no questions asked. I trusted her with my life; she trusted me with hers. Such is the necessity of police work. This is similar to the military where soldiers experience close-knit relationships in dangerous, life-threatening combat situations. Personal differences most often are pushed aside and the job is accomplished. It is as simple as that.

"I need to take a potty break," Trooper Valerie announced around 2 am during the first week of patrol together, her voice suddenly breaking the silence of the quiet evening.

"Great timing," I responded, realizing that I needed to stop as well.

We were in rural farm country with only fields and woods surrounding us. There were no restaurants, rest stops, or any other formal place that would suffice as a bathroom out in this rural setting. As was usual, I stopped the car, walked to the side of the road and relieved myself making sure no one was coming down the road. When I got back into the patrol car after my potty break and sat behind the wheel getting ready to pull away she just looked at me with a blank stare. She had not even gotten out of the patrol car.

"What do you expect me to do, go right here?"

"What?" I responded, not quite sure what she was saying.

At first I didn't realize what she was talking about. My previous six years in police work and nine years in the National Guard had been spent with only males. Like most things in police work, my actions and reactions become automatic. Little thinking was necessary. I just did things as I had learned to do, out of safety and out of repetition. Trooper Valerie was the first woman that I had worked with. She must have realized that I just had not thought about it. Slowly the light came on in my head.

"I'm really sorry, I am so used to working with other male troopers, I just didn't think."

"Geez, take me to a bathroom." She rolled her eyes at me, smiled, and let out a laugh that I would come to know, and that would come so easy to her on many occasions.

We worked together for over a year. I had been taught by my training officer, Trooper Mike, to wade right into situations and stop things before they could even get started or at least before things got out of control. Even in the most dangerous situations, I was taught to quickly take control and put a stop to whatever we came across no matter how potentially dangerous the situation was. He was a Vietnam veteran and had seen combat. That was his style and it had worked for him in Vietnam, as well as on the roads of Michigan. As is often the case, I was a near clone of my training officer and took on his style to a large extent, flavored only by some of my own nuances sprinkled in here and there. My new partner was not a military veteran and her style was more easy going and less confrontational. She tried to reason with people even when immediate action might be dictated by training and experience. We used our differing styles to our advantage depending on how the person we were dealing with acted toward us.

As often happens, we, or more accurately, I, began to become agitated with our differing styles of handling situations that we encountered when I felt a more direct approached was called for. Too often for me, when an agitated motorist we had stopped started a tirade directed at her, she just stood there and took it. How could she just let people yell at her with all of those cars going by watching us? Wasn't she embarrassed to let the offender control the situation? I had been trained that when force is used against you, even verbal force, you use only that force necessary to overcome the situation, but you do use it.

It all culminated in me boiling over one day on the side of a very busy freeway in the City of Southfield. It was early afternoon and the dangerous traffic whizzing past us was heavy. The very tall motorist she had stopped for exceeding the speed limit immediately jumped out of his car the moment his car came to a rest. He ran toward our car, and we met him halfway between our cars. He immediately started to scream at my partner.

"Why did you stop me?" he demanded.

"Speeding," my partner told him.

"Why don't you find a real criminal to arrest rather than harass me? Don't you have anything better to do? I bet you are feeling really proud about stopping me, eh?"

"Sir, just relax and take it easy. You were only speeding," she told him. She went on to explain that by enforcing the traffic laws, many accidents, injuries and deaths are prevented.

"I'm a busy man. I don't have time to waste on your bullshit stop," he said angrily, hunching up his shoulders at my partner.

"Look, this won't take long. I'll make a quick check of your driving record and let you know what I am going to do," she said.

"What a bunch of crap. Check my driving record?" he retorted.

"Just calm down. I'll be right back with you. Have a seat in your car," my partner told him.

"I won't calm down. This stop is bullshit. Give me my driver's license and let me go, right now," he demanded.

"I need to check your driving record first," she replied.

"Listen, Trooper, give me my license back right now," he again demanded, angrily waving his arms around. He was now standing over my partner continuing his tirade.

I initially just stood silently watching and providing protection for my partner because it was her stop as she was driving that day and she was the senior officer. But I had just about had enough of this guy's guff. I was so embarrassed watching this offender dress down my partner. Besides, I was sure this guy was going to take a swing at her any second, and then I would be able to take control of the situation in the blink of an eye.

I saw the looks of passing motorists staring at these two state troopers being harangued by an angry motorist. I was ready to explode. She slowly became a bit agitated herself, not with the angry motorist, but at me, her partner who wasn't agreeing with her handling of this unruly motorist. I saw my partner and the angry motorist pushing his chest against hers and leaning over her so that she was actually bent backwards at her waist. I lost it. The motorist was wrong; my partner had tried to use reason with him, but it was not working. So controlling myself the best that I could, I walked up to them, physically wedged myself between them and forced the motorist slightly back. His eyes suddenly opened wide glaring directly into my eyes with a cold hard look. I sensed he did not want to hit a woman, but his quickly changing demeanor suggested he might not hesitate to hit another man, even a trooper.

I was nearly as tall as him and my icy unflinching stare into his eyes quickly deflated his state of rage; he immediately sensed harm was about to befall him. I simply whispered very quietly to him so he could barely hear me, which instantly made him pay very close attention to me.

"What, what?" the driver stammered unable to think of anything else to say.

"Get back into your fucking car or you will be going to the hospital," I quietly whispered to him, instantly making him pay very close attention to me so that he could hear me above the noise of the passing traffic.

"Yes, Trooper," was all he managed to mumble as he turned toward his car.

I know my language was inappropriate, but as we were taught at the academy, the use of force continuum dictates that verbal control is the first and least application of force. In other words, using profanity to gain control in this escalating situation was better than punching him or worse. And besides, it worked. He actually gasped, the air suddenly gushed from his lungs, his red face drained, and he scampered back to his car and his waiting family who had questioning looks on their faces.

I don't know who was angrier at me, the motorist or my partner. I had saved her from an almost certain punch or worse, but she had not seen it that way. To make matters worse she let the motorist go without any enforcement action. Now I was really mad. She slowly turned to me once we were back in the patrol car and yelled, "It was my stop, my decision, and you had no right to interfere!" Up to that point, we always worked well together, even with our differing styles of handling situations. I didn't understand at that time why I chose to usurp her authority so blatantly during that traffic stop. Following my actions that day, we both requested and were granted a change in partners. A short time after our parting of ways was the first time that I met John Wayne.

Shortly after that encounter she transferred into narcotics as an undercover officer. I had seen her only occasionally after that. When we ran into each other, we were cordial but short with each other. Neither of us apologized or discussed our previous working relationship or all of the things we had shared over the year or so when we had worked so closely together. We were no longer the friends we used to be, or so we thought.

I would later learn, following Trooper Valerie's death, that there was more than one way to handle most any situation. This reflection taught me that the circumstances of any given encounter would best dictate the method of successfully resolving the situation. In other words, there is more than one way to handle any situation on the road depending on the circumstances encountered. The regret that I live with every day now is that I never had the humility at that time to realize it and apologize and make up to stay friends with my partner. Little in this life is as important as family and friends. Police officers are both family and friends rolled into one.

I do suspect that with her gracious personality she realized that I was sorry long before she left this world on that lonely night on the shoulder of the freeway, all alone. At least I hope so. I regret that I had not been there, working with her as her partner once again, when she went on her final patrol.

Her life reminds me of the poem that had circulated in the police grapevine and that I kept with my collection of poems to help me. It seemed appropriate to reread after losing my partner.

COP ON THE TAKE

First he takes the oath.
Now look at all he takes.
He takes it in stride when people call him pig.
He takes time to stop and talk to children.
He takes your verbal abuse while giving you a ticket you really
  deserved.
He takes on creeps you would be afraid to even look at.
He takes time away from his family to keep you safe.
He takes your injured child to the hospital.
He takes the graveyard shift without complaint because it's his turn.
He takes his life into his hands daily.
He takes you home when your car breaks down.
He takes time to explain why both your headlights have to work.
He takes the job no one else wants telling you a loved one has died.
He takes criminals to jail.
He takes in sights that would make you cry.
Sometimes he cries, too, but he takes it anyway because
  someone has to.

If he is lucky, he takes retirement.
He takes memories to bed each night that you couldn't bear for
even one day.
And yes, occasionally he may take a free cup of coffee.
Sometimes, he takes a bullet.
Then he pays for all he has taken, and God takes him.

My partner never had the opportunity to take the retirement that she had worked so hard to earn. She did take on her share of the dangers she steadfastly and unflinchingly faced to help others, all the while displaying her trademark smile and laugh. Such are the dangers of police work. I learned from years of police work and from losing my partner that life is fragile, often lost in the blink of an eye. It is truly to be lived, enjoyed and treasured. The wisdom I gained from my experiences is simple: do whatever you can for others, and those helping gestures will come back to you in unforeseen ways when you least expect it. I know this because I have experienced it many times when I needed help the most.

23

THE DEAD PARTNER

It was a Thursday in July some 30 plus years ago. I was working desk duty at the Northville Post because my partner, Trooper Denny called in sick. We worked two officer cars after dark back then, so policy prevented me from going out on patrol alone. That was a welcome change of pace for me on this lonely midnight shift working on the quiet front desk at the post. No drunk drivers to puke or urinate in the back seat of my patrol car. No arrestees to swear at me, call me names, lie, scream, or spit on me.

There was always the potential for some character walking into the post with a bizarre issue, complaint, or just wishing to talk to someone who would listen in the wee hours of the morning. Yep, they do that even in the middle of the night. There were papers to shuffle, investigative reports to read, traffic tickets to file, telephones to answer and reports to file. Then there were the callers asking if it might be raining or snowing outside. They likely could not get to their windows to look outside to see the weather for themselves. Around midnight my eyes were growing tired from all of the reading.

The lone car stopped in at the post so the troopers could drop off reports and they asked if I wanted to accompany them to get some dinner. The sergeant nodded his assent and I grabbed my gun belt and hat and jumped in the backseat of their patrol car. It had been a slow night for them also, but we all knew how quickly that could change. We discussed which restaurant was still open at this late hour and could provide the best table fare on a Thursday in our post area. In reality, most any place open at that late hour would be offering the same options. We headed north on the freeway enjoying the quiet evening.

"21-10, 21." That sudden foreboding jumped at us once again.

"21, 21-10, go ahead."

"Check on a possible P.I. at I-275 near the Grand River interchange."

"Roger 21." *Here we go again*, I thought, as we went from being relaxed and carefree expecting a quiet midnight dinner to full alert in a matter of seconds. A P.I. calls on all of your training, skills, mental ability and compassion long before you arrive on scene. Out of habit, the mental preparation began as the speedometer shot past 100 mph, 110, 120. The screech of wind roared past the patrol car howling in my ears. Should I grab the first aid kit from the trunk of our car when we arrive? Will we need to protect against other drivers crashing into the accident scene? How many victims might there be? Will we need an ambulance? Will gasoline be leaking from the car's gas tank? Will fire trucks be needed to put out a possible fire or to extricate the victims? Will we need a wrecker to tow the car if it's inoperable? What about backup officers to handle traffic around the scene? The mental checklist of what might be needed, honed to a well-practiced routine by my training and experience, was running through my mind.

My mind kicked into slow motion when I first saw the car on the grass of the right shoulder away from the travelled portion of the freeway. The patrol car took so long to travel those last 30 yards it was as though we were driving through clear Jell-O which

seemed unwilling to part and let us pass. As we slowed to around 30 mph, I released my seat-belt and I already opened the rear door of the patrol car as I was ready to respond to this unknown carnage. I stepped onto the grassy shoulder of the roadway as the patrol car lurched to a sudden stop and I was propelled forward around the front of our car from the momentum.

As I instinctively began scanning the area, my eyes gathered images in rapid succession and forwarded them to my brain for analysis. Images of 8 x 10 manila envelopes scattered around the victim's car registered in my mind. There was only one car, a single vehicle accident. A hole no larger than 14 inches in diameter puckered outward on the windshield on the driver's side of the car with a few dangling strands of hair stuck in the glass. Some of the large yellow envelopes were upside down while others lay right side up. "MSP Evidence" the envelopes announced. Only a state police officer would have those envelopes. My brain was struggling to take in the significance of what I was seeing. Then I saw a human form was lying face down on the paved shoulder of the freeway. I saw that it was a female in civilian clothes.

At that time a screaming siren skidded up to us from the opposite direction. A local police officer from Novi Police Department responded to the P.I. also. Red and blue flickering lights bounced off of the freeway overpass creating an eerie effect to the surreal thought that was forming in my slowly working brain. The words MSP Evidence bounced around my brain. The criminal investigation division (or CID, Narcotics Section, as we knew it) had only two females assigned to it at that time. I knew both of them, and one was my past partner, Trooper Valerie, who had transferred to a narcotics enforcement team as an undercover officer.

I approached the body with trepidation. When I rolled her over, her eyes looked directly into my eyes as though she was about to speak to me. I saw that she was Valerie, my former partner. My heart leaped to my throat choking me. I tried to deny what I was seeing, but the images did not change. No pulse, no heartbeat, little bleeding from the wounds. The words that I thought she was about to speak were never uttered. I waited for that telltale laugh I came to know when I worked with her on so many shifts, but it never came. Although she looked alive, she was forever gone.

It was gut wrenching to watch that ambulance pull away with her lifeless, broken body neatly stored inside and wrapped in the sanitary white sheet. Unbelievable, unimaginable, a feeling of complete emptiness and total loss enveloped me as the ambulance faded away in the night. It was a loss just too painful to bear. My past partner, with whom I had shared so many experiences, arrests, chases, meals, and laughs, slowly faded into the darkness on that freeway. The loss cannot possibly be put into words, but that crushing emotional cost was just the beginning. She was married to another trooper whom I knew very well.

The death message we delivered to her husband was so terribly difficult that it is indelibly embedded in my brain. Having delivered his share of death messages, her husband knew immediately what he had just lost the moment we knocked at his door in those early morning hours and he saw us with solemn looks on our faces. What can one say and what can one do in such a situation? A fellow trooper had just lost his wife, his friend, his colleague and companion.

Police funerals are difficult. As with most such funerals, officers attend in full dress uniform. Meeting with my partner's family was very difficult to bear even with the support of my own family. There was nothing I could say or do to bring her back or ease her family's pain. My former partner's mother and I hugged and cried together for an eternity. She wanted details to help her put this behind her, as much as possible. With a great deal of difficulty on my part, I gave her the information she so desperately needed, but just that; some details would stay at that accident scene never to be revealed.

Police funerals are meant to honor the fallen. They are quite something to watch and very impressive if you don't know the honoree very well. If they were a close friend or your partner, they are unbearable. The officiating officer explains the risks police officers face every day and thanks the family for the sacrifice their officer gave in service to the citizens they had sworn to protect. The deceased officer's life is celebrated with descriptions of the officer's merits and sacrifices. The Director of the Michigan State Police gave a moving speech, as did the family clergy. Hundreds of police officers from the Michigan State Police, local police agencies and sheriff's departments stood in solemn tribute wearing their Class A uniforms to pay their respects. Many of these were friends of Trooper Valerie.

I was there with Valerie at her funeral, our last patrol together, her in her casket and me trying to hold it together, with little success. As I rapped my knuckles on her casket out of respect and to say my final good-bye, I swear that I heard her carefree laugh one last time telling me not to worry as she was going to be okay on this, her last patrol. My tears just would not stop.

At times I dream that we are again together on patrol, her laughing that laugh with that famous "Geeeez" she uttered so often. I am once again with my partner protecting the citizens and visitors of Michigan. We always handled all that was sent our way using her easygoing manner to get offenders to do what was requested of them without having to resort to physical means in most cases, but she was tough when she needed to be. She missed very little and handled investigations with a level of skill that taught me a great deal. She treated even serious offenders with professionalism and common courtesy that enhanced the reputation of the MSP. Most of all, we communicated during traffic stops and investigations with very little need to actually talk, just a quick look, nod of the head, or other gesture to communicate a threat or that we saw a violation without tipping off the suspect. That is when I realized how close we were. I learned a great deal from her while we worked together. Then I awaken and once again remember that she is gone, gone forever, except in those dark recesses of my brain and those lonely quiet nights when sleep just eludes me.

Her death reminded me of some words of wisdom, the source now long forgotten, that I read about, written regarding those who served in the military. Those same words so aptly apply to police officers. Though I don't remember the exact words, the version that I transformed to apply to police officers goes something like this.

Every person who becomes a police officer, full or part-time, for a police department, whether operated by a state, county, city, or township, at one time in their life, signed a blank check to the governmental entity for whom they worked, made payable in the amount, up to and including their life.

The State of Michigan cashed that check written by my former partner, Trooper Valerie, that night when she lost her life transporting evidence for court the next morning.

24

THE DAY I MET
JOHN WAYNE

Just after my former partner, Trooper Valerie and I decided to stop working together due to a difference of opinion on how to handle the various situations we encountered, I first met him.

Since I was a young boy I had watched John Wayne in the many movies that he starred in. He was a take-charge, win-at-all-costs hero, to be admired and emulated by all. He had beaten, almost single-handedly, the Japanese during WWII, and he cleaned up many western cowboy towns ridding them of robbers and thieves. He had a strong sense of right and wrong and made quick decisions to win the day. No one had to tell him what to do and when to do it. He instinctively knew how to handle every encounter and he quickly and decisively prevailed in every situation. He was always right, no questions asked. I certainly looked up to him as my role model as a young boy long before I considered becoming a police officer.

I saw him staring at me one day for the very first time in my own bathroom mirror. He looked at me intently, trying to figure me out and to understand who I was. I studied him to figure him out and determine why he was in my mirror. We stared at each other for a long time, neither of us moving. Slowly, as if my brain was grappling to understand, his facial features started to morph into my facial features. It was as though I was watching an apparition. John Wayne was slowly transforming to look just like I did.

I began to understand that the young man with the meager past who had been raised to be honest, respectful, caring, and helpful had somehow transformed into someone I didn't recognize at first. Who was this strange person staring at me in my own mirror? I was the one, like John Wayne, who fought criminals and won on a daily basis. I was cleaning up *my* patrol areas ridding them of the bad guys. I had a strong sense of right and wrong and made quick decisions to win the day. No one had to tell *me* what to do and when to do it. I was always right, no questions asked. I was the take-charge, bull-in-a-china-shop, win-at-all-costs guy. I was the hero to be admired and emulated by all. That new person had blazed a wide path in dispensing law and justice in *my* post area.

I realized I had morphed into a John Wayne character over a year ago but I had never noticed it before that day. It slowly sank into my confused mind that I had been the reason my partner and I did not work together any longer. I had started to run roughshod over the very citizens I had sworn to serve and protect. However, this was not a movie and I was not a movie character. What I had done and how I had started to treat others I encountered affected real people. Thankfully I can say that I never outright abused anyone with my authority. I did treat some people less than civilly and made arrests or wrote tickets when they weren't entirely necessary. At times, the end result may have been better had I made more reasonable decisions. I did retain enough of a sense of right and wrong while I played the role of John Wayne to curtail my brash new persona. After I came to realize that I had taken on the role of John Wayne, I turned the corner necessary to start the slow transition to becoming the true professional and caring police officer I intended when I first pinned on my badge.

In the years following that fateful day I have seen many other police officers transition into what I and many other officers have come to call the John Wayne Syndrome. Officers mean no disrespect to the real John Wayne, only using his many movie characters to refer to phase three of the typical evolution of most police officers as they move through their careers. From what I have seen in many other officers as well as myself, the transition goes something like this.

Phase One — new officers are scared of their own shadows, make few decisions, cannot remember what the law is on a particular point or how to fill out that form, possess little self-confidence, are not sure how to handle violators or innocent people, and face danger praying to survive another day. The time frame varies with the individual but usually starts on day one and lasts for a year or a little longer.

Phase Two — officers in this phase feel somewhat comfortable in most duties and situations thrown their way. They are normally at ease dealing with the public in situations where enforcement action must be taken. There is still much to be learned, but officers can operate independently in most situations without close supervision and are comfortable in asking for guidance from more senior officers or supervisors when necessary. When engaged in a traffic stop or investigation the officers focus on the matter at hand and handle it with a level of competence. However, they may initially miss small indicators of criminal activity or of impending assaults. Eventually, as many functions become routine, officers start to see the small things that lead to additional arrests previously missed.

They start to learn to look beyond the immediate situation to tie in other recent crimes and help other agencies solve unsolved cases. This phase lasts from around a year or so until three or more.

Phase Three — officers now know all that there is to be known. They have seen it all. Just ask and they will tell you so. There is only one way to do anything, their way. Officers in this phase will tell everyone they just made the perfect arrest, wrote the perfect violation, obtained the confession no other officer could have possibly gotten, found the concealed gun or drugs no one else could have found, provided the flawless courtroom testimony, and the list goes on.

If selected to be a training officer for a new officer fresh from the academy, they consider themselves the perfect but very demanding training officer. In actuality they will treat the new officer like a criminal suspect or worse, finding the most insignificant faults and readily pointing out the many errors of the new officer (of course the phase three officer never has and never will make those same mistakes). This phase three training officer often cannot help transition the new officer from academy theory to practical application on the street or to help the new officer become the best officer possible. Unfortunately, the phase three officers do not know they are in phase three and would never believe anyone who tried to tell them so. Remember, they know everything and if it were true, they would already know it. This is the ultimate state of arrogance; hence, meet John Wayne at his worst.

This is a dangerous time for the phase three officers. This is when they will usurp their authority, take charge of *their* streets, *their* patrol area, and conduct *their* investigations. During this time they will make bad arrests in the interest of justice and use excessive force or assault suspects because they deserved it. These officers will demean, abuse and be unfair to new officers, fail to share their experiences, and run their own program rather than follow their department's directives.

Lawsuits against the officer and department can be expected while the officer is in phase three. In my experience, this is when disciplinary action often arises from this officer's aloof conduct that violates department policy or infringes on citizen's rights. The onset of this phase depends on the officer, but generally can be expected around three years on the job or more and extend until the officer comes to realize how wrong this behavior and attitude are. I have seen officers with many years on the job who have never left this phase because they refuse to acknowledge that they have taken up the character of John Wayne.

Phase Four — officers have come to realize that they are in phase three and they are functioning as a John Wayne imposter, and they need to get to the place they originally wanted to be as a police officer. This is the first and very necessary step in leaving phase three and growing in to phase four.

Phase four officers start to retake the attitude that they are only one spoke in the wheel of justice, albeit an important one. They again realize that there are reasons for the orders superiors give to them, and whether they agree or not, they carry them out to the best of their abilities. They gather and consider all evidence and information before making decisions whether to make that arrest, issue that citation, or condemn someone's actions. They realize that maybe giving a break is just what is needed to help a person going through personal difficulties. Of course when the facts dictate, the arrest is still made and the citation is written, but with a purpose that is explained to the offender and for a valid reason.

Officers now look for connections between a current case and other unsolved cases handled by their own or other agencies. On traffic stops, where evidence of a crime is uncovered, the officer tries to tie it in to an unsolved B & E where the property stolen may match what the officer sees, or pill vials with prescription drugs that have been recently taken from a larceny or robbery at a pharmacy. During a CCW arrest, the officer checks to see if the gun had been stolen, possibly solving a B & E or robbery. The officer has learned that a well-placed telephone call or an area broadcast often results in solving crimes that would otherwise go unsolved and aids in bringing justice to the victims and suspects.

When phase four officers are entrusted with the sacred role of training a new officer, they show patience, understanding, and openly share knowledge with explanations for any directives. Phase four training officers realize the new probationary officer is not the enemy, but a brother or sister officer who has been entrusted to their care to mold and polish to the very best of their ability and is thus a reflection of their efforts. These officers realize it is sometimes a difficult transition from police academy theory to the real world of working as a police officer for a new officer. They also realize that different people learn in different ways and at different speeds and focuses on the new officer's strengths and abilities.

They remember back when they were new and what they wished their training officers had been like and act accordingly with the new officer. They know that there is more than one way to handle a situation, and when the new officer handles a situation in a way different than the phase four officer would have, credit is given as long as the method was safe and legal. They work to help the new officer become the very best officer possible to the credit of the department and the citizens they will both serve. These officers beam with pride every time they see the trainee later in their career and share the enjoyment when the now seasoned officer conducts an excellent investigation, knowing that they helped in some small way to develop another caring, dedicated and professional police officer to carry on.

These seasoned officers now demonstrate good judgment, common sense, well-reasoned decision making and compassion. Good deeds are performed for citizens like helping change a flat tire, helping find the lost dog, buying coffee for the drunk in the restaurant where the officer just ate and telling him not to drive to avoid being arrested. They take those extra minutes to console those in need, to give that ride home to the stranded victim, to explain to offenders the wrongness of their actions and to simply be human. With their vast experience, knowledge and compassion, they also remember to guard against those very few offenders that would harm the public as well as them and they never let their guard down.

Phase Five — The last phase is one that officers need not graduate to, and hopefully they never will. Officers call this the "retired in place" or RIP phase where the officer does very little, hides from responsibility and simply collects a paycheck. An officer should never become complacent because to do so is dangerous to the officer and is a terrible waste of resources. There are always problems that can be ferreted out and solved, an existing program that can be improved, a new program to be initiated, an impending tragedy to be averted, or something in the community that can be achieved. It is up to all officers to move forward and contribute until it is time to hang up their uniforms in favor of fresh bodies and fresh minds from the training academy.

As officers evolve from phase one to phase five, officers move from performing "by the book" to using their now well-honed judgment. It initially seems hard to know who deserves a traffic ticket and who needs a break when all has been going badly in the offender's life. It takes some time, it takes many emotional experiences, and it takes a true desire to evolve into an excellent police officer. Once officers learn to talk to people they come into contact with in an easy and friendly way, they are able to learn a little about them in just a few seconds. That information can then be used to decide on the proper actions in each case. Experience teaches officers that just one break to the right person at the right time can turn someone around.

On the other hand, officers must know when to hold an offender accountable to protect the offender and the public. I made that difficult decision when I decided to make an arrest for drunk driving on Christmas Eve. I had to decide between letting the guy go with a simple warning probably to enjoy Christmas with his family, but possibly to harm others on the road that night depriving them and their family of a happy Christmas celebration. Because of the arrest that I made, the drunk driver spent the Christmas holiday behind bars rather than with his family. I felt like a world class jerk as I thought about Christmas with my family. A few months later I received a card from the wife of the intoxicated driver that I had arrested, thanking me from the bottom of her heart because all of the grief the family experienced on that cold lonely Christmas Eve was the one thing that turned the driver around to never take a drink of alcohol again. She wrote that I had given them the husband and father that they had previously known back to their family.

That thoughtful woman blessed me by affirming that the terrible deed I knew I had to do not only helped to protect other families scurrying to enjoy the holiday who might have been injured by him, but ultimately helped her husband and her. I will never know whether another family would have been injured or killed by the drunken driver had I simply turned my head and let him drive on that Christmas Eve. Police work is full of what-ifs and unknowns that will never be revealed to the officer who must live in the present.

Above all, police officers must always remember each day when they pin on their badge, that they are no longer Bill Smith or Betty Jones the private person. In most other types of employment this strict requirement does not exist. When they are working, and to an extent even when they are "off duty," they are representatives of a governmental entity and must always act and speak with that fiduciary duty in mind, especially in times of stress or anger. There is no place for personal viewpoints or "street justice" for professional officers. How a situation comes out in the end ultimately is not for the officers to decide. This can be very difficult when a suspect's behavior involves name calling of the worst names imaginable, demeaning family members, spitting, threatening to sue, or attacking physically. Even in these extreme cases, when an officer forgets that cardinal rule and crosses the line, the officer puts himself in jeopardy of criminal prosecution, civil lawsuits, and agency discipline, not to mention placing the agency in a bad light with the public.

The two critical phases in a police officer's development are phase three and phase four. Good phase four cops are always assessing what they have done to see if it was the right thing to do, so they can make corrections in the future when they encounter a similar situation. Officers stuck in phase three are too arrogant to waste their time looking back at what they have done to see if they can improve themselves because they know they were always right. These officers are always looking for adulation or spending their time grooming themselves for that next promotion with the increased pay and increased power over others or that sought after assignment. They don't waste time taking care of the officers they are responsible for as that takes away from time spent buttering up their superiors by playing golf with them, going out for drinks, or attending baseball games to curry favor for their next big promotion. They do whatever it takes to get noticed by their supervisors and feel no shame in such calculated attention-getting activities. Rather than truly being professional police officers, they are only masquerading by wearing a police uniform and greedily grabbing their increased pay and pensions. In my opinion, they never truly earned the right to wear that uniform and they acted the part just enough to get the promotion.

Good cops simply do their jobs to the best of their ability, with wisdom, compassion, and good judgment in deciding whether to write the violation or give only a warning. Rather than remaining stuck in phase three, phase four officers realized they needed to mature and move on to serve others rather than themselves. They rise to supervisory positions due to their skills and ability without need to resort to politicking, glory-seeking and artificial gamesmanship. These are truly professional police officers to be admired and I salute them and all they stand for.

25

AN EASY DAY

Trooper Maurice (Mo) and Sergeant John had been assigned to a Presidential protection detail. These assignments came along fairly often when the President of the United States had some political engagement in Michigan. The state police often provided extra man power (ok, officer power) when he came to town. Advance work for a presidential visit was being conducted by the U.S. Secret Service. Mo and John had been assigned to assist with that pre-visit work. They were enjoying the assignment that provided for some down time, although it required meticulous planning and footwork.

Located in Canton Township, Ford Road was a five-lane affair with a center turn lane with many businesses lining both sides of the road. Cars and pedestrians cluttered the road as well. Mo and John were stopped in the turn lane after their errand when suddenly a BOL (Be On the Look-out) came out over the police radio announcing that a shooting had occurred minutes earlier in the nearby city of Wayne. The BOL reported the suspect and his white pickup truck were being pursued by a police officer from Wayne Police Department where the shooting occurred. The victim who had been shot by the suspect was believed to be dead.

About that time Mo and John saw the white pickup truck barreling down the road aiming directly at the stationary state police car which now had the emergency lights activated. Thinking the suspect intended to drive into the patrol car, Mo and John jumped out of their car with Mo pointing his service revolver down the road and John pointing the shotgun at the approaching pickup. The truck slowed down almost to a stop, then suddenly without warning roared past them. The driver had a shotgun pointed out of his window at the officers and fired a single shot at them. The pickup fled at high speed as the troopers (trooper and sergeant, but once a trooper always a trooper) jumped into their car and gave chase. The troopers could not risk shooting at the murder suspect for fear of hitting an innocent civilian. Generally only bad guys shoot in such situations since they don't care who they hurt.

The line of police cars following the suspect grew as police cars from many local police departments and deputy sheriff's joined the effort to apprehend this murderer. The sight was reminiscent of a high-speed lighted Christmas display. Sirens screeched and wailed, alerting all that it would be wise to quickly pull off of the road and let the caravan pass. I heard the radio traffic from my position only a mile or two away. It was a warm and sunny day and I had seen very little activity in the rural area that I was patrolling. I had only made a few stops of minor violators letting most of them go with only a warning. This was one of those days that allowed me to recharge my batteries, providing a break from the days when non-stop calls wore me down. My mind drifted with positive thoughts.

The radio traffic startled me into full consciousness and it was so intense that it was difficult to ascertain where the pursuit was and where it was headed. I finally gleaned enough to determine the pursuit was entering the US-23 freeway northbound toward the town of Brighton. I entered the freeway behind the long collection of police cars and the white pickup truck farther down the freeway.

Radio traffic reported that various police officers were stopping at each freeway overpass to take cover behind the concrete columns. I later learned that as the suspect neared each overpass, the suspect shot at the officers with his shotgun. The officers would duck behind the concrete, let the suspect pass, ensure no civilian cars were in the line of fire then step out and fire at the suspect's fleeing white pick-up truck. Later when I looked at the vehicle, I saw that many of the officer's bullets struck the suspect's pickup but the suspect miraculously avoided being struck himself. This may seem strange to the average person, but a person in a metal vehicle that deflects bullets, driving 100 mph zig-zagging down the road, is difficult to hit, especially when the suspect is firing at the officers who are trying to hit him. This went on for several miles and at each of the overpasses.

Finally, with Mo driving in excess of 100 mph, Sergeant John actually climbed outside of the speeding police car and sat on the edge of his open passenger's window to shoot at the suspect's vehicle. He aimed at the rear window of the pickup directly behind the suspect's head. The rear window of the suspect's pickup shattered on his second shot and the suspect twisted around in his seat at 100 mph and pointed his shotgun at the sergeant. Mo, seeing what was about to happen, grabbed the gun belt of Sergeant John and yanked him back into the police car affording some protection behind the car's windshield. Mo was a very large trooper with arms like many other people's thighs, so pulling Sergeant John back into the patrol car wasn't too difficult.

In this situation, the weapon of choice might have been a rifle that accurately shoots a single bullet, however, each trooper choses either a shotgun or rifle when they begin their shift based on what the officer thinks is best for that patrol. Trooper Mo had chosen a shotgun that day. Again Sergeant John climbed back out onto the window edge and fired, this time striking the suspect in the back of the head with some of the buckshot pellets. The suspect's vehicle veered left onto the grassy median, which made his pickup truck bounce violently due to his speed. That momentarily stunned the suspect and caused him to drop his shotgun out of the driver's window where he had been aiming it. His truck swerved into the center grassy median of the freeway, across the freeway southbound lanes, and came to rest up against the grassy slope of an exit ramp. I could just see the suspect's vehicle leave the northbound lanes and cross the southbound lanes and slide to a stop from my position in the line of police cars. I thought I had seen something fall from the driver's window of the pickup but I could not be sure what it was.

I heard shots fired as I skidded to a stop next to a stationary state police car where a young trooper was standing outside of the car holding his shotgun with a wisp of smoke curling up out of the barrel. The trooper had fired his shotgun at the suspect moments before, and I had to take the gun from him and put the safety on as he was dazed from the encounter. The trooper told me the suspect's shotgun had fallen from his truck when he crossed the freeway median and the suspect had reached behind his truck seat for another shotgun. As I quickly scanned the area I could see a rough semi-circle of police cars with police officers, guns drawn, pointed at the suspect. I could see the suspect seated in his truck with his head slowly moving, but appearing to be looking at nothing in particular. None of the officers moved, apparently waiting for the suspect's next move. I decided to close in on the suspect before the suspect had an opportunity to fire on the officers encircling him.

I ran that 20 or so yards of open grass coming up to the suspect's pickup from behind. As often happens in stressful situations, I felt like I was running in slow motion trying to close that dangerous open distance to reach protective cover if he came out shooting. As I ran, my mind slowed down to a crawl and took in all of the images that my eyes were sending to my brain. I saw the large number of bullet holes in the driver's door and the bed area of the pickup truck as I ran to the vehicle and noted the back window of the pickup had been shot out. My mind tried to pick up clues to determine if the vehicle had been disabled due to gunshots or if the suspect had been wounded. That important information would tell me if the suspect would still be an immediate threat.

When I arrived at the back of the suspect's pickup truck, I aimed my handgun at the driver's door where I could see his face in the rearview mirror through the shattered back window. He was looking directly at me. He was wavering inside of his pickup, and I didn't know if he was getting out of his pickup to shoot at me or if he might shoot at me from where he was. I remembered being told by the other trooper that the suspect had another shotgun he had retrieved from behind his seat of the pickup.

At that moment I felt fear. I was not afraid of the suspect; I was much more afraid of the many police officers with their guns pointed at my back who had been too transfixed to move. I felt that if the suspect came out shooting, those officers would do what they had been trained to do, and that would be to unleash a wave of bullets at the suspect even though he was only a foot or two away from me. I felt confident that I could handle the suspect, but

I had absolutely no control over those officers who were definitely feeling the stress of the moment. Also some of the officers aiming at the suspect had shotguns loaded with buckshot that spread out in a cone-like pattern farther from the gun barrel increasing the likelihood of hitting me. I wondered, *should I move in on the suspect and possibly trigger the unleashing of a wall of lead aimed at my location*? As I had been trained to do by my training officer, Trooper Mike, and without much additional thought, I slid around the rear of the pickup and quickly but cautiously stalked toward the suspect's door to resolve this situation.

I popped my head into the edge of the driver's window opening and saw him. He was an older man, maybe mid-fifties, with longish dirty hair and disheveled clothes, with a bright red frothy pool spilling down his shirt. A bullet from one of the police officers had found its mark and weakened the suspect from a loss of blood. He turned his head toward me and he looked directly into my eyes with a dull look as I pulled open his door. My experience instantly told me that that dull look was caused from either near death, extreme exhaustion or both. His second shotgun fell onto the ground as I grabbed his bloody shirt with my left hand and pointed my pistol squarely at his chest with my right and yanked him out and onto the ground in one powerful and swift motion. He grunted as he landed on his back and stared up at me with a faraway look in his eyes. My gun was now aimed at his face. I saw the red, frothy blood, bubbling from his chest where the bullet had obviously passed through his lung.

By now a circle of police officers had joined me and gathered around the suspect who looked up at them but said nothing. He couldn't. He was nearing death. Suddenly the circle of police officers was parted by a woman who yelled that she was an off-duty nurse on her way to work. She had no idea how this man had been injured, but she was going to use her skills to help to the best of her ability. She directed us to help her apply first aid to this man who was leaking his life-sustaining blood onto the grassy freeway shoulder. In spite of direct pressure on the wound by this nurse, the blood kept running from the suspect's back as the gunshot was a through and through wound.

Within a few seconds the suspect took one last deep breath and exhaled. The sound of his death rattles could be heard in the stillness. What little life had been left in his eyes faded away and his eyelids slowly closed for the last time. I later learned that he and a buddy had been drinking and had gotten into a fight at a motel in Wayne which led to this suspect shooting and killing him. A Wayne police officer arrived and a shoot-out between the suspect and the officer resulted in the suspect being shot in the chest. This wound ultimately resulted in his death, but not before he had the chance to cause an enormous amount of trouble. My mind flashed to my dad in Germany hunting down fleeing Nazi SS Troopers at the end of the war. Now I understood my dad's vacant stare just a little bit more.

The adrenaline flush from the group of police officers standing over the suspect slowly drained away as the officers realized they had survived yet another life and death encounter and they had the good fortune to be able to hug their families once again at the end of their shifts.

After helping load the body into the ambulance, I took one last look around. The bloodstains would soon be washed completely away by the next cleansing rain, but not the images captured by my mind. I drove back to the post, changed my clothes, and went home for the day as my shift had ended hours ago. Mo and Sergeant John waved as they returned to their assignment of preparing for another Presidential visit. For knowingly exposing themselves to the suspect's gunfire without backing off, they would later be awarded the department's Bravery Award for their actions on that day.

Police work is full of surprises. The only constant in police work is the sudden and unexpected events that erupt in your face when you least expect them. This incident reminded me of the potential dangers I face when I get ready to go to work each shift, wondering if I should turn left or right when leaving the post parking lot and whether that would make any difference at all.

26

THE SUSPECT

It was early fall. The tree leaves wore their brilliant colors and started to litter the ground. The days were warm but the nights were cooling with some mornings displaying frost on the ground. Winter was surely on its way. I was working in the east side of Washtenaw County on the 8 p.m. – 4 a.m. shift, an overlap shift to ensure police coverage during the change from afternoon shift and midnight shift. The area is sparsely populated with many farms but few houses. Vehicle traffic was usually very light on the country roads. Not too much happened in this quiet community of mostly hardworking, honest people. Occasionally the routine would be broken by stopping a suspected drunk driver, or apprehending someone on an outstanding warrant, or just someone wanting to chat.

"21-16, 21," called the dispatcher.

"21, 21-16, go ahead." I was startled into action as I grabbed the radio mike and instinctively replied.

"We have a report of a B & E in progress at the Salem General Store."

"21, I am only five minutes away," I responded.

"Affirmative, 21-16," the dispatcher answered.

"21, put me out at that location," I announced as I slid to a stop, jumped out, drawing my gun.

Earlier that night, I stopped by Salem General Store to buy a snack and beverage. There was not too much of any significant value in that store and not much could be anticipated in the cash register. The quaint village consisted of a population of less than 500 people, one general store, a volunteer fire department, and a handful of houses. I couldn't imagine who would break into that store.

I instinctively scanned the front of the store. A metal 55-gallon steel drum that was usually sitting out in front as a trash receptacle was protruding out of the shattered front window. An older black man wearing tattered clothing was sitting on the steps to the general store holding something in his hands. The population in this village is all white. *Strange, the store was being burglarized and a witness was just sitting on the front steps*, I thought. Maybe he saw who broke into the store and could tell me which direction the suspect or suspects had run.

As the man's eyes met my eyes, I saw that he was holding a candy bar in his hand. As soon as he saw me looking at him, he slowly and methodically opened the candy bar wrapper and took a large bite of the candy bar, continually looking directly into my eyes. Based on what my mind had cataloged in those first few seconds at the scene of the crime, my experience told me this man was not a witness, but the burglar himself.

Was he armed and would he rush me in an effort to escape? Would I soon be involved in either a fight or a foot chase to run down and arrest him? He sat motionless looking at me with a mouth full of candy bar, methodically chewing the candy. I approached him with my gun held to my side as the potential burglar never moved. Very odd indeed.

"Sir," I started to speak to him.

"I threw the barrel through the front window, went into the store, and took this candy bar that I am eating," he simply looked at me and said.

"Sir, stand up and turn around and keep your hands in sight," I ordered.

"Anything you say trooper," he quietly responded, raising his hands above his head.

Now I was confused. He had just confessed to felony breaking and entering. To prove that crime I needed to have evidence beyond a reasonable doubt that: 1) a breaking had occurred, 2) the suspect had entered the building, and 3) the suspect had at the time of the breaking had the intent to commit a larceny or felony within the store. He knew all he had to do to commit a breaking and entering was to use force to gain entry, enter the store, and commit a larceny by taking the candy bar. When he started to eat the candy bar in my presence, he showed that he had the intent to permanently deprive the store owner of the candy. Given the evidence I saw coupled with the suspect's confession, the burglar had just given me an airtight case. Still the suspect had not moved an inch.

I arrested him, searched him, and secured him in my patrol car. My backup had just arrived and watched the burglar while I took photographs and examined the store. Nothing else was obviously missing or otherwise disturbed. The owner had been called and upon his inspection of his store, confirmed that nothing else seemed to be missing. The cash register was not tampered with. It seemed unbelievable that the suspect had committed a felony in order to get a candy bar, but at the time I couldn't find any other explanation for his unusual behavior.

I read the suspect his Miranda Rights and he acknowledged that he understood them and that he did not have to talk to me and that he did not want to talk to an attorney before I asked him questions about the breaking and entering. He then proceeded to ask me to take him to jail. That was the extent of our interview. Checking the suspect's criminal history on the law enforcement computer system revealed a long list of previous convictions, but nothing involving violence.

Judge Dunbar was tall and thin with snow-white hair and piercing blue eyes and presided over his District Court. He was also a seasoned, understanding and fair judge. He always wore string ties under his judicial robe. He never missed any testimony and he could see through the best attempts to hide the truth, though often his eyes closed during trials.

When the suspect's case was called for his arraignment, Judge Dunbar asked him how he would like to plead. "Guilty, your Honor." The judge informed the burglar that he would enter a not-guilty plea on behalf of the defendant and bind the case over to the circuit court for a preliminary examination. However, the defendant emphatically told Judge Dunbar that he was guilty of breaking and entering the general store and that he had in fact committed a larceny in the store by taking the candy bar. District courts have jurisdiction to handle criminal matters that carried a possible sentence of one year, including some crimes up to two years. In felony breaking and entering cases like this one, the defendant is arraigned in District Court where the formal charges are read and a determination is made whether the prosecution has established that probable cause exists that a crime was committed and probable cause exists that the defendant committed that crime. If probable cause is found, then the defendant is bound over to the circuit court for trial. The defendant stated that he did not want or need a preliminary examination or a trial.

When questioned further by Judge Dunbar as to why the defendant wanted to skip all of his due process rights, the defendant told the judge that it was getting close to winter. He did not have a job or enough money to house or feed himself. He told the judge that he had been in the Detroit House of Corrections (known as DeHoCo) before and he knew it was warm there with three hot meals per day. Judge Dunbar, drawing on his years of experience and compassion, realized the defendant never intended to injure anyone or commit any serious crime; he only wanted a warm place for the winter. The judge allowed the defendant to plead to a lesser crime and sentenced the defendant to six months in DeHoCo. The defendant politely thanked Judge Dunbar, smiled at me, and was led away to serve his sentence over the winter months.

That incident taught me that not all "criminals" are bad people. People do things for a variety of reasons that might not make sense until the whole story is known. Police officers usually do not initially know all the information that eventually comes out during the investigation. The defendant in this case turned out to be a decent, though clearly desperate person, but it just as easily could have turned out much differently in a different situation because desperate people often commit terrible acts.

27

BAND-AIDS

It had been some five years since I had graduated from the State Police Academy. My eyes had seen so much hurt, misery, tragedy and death. It seemed that each day was a repeat of the previous ones with changes only in the names and places of those involved in the calls that I was sent to handle. I always worked hard to not become complacent. I had learned that to do so meant that in the wrong situation I could be hurt or killed because of it. I also tried never to become apathetic toward the people I encountered, either those I helped or those I ushered into the criminal justice system. That is a tough balance and something that the individual officer must consciously work on every day. I still cared. But the routine of the everyday mistakes of people and the intentional wrongs committed toward others weighed heavily on me. Why do people intentionally hurt others? I suspect I would never fully understand the answer.

I was in a funk feeling depressed for no particular reason on that sunny day. Maybe it was from the continuous stream of traffic offenders I had dealt with who berated me for stopping them. Maybe it was from the criminal defendants that I arrested and watched get off with only a slap on the wrist for their offenses. Maybe it was just the lack of sleep due to working the seven afternoon shifts followed by seven midnight shifts and then the seven day shifts, so my body never knew if it was day or night, breakfast or dinner time. Or maybe it was just the routine of the criminal justice system. I could have been falling into the trap of apathy, which was dangerous for police officers. I found myself just going through the motions trying to keep busy to head off being depressed.

I was working Hines Park in Wayne County where people from all strata of life frequented.. It was beautiful with the miles of cut green grass shaded by tall trees along the gently flowing Rouge River. As I rounded the bend of a curve I saw an intersecting road coming down a rather steep and high hill. A bicycle was lying on the shoulder of the road on the grass. A small boy was sitting next to his bike with his head down. I was a quarter of a mile away, but I could see something was wrong. I sped up a bit and turned toward him. When I pulled up next to him I saw he was really crying hard with tears running down his cheeks. His right knee was up and bright red blood sparkled in the sun as it ran down his leg. I immediately saw that the wound was not life threatening and there were no compound fractures. I felt a wave of relief wash over me.

In fluid motion from years of repetition, I flung open my driver's door while the patrol car was still slowing, pressed the trunk release, and ran to the trunk to grab the first aid kit. It was times like these that I was grateful for that first aid training we were given so long ago in the academy. The yearly updates also helped my confidence as I ran up to the boy who looked all of eight years old. As I neared him, I instantly saw the gravel on the asphalt with the bicycle tire skid mark. I easily envisioned how this accident had happened. The boy had gained speed going down that steep hill and as he applied his brakes the bike had slid in the gravel that was lying on top of the asphalt and he lost control of his bike. The bike slid out from under him and he fell forward onto his knees and the palms of his hands. As he was wearing shorts, the gravel produced some nasty, but not too-deep cuts. I saw bits of gravel embedded in his wounds. I knew these cuts were painful for the small boy.

Seeing me running up to him changed his facial expression from fear and pain to relief and even a slight smile. Experience had taught me that getting his mind off of his injuries would help him regain his composure so he would not focus on his pain. I talked with him about where he lived, where he was going, and how pretty it was in the park that day. I noted that his bike was not badly damaged and only had a few scratches on the fender. He was easy to talk to, and he seemed to enjoy talking with a police officer. I took out a sterile gauze pad and wiped the tears from his cheeks as he puffed out his chest a little. His fear was mostly gone.

I told him that I would wipe off his cuts to remove the small bits of gravel and dirt and apply iodine that would sting but would kill the germs in his cuts. He said it was ok for me to do that for him. I gently wiped the dust, dirt and gravel from the cuts. He grimaced a little but stayed still. Then very carefully I applied the iodine with the gauze tip on the vial. He jumped from the immediate sting and a few tears welled up in his eyes, but he sat still. His trembling lip told me he felt the pain from the iodine as it cleansed the wounds.

"I'm sorry I got some of my blood on your pants," he said smiling up at me.

"That's okay, I am just glad you weren't seriously hurt," I told him as I smiled back at him.

I peeled off the paper holding the Band-Aid and placed it across the now clean cuts on his knee then applied a second Band-Aid to some lesser cuts. I helped him up. He suddenly and without warning stood up and gave me a big hug and said simply, "Thank you." We smiled at each other and I knew that things in the world at that moment and in this place were at peace. I thought of all the times I had put Band-Aids on my own children's cuts and how, for some reason, helping a child seemed like the most significant impact I could make.

As he rode away on his bike, I drove away in the opposite direction. I watched him in my rearview mirror slowly pedal up the steep hill as we waved good-bye to each other. A smile grew across my face that I just couldn't suppress. The sun seemed brighter, the grass more green, the breeze was cool and steady and I felt goodwill toward all the world. I realized that this was probably the most important thing I did in the last few years, and for this young man, this was a serious situation demanding all of the expertise and compassion I could bring to help him. No serious felony arrest, no major crime solved, no serious or fatal accident investigated, or no gripping courtroom testimony provided could compare to the importance of helping this scared young man in his moment of need.

Now that I have long since retired, I wonder what has become of him and how he turned out as a grown man. I will never know what impression I made on him or if I might have changed him in some small but helpful way. I do know that encounter made a huge impression on me, and I was changed in some big way that day. Every day since that incident I have looked forward to helping people, both at work and in my private life, which has kept any potential apathy at bay. I will never forget the day that brave young man came to my rescue.

Approved, SCAO

STATE OF MICHIGAN JUDICIAL DISTRICT 3rd JUDICIAL CIRCUIT COUNTY PROBATE	SUMMONS AND COMPLAINT	CASE NO. 83-12329-NO

Court address

Court telephone no.

2 Woodward Ave., #711, Detroit, MI 48226

(313) 224-5360

Plaintiff's name(s), address(es), and telephone no(s). Richard Roscoe 1234 Main St. Livonia, MI	v	Defendant's name(s), address(es), and telephone no(s). Trooper Robert Muladore 4321 Center St. Livonia, MI

Plaintiff's attorney, bar no., address, and telephone no.
Dewey C. Howe
3432 Middlebelt
Livonia, MI

SUMMONS **NOTICE TO THE DEFENDANT**: In the name of the people of the State of Michigan you are notified:

1. You are being sued.
2. **YOU HAVE 21 DAYS** after receiving this summons to **file a written answer with the court** and serve a copy on the other party **or take other lawful action with the court** (28 days if you were served by mail or you were served outside this state). (MCR 2.111[C])
3. If you do not answer or take other action within the time allowed, judgment may be entered against you for the relief demanded in the complaint.

Issued	This summons expires	Court clerk

*This summons is invalid unless served on or before its expiration date. This document must be sealed by the seal of the court.

COMPLAINT *Instruction: The following is information that is required to be in the caption of every complaint and is to be completed by the plaintiff. Actual allegations and the claim for relief must be stated on additional complaint pages and attached to this form.*

☐ This is a business case in which all or part of the action includes a business or commercial dispute under MCL 600.8035.

Family Division Cases

☐ There is no other pending or resolved action within the jurisdiction of the family division of circuit court involving the family or family members of the parties.

☐ An action within the jurisdiction of the family division of the circuit court involving the family or family members of the parties has been previously filed in _____ Court.

The action ☐ remains ☐ is no longer pending. The docket number and the judge assigned to the action are:

Docket no.	Judge	Bar no.

General Civil Cases

☐ There is no other pending or resolved civil action arising out of the same transaction or occurrence as alleged in the complaint.

☐ A civil action between these parties or other parties arising out of the transaction or occurrence alleged in the complaint has been previously filed in _____ Court.

The action ☐ remains ☐ is no longer pending. The docket number and the judge assigned to the action are:

Docket no.	Judge	Bar no.

VENUE

Plaintiff(s) residence (include city, township, or village)	Defendant(s) residence (include city, township, or village)

Place where action arose or business conducted

Date

Signature of attorney/plaintiff

If you require special accommodations to use the court because of a disability or if you require a foreign language interpreter to help you fully participate in court proceedings, please contact the court immediately to make arrangements.

MC 01 (5/15) **SUMMONS AND COMPLAINT** MCR 2.102(B)(11), MCR 2.104, MCR 2.105, MCR 2.107, MCR 2.113(C)(2)(a), (b), MCR 3.206(A)

28

THE LAWSUIT

My partner Trooper Chuck and I had stopped the car before midnight for some minor traffic violation on the freeway in the city limits of Livonia. The sunken freeway, known as a "ditch," was some 20 feet below the ground surface looking like a giant trench, reducing traffic noise for local residents. We had stopped the offender for a speeding violation when we heard a terrific metal-to-metal screeching above us. We looked up into the warm night air and saw a car driving along the drop-off to the ditch, shearing off the freeway fence posts. The chain link fence danced up and down like a huge ribbon waving in the breeze as it was pulled away from the posts by the car. Finally the car stopped, but I saw the driver spinning his tires in an attempt to escape the clutches of the freeway fence that had ensnarled his car almost like a spider web with a fly entrapped. We sent the offending motorist on his way and raced to the next exit ramp and turned toward the car above. Certainly the driver would be injured and would need our medical skills to help him.

As we approached the accident scene we saw broken car parts of metal and plastic littering the roadway above the freeway. A long portion of the freeway fence was lying on the grass. The car appeared to be stuck in the shoulder where the tires dug deeper into the deep moist grass. The driver's door was open but the driver was nowhere to be seen. A glass with a liquid that smelled of alcohol sat in the console of the car. The hood of the car was hot to the touch. A quick check of the license plate showed the registered owner lived only five blocks away and there were no reports that the car had been stolen. While we conducted our initial investigation, dispatch advised us that a nearby homeowner reported a male running from the car in a northwesterly direction, the same direction as the home of the registered owner. When backup arrived, we immediately drove to the registered car owner's home.

Just prior to that time, the law regarding drunken driving arrests required the officer to actually see the driver operating the car while intoxicated. The law had just changed to allow arrests for drunk driving at the scene of an accident even when the accident was not actually observed by the officer so long as probable cause existed that the suspect had been the driver and was intoxicated.

We drove into the driveway of the home where the registered owner of the car lived. We knocked on the door. No answer. I saw the front window curtain move ever so slightly as though someone had just peeked out of the window to see who was at the door. We knocked again with the same result. We had dispatch call the home. The dispatcher advised that the owner would be coming to the door as she had told him the police wanted to talk to him. When the door suddenly opened, the young male stood before us wearing only underwear. His hair was disheveled, his eyes were very blood-shot, his speech was slurred, his breath smelled of alcohol and his balance was unsteady, all signs of an intoxicated person. I asked him if he had been driving his car that evening. He stated he had not. He then looked out of his front window toward his driveway with a feigned look of utter surprise and said, "My car has been stolen!" I asked him if we could come in and take the stolen car report. He stood aside and said, "Come on in."

Once inside of the house and after reading him his Miranda Rights and receiving his waiver of those rights, I asked him if he wanted to make a stolen car report. He stated that he did. I asked him if he had been in an accident this evening and he told us in no uncertain terms that he had not. I reminded him that making a false police report was a crime but that if he wanted to file a stolen car report we would take that report.

"Well, I don't think I want to do that," he said, looking at me and then my partner. I told him that I could smell intoxicants on his breath.

"Where have you been this evening?" I asked him.

"I've been at home all night," he hesitated before answering.

"I can smell intoxicants on your breath, what have you been drinking?" I asked.

"Tequila," he quickly responded.

"May I see the bottle of Tequila?" I sternly asked him.

"Oh, that's going to be a problem, the only bottle I have here has not been opened," he said.

Clearly he was lying and I knew that he had been driving when he crashed his car into the freeway fence that we had witnessed. He was given sobriety tests typically given in drunken driving arrests and miserably failed each one. We arrested him and took him to the Northville Post where he blew a .13 on the breathalyzer. At that time .10 was the presumptive level of intoxication for drunken driving (now it is .08). My partner and I celebrated that another drunken driver was taken off of the road helping to make driving safe for the motoring public.

We were notified of the criminal case against the drunken driver. The prosecutor was known for being one to avoid a courtroom fight. Even knowing that the prosecutor didn't like to take cases to trial, I was shocked when I was told that he was dismissing the criminal charge of drunken driving. As the drunken driving law change was so new, he did not want to try our case with that new law. I had an ominous feeling when the criminal case was dismissed but I tried to put it out of my mind.

It was some months later on a quiet Sunday morning when I heard a knock on the door of my house. It was very early in the morning and the knock concerned me. I opened the door to see two men in sport coats and ties standing on either side of my door. *They look like police officers*, I thought.

"Are you Trooper Bob Muladore?" the first one said. I told them that I was.

The second one said, "Sorry to have to do this but we are U.S. Marshals and we have a Summons and Complaint for you. You are being sued in federal court." What? I had no idea what I had done to get sued. As they returned to their car parked in my driveway, I opened the paperwork. I saw my name, United Stated District Court, and then I saw $12,000,000.00. My mind only saw the dollars that I was being sued for. I saw nothing else about the lawsuit.

Once the shock wore off a little, I forced myself to look at the name of the person suing me. I realized it was the drunken driver who had sheared off the freeway fence some months ago. I saw that my partner and I, and the MSP, were being sued for false arrest and violating his Fourth Amendment rights (entering his home without a warrant). My guts churned, my wife asked what was wrong. I told her and she too looked scared. Most police officers are not rich people. I told her not to worry and that this would be handled at work. I was not so sure of that at that very moment but I didn't want her to worry with our three small children in the house.

Police officers are taught how to do their job in the academy to ward off lawsuits. We were taught to follow the law, which we had done in this drunken driving accident case. Anyone can file a lawsuit by simply making allegations and paying the filing fee at the courthouse. I knew I did not do anything wrong. The months dragged on with my deposition, my partner's deposition, and the deposition of the drunken driver. Depositions can be nerve-wracking for the witness as the attorneys try to catch the witness in lies or to get the witness to say something helpful to their case. Needless to say, this whole process wore on my nerves over the year it took to unfold.

The Michigan Attorney General's Office (AG) handled our case as it occurred in the line of duty. As the case neared the trial date, the assistant AG who was handling our case called my partner and I into his office.

"Plaintiff's attorney said that his client would settle this case for twenty thousand dollars and dismiss the case, what do you think?" the assistant AG asked.

"Well I don't know. We were sued for twelve million and he'll settle for twenty thousand," said my partner. "That seems like there is something fishy going on."

"No way, we did nothing wrong, I don't want to settle," I answered.

"You might lose," counseled the assistant AG.

"We followed the law. I don't want to settle," I again told the AG.

"Okay, I'll tell plaintiff's attorney you won't settle," the AG told us.

"Let us know what the attorney says," I said. I was adamant that the case not be settled for even one dollar as we did nothing wrong. The entry into the suspect's house was with his permission so there was no Fourth Amendment violation as the lawsuit alleged. The arrest was valid with the recent law change allowing us to effect the arrest on the probable cause that the suspect had been driving while intoxicated.

"I'll let you know as soon as I hear back from the attorney," the AG told us as we were leaving his office.

A few weeks later, the assistant AG called us and informed us that the suspect/plaintiff had moved to Colorado and did not want to come back to Michigan for trial. Finally the plaintiff's attorney, after realizing we would not pay any money to settle, and he had no chance of winning at trial, agreed to dismiss the lawsuit. The whole time we went through the lawsuit, I expected the dismissal to be a huge relief. That was not the case as I realized I would always be at risk for a lawsuit just for doing my job. It felt like meager thanks for protecting the public. I tried to console myself that at least the case resulted in one drunken driver that didn't kill an innocent family. I learned that anyone can sue me, but if I followed the law, the lawsuit would likely end favorably for me, as it did in this case.

29

THE BANK ALARM

Bank alarm calls are common, in fact, all too common for police officers. They are almost always false. Careless tellers, bad weather, system malfunctions, or other simple mistakes are the culprits in setting them off on most occasions, but not always. It is that rare actual robbery that police officers keep in mind when they rush to all bank alarm calls.

"21, 21-16."

"21-16, 21"

"21-16, report of a bank alarm, South Lyon State Savings Bank."

As the patrol car shot past 100 mph, my mind flashed back to one such bank alarm in Houghton, Michigan during the winter. The sole robber took his shotgun into the bank, shot one teller in the arm, permanently severing it from her body. She was the wife of the police chief. The robber took another female teller hostage but he was stopped not far from the bank when the tires on his car were deflated by gunfire. The robber had strapped a bomb on the teller to prevent her rescue and to use her as a human shield to protect himself. The standoff lasted all night in the sub-zero weather. As morning began to dawn, the suspect took a large knife and started to cut handfuls of hair from the hostage screaming, "I won't let her go, I will blow her to hell." With the road beginning to fill with people heading to work, the threat of injury to other innocent citizens greatly escalated, necessitating drastic action. The MSP hostage negotiator, also a psychologist, advised that in his opinion, serious harm or death to the hostage was imminent. Three MSP snipers simultaneously fired on the robber instantly killing him before he could detonate the bomb. The MSP bomb squad members deactivated the bomb rescuing the distraught woman.

"21-16, 21, copy the last transmission?" the dispatcher sounded concerned and my mind was snapped back to reality.

"Roger 21, I'm on I-96."

"21-16, I tried calling the bank but no one answered," added the dispatcher.

"21, 21-16, start a back-up unit," I told the dispatcher.

"21-16, 21, I tried but there are no other available units at this time." *Hmmm, no back* up, I thought as I stomped the accelerator to the floor.

No one answering the telephone at the bank. It seems unlikely that this alarm is false, I thought.

It was January, so the freeway was clear and it was very cold outside. I had on the emergency lights but no siren to avoid warning the bank robbers if the alarm proved to be valid. The patrol car was a dud, only capable of a top speed of 122 mph. I was going all of that. I was some 10 miles away and nearing the bank quickly.

When I came up on the overpass of the freeway my steering wheel suddenly lost all tension. It felt as if I was floating on the air. At that speed, decisions had to be made quickly or something terrible would happen. It immediately dawned on me that the overpass, which freezes before the road surface, was glare ice. The rubber tires no longer had any grip on the road surface, but were sliding on the glare ice. I did the only thing I could do, nothing. If I tapped the brakes or turned the wheel, I would go sideways. A crash at 122 mph would have meant certain death for me.

The car slowly turned to the left and continued to slide. As the sweat began to flow I hit dry pavement and the car jerked straight again as the tires bit into the dry concrete. It all happened in less than 3 seconds.

I left the freeway and quickly negotiated the last few miles, silently entering the parking lot of the bank. I looked for a running vehicle with a driver behind the wheel who might be a getaway driver in the group of cars scattered around the parking lot, but I saw none. No cars were parked close to the entrance of the bank.

Grabbing my shotgun and racking in a load of buckshot, I silently approached the bank, careful not to pass by windows without first looking inside for would-be robbers that might notice my approach. When I arrived at the glass door, I peered into the lobby of the bank. I saw no one in the lobby other than the tellers on the far side of the counter. A quick scan of the back of the bank failed to reveal anyone.

I slowly opened the door of the bank with my shotgun at the ready. One of the tellers immediately noticed me, and her face broke out in a sheepish smile.

"Oh officer, I am so sorry, I accidently tripped the alarm," she managed.

"Is everything okay?" I asked, looking at the other tellers.

"I am sorry officer. I am the manager, and I was just going to call to report the false alarm, but I finished putting my lunch in the refrigerator before I could call," an older woman stated as she came from a back room.

"Okay if I have a quick look around?" I asked.

"No, please go ahead," the manager said.

After checking behind the counters and in each office, I quickly checked the bathrooms. Satisfied, I told the manager and teller that I would be leaving. The errant teller and manager thanked me as I walked out the door.

"21, 21-16, false alarm."

"21-16, 21, Okay, I just got off of the phone with the manager. She told me to tell you 'thank you' again," replied the dispatcher.

"21, 21-16, I will be clear of the bank."

As I drove away my mind replayed that call and I thought, *another false bank alarm by a careless teller. She will never know how close of a call I had responding to that carelessly tripped alarm.*

30

PARKERS OR A RAPIST

Police officers have an innate distain for wife beaters, child molesters, and rapists and they are always on the lookout for them. While attending the police academy, staff instructors provided examples of cases that either they or other troopers were involved in to provide indirect experience to members of the recruit class. The experiences shared helped me immeasurably in understanding what I would face once I started working the road.

One evening just as dusk was settling in, my partner Trooper Chuck and I were in Northville Township patrolling near a large office building when I spotted a lone car parked in the far back of the parking lot. An uneasy feeling crept over me and I felt that the car did not belong at that location.

My mind flashed back to the police academy and I vividly recalled one such story about a trooper checking on a routine couple parking in a drive-in movie lot. Assuming that this would be just another couple making out, he contacted the male driver of the vehicle. The academy instructor told us the driver told him that they were just parking and enjoying the evening. The woman sitting next to him confirmed that story and the trooper went on his way.

Later, that trooper learned that the male had a pistol pointed at the trooper when he approached below the window out of sight of the trooper. The man had kidnapped the woman and was about to rape her. He told the woman if she cried out, he would first kill the trooper and he would then kill her so she played along with her kidnapper and was ultimately raped and released. The instructor had a difficult time relaying the story to us as it had affected him a great deal, knowing that he had allowed the kidnapping and rape to continue, though he had no way of knowing it was happening when he talked to the man and woman.

Those stories from the academy made a deep impression, especially when similar suspicious situations occur. As I approached the vehicle, I had an uncomfortable feeling.

I had snuffed out the patrol car headlights long before I approached the car so as not to alert the occupants of my approach. I had also shifted my car into neutral and turned off the patrol car's ignition switch to eliminate the noise of my approaching car and silently rolled up behind the car. I heard muffled cries escaping partially open windows of the car. When I was just behind the passenger's front door, I saw the two were clearly engaged in intimate sexual activities. The question was whether both were consensually engaging in those sexual activities. I looked at my partner and we both nodded in agreement to investigate.

When I clicked on my flashlight I saw the woman was on top of the man. She looked at me and quickly jumped off of the man, pulled down her skirt, and rolled the window down.

"Is everything okay," I asked the occupants.

"It's okay, we're engaged," she blurted out.

"Are you sure?" I asked the woman.

"Oh yes, officer," she replied in a calm but excited voice.

"Please step out of the car, miss," I asked. She stepped out of the car, smoothed her dress and walked to the back of her car. My partner watched the male and asked him for identification.

"Are you sure you are here of your free will?" I again asked.

"Yes, we are getting married soon, and, well, you know," she said.

"May I see your identification, please," I asked her.

Yes, I felt a wave of relief that everything was "okay." Her response hit me as being very funny, as though being engaged was a prerequisite to participating in consensual sexual activity. As long as it was consensual between adults it was legal.

Her comment brought out an uncontrollable laugh out of me that I just could not stop. Fortunately, both parties in the car also saw the humor in the woman's comment and laughed along with me. The woman and man both thanked me for checking on their welfare. I'm not sure they understood what had motivated my partner and me. Many people would have been more upset about being interrupted. Whenever I have to do something intrusive and uncomfortable for others, I remind myself that I can never know all of the details of a situation, and I don't want to walk away from someone in danger. In this case, what might have turned out as a serious sexual assault and kidnapping, ended up providing a little levity.

31

ROUTINE DANGER

I learned early in my career that a patrol car is just another tool in the police officer's toolbox. While most citizens value their car and drive them carefully and treat them well due to their cost, police officers learn that they must push police cars to the limits countless times each day in order to perform their duties.

During my first week on patrol fresh from the academy, my training officer Trooper Mike directed me to stop a car for a traffic violation. The car had turned down a rut-filled gravel road and accelerated to 45 mph. I tried to catch up to the target vehicle but the patrol car was bouncing badly and I slowed down so as not to damage it, the same as I would in my personal car. Trooper Mike looked at me with a wild look and said, "What are you doing?"

"I don't want to damage the car," I replied.

"What? How long do you intend to follow that car before you stop it? Stop that car now," he demanded.

"Okay," I said and sped up causing our car to bounce almost out of control until I had caught up to the violator, initiated a stop, and ultimately released the offender with a warning.

"Look, the patrol car is just a tool, like your flashlight, handcuffs, or gun. Use it like one," he instructed.

Some years later, Mike and I were sent to a fight in progress at a rest area on the I-275 freeway in Plymouth Township one early afternoon.

"21-8, 21," the dispatcher called.

"Go ahead, 21," I replied.

"21-8, we have a report of a fight at the I-275 rest area in Canton. A male victim is being badly beaten by a male subject," the dispatcher said.

"21, 21-8, we are only a five miles away. We will be there in a couple of minutes, will advise when we arrive," I said.

Traffic on the freeway was heavy, but Trooper Mike was driving, so we were, of course, pushing it, all out, topping 130 mph when a deafening explosion erupted from the rear of our patrol car. It sounded like a howitzer shell exploded in our trunk. The car lurched back and forth. My partner fought the spinning steering wheel. Cars around us sought safe haven away from the screeching, whining, shiny blue State Police car with siren blaring and the emergency lights flashing wildly.

My mind flashed images and thoughts of my wife and three small children. I wondered what they might think when they received the call that I had been seriously injured in this car crash, or worse. I remembered all of those times I was too busy to read a book to my kids or stop to help my wife with some small task. These small things in my life now seemed so important as the car wildly continued on.

The gears in the rear universal on the back axle had disintegrated. I just knew that at the least, we were going to crash and suffer serious injuries due to the high speed we were traveling. He fought it until he had slowed down to about 35 mph when our car's rear axle locked up solid and we slid into the grassy median.

To this day, I still don't know how we did not crash, flip over, or get hit by another car. Luck was on our side and that didn't happen and we didn't get hurt. My partner had wrestled the car with an amazing amount of skill to bring us to a safe stop. This was just another close call that could have ended much differently but for a little luck, my partner's driving skills, and maybe a little help from some higher authority who had been watching over us as we ended another shift safely.

When I went home at the end of my shift, I hugged my wife, I found time to read a book to my three eager children and I quickly helped with a few odd overdue projects around the house. I never forgot how the simple, routine things I do have the potential to make all the difference in my life.

32

HIDDEN GUN/ HIDDEN INTENT

It was late afternoon with plenty of daylight remaining in the day. I stopped a car for weaving on I-275 in the city of Livonia, an indicator of an intoxicated driver. While many drunk drivers are apprehended during the night, it isn't uncommon to find them during the day like this one.

This suspected drunk was like many of the other drunks I had arrested. He was belligerent, loud, slow to respond to directions, and denying that he was drunk. However, I noted that he seemed to be watching my every move, more than the average person stopped for suspected drunk driving. I saw him looking at my uniform, but I thought he might simply be curious. Given his actions, I too kept a close watch on him.

I told him that I would be asking him to perform some routine sobriety tests to determine if he could continue on his way or if I would be arresting him for drunk driving.

"Do you know the alphabet?" I asked the driver.

"Of course, I graduated from high school," he responded.

"Go ahead and recite it for me starting at the beginning," I said.

"A, B, C, E, G, oh I forget it sometimes," he said.

"Count on your fingers by touching the tip of each one to the tip of your thumb, starting with your little finger and counting on each starting with 1 through 4 and then back down to 1 again," I directed.

"1, 2, 3, 4, 1, 3, 2, 4, I did okay on that, right?" he said. I slowly shook my head, indicating he had not.

"Do you have anything wrong with your legs or have any problem with your ability to balance?" I asked.

"No," he answered.

"I want you to walk heel-to-toe, touching the heel of your left foot to the toe of your right foot, taking seven steps forward in a straight line then turning around and taking five steps back toward me in a straight line, counting each step out loud," I said.

"One, two, three, four, five, okay, I am turning around," he mumbled. I caught him as he turned to keep him from falling. "One, two, three, and four," I saw that he missed touching his heel to his toe on several steps as he walked in each direction.

"How did I do?" he asked.

"With your hands at your sides, keep your right leg straight and hold it up about a foot off of the ground."

"How's this?" he asked as he wobbled.

"Try the same with your left leg," I requested as I watched him nearly lose his balance almost falling.

"I guess I didn't do so well on that test," he sheepishly mumbled.

"I want you to blow into the PBT as long and hard as you can. Can you do that?" I asked.

"Yep," he replied. I had him blow into the PBT and he stopped after a short blow.

"Keep blowing, keep blowing, okay, stop," I told him.

"Can I go home now?" he asked.

"No, you are under arrest for operating a vehicle under the influence of alcohol," I told him.

"I am not that drunk. What is the limit?" he asked me.

"You blew a .13%. At .10% the law presumes that you are too drunk to drive," I said.

After I told the driver that he was under arrest, I handcuffed his hands behind his back. I conducted a search following his arrest of his clothes and body (one of the 10 exceptions to the search warrant rule to the Fourth Amendment of the U.S. Constitution) and found a small, fully loaded, semi-automatic pistol in an inner breast pocket of his leather jacket. After securing him in my car, I searched his car, called the wrecker to have it towed, ran LIEN (computer) checks on the driver and car and other routine duties of completing arrest forms. The response from the LIEN check revealed the driver had a lengthy criminal record including several stints in prison.

I arrested him for the felony of carrying a concealed weapon and for the misdemeanor of operating a motor vehicle while intoxicated and drove him to the post for a breathalyzer test to determine the exact level of his intoxication. While the sergeant administered the breath test, the suspect told the sergeant that if he got the chance, he would have shot me because he did not want to go back to prison. The sergeant asked him if he was serious and the suspect told him he was dead serious, but that I had never turned my back to him or looked away from him long enough to give him a chance to get the gun out and use it on me. He said he knew if I had seen him going for his gun, I would have shot him first because he had looked for and saw that I wore a distinguished expert pistol badge on my uniform.

There have been at least four other incidents (that I know of) where suspects have threatened to kill not only me, but my family as well, in addition to the 12 or so times suspects had grabbed for my gun in its holster. My wife and children have had to live with that reality for things they had nothing to do with. I suspect that they continue to carry that fear with them (although they mask it well) never knowing if and when such threats might become a reality, yet they still question me about why I always carry my gun years after I have retired. Each threat was very credible and potentially very real. I have been stalked by gun toting suspects on more than one occasion while I worked the road. Such is the nature of police work.

33

SALIVA SURPRISE

I was working the 8 p.m. to 4 a.m. shift in the early fall with another trooper. The weather was clear and warm. It was a great day to work. I had stopped many offenders for minor traffic violations and each had graciously accepted either a verbal warning or citation as I felt the situation warranted. I was feeling good about my efforts at trying to keep the roads safe for all to travel.

As darkness set in, I noticed a car that was driving below the speed of other cars around it. When stopped for a traffic light, the driver delayed moving forward when the light turned green for him. When he veered to his left nearly bumping the car next to him, I knew the driver was having some problem that I needed to investigate, so I pulled him over.

As usual, I positioned my patrol car to provide a corridor of safety from cars approaching from behind my location. My partner Trooper Chuck walked up to the passenger side as I approached the driver. I noticed that he did not look in his outside rearview mirror to watch my approach; rather he continued looking straight ahead, which was somewhat unusual. My partner motioned to me that he saw an open beer can on the floor between the driver's legs. As soon as I greeted him, the driver began his vulgar verbal attack on me.

"What the fuck did you stop me for?" he asked with a slurred voice. His clothes were disheveled and a urine spot was obvious on the front of his pants.

"Sir, I stopped you for suspected drunk driving," I explained.

"Bullshit, I wasn't drunk driving. I only had two beers," he said.

"May I see your driver's license, registration and proof of insurance?" I asked. He fumbled for his wallet, then flipped past his driver's license four times before he found it and handed it to me.

"Do you have your registration and proof of insurance?" I again asked.

"What, let me see, why did you stop me?" he asked me again. He tried to open his glove box but missed the release button several times before he finally found the button and opened it. He grabbed a stack of paper and handed it to me.

"Here is the shit you asked for, look for it yourself," he said in a nasty tone.

"Sir, please step out of your car," I said.

"You asshole, you some kind of bastard or what, why do I need to step out of my car for, I ain't done nothing wrong," he slurred.

"Let's go," I said as I opened his door and pulled him out of the car by his arm.

"I'm going to have your badge. I pay your salary. Why aren't you trying to catch real criminals? I'm just trying to get home," he said as he glared at me.

This drunk was worse than most. After he performed, or I should say tried to perform, field sobriety tests, I arrested him and placed him in the patrol car in the back seat. Unlike many other police departments, state police cars are open like civilian cars with no glass or barriers of any type between the back and front seats.

While I was filling out the forms, I heard the sound of spitting. A large, warm glob of spit hit the back of my neck and started to run into my shirt. As I turned around, a second glob struck me in numerous places on my face.

I exited the car, went into the trunk and took out a large gauze bandage from the first aid kit and stuffed it into his mouth. He recoiled as I wrapped a second gauze bandage around his face to prevent further spitting. Evidently he thought I was going to punch him in the face for what he had done to me. It wasn't that he didn't deserve it in my opinion, but I would not have been justified in hitting him. I would only have gotten myself into trouble and likely sued in civil court by the drunk.

I took him to the post and finished processing him before I went to the bathroom and washed my face and neck with soap and hot water and changed my shirt. There was nothing else I could do. This was not the first or last time that I had been spit on by people that I had arrested. Each time I had been spit on I only hoped that the person spitting didn't have hepatitis or another serious communicable disease. I learned that not all dangers a police officer faces involve guns, knives or accidents. This drunk driver reminded me that contracting a serious disease is a real threat in policing and whether the suspect is infected often remains unknown until long after the event is over.

34

BEAUTY AND THE BARF

My partner Trooper Richard was driving on I-696 in Farmington Hills one warm summer evening with traffic moving at 75 mph. "Look at that van right ahead of us," he said.

"Yep, driving on the shoulder. He's probably drunk," I replied.

"Let's take a look at him," he said as he turned on the overhead right light. The driver took more time than usual to stop, an indicator of a possible drunk driver.

My partner approached the driver and I walked up to the passenger front window. I motioned to the passenger to roll down her window so I would be able to hear my partner and the driver talking in case things started to become heated. As she did so, my eyes were immediately drawn to this stunningly beautiful woman. I saw that she was wearing a low-cut thin white dress with spaghetti straps. Her make-up was flawless, accentuating her naturally beautiful facial features. Her blond hair flowed in the cool evening air as the passing cars zoomed by on the freeway.

"Good evening officer, may I help you?" she asked in a soft and sleepy voice as she leaned out of the window. I noted that her speech was slow and her words were slurred. I also noticed that she was very well endowed. Well you have to look for possible weapons or drugs, right? I placed my left (non-gun) hand on the edge of the door of the vehicle while I looked into the car, but I did not see any open alcoholic containers, drugs or weapons in the van.

"Good evening, ma'am, where are you headed tonight?" I asked to start a dialogue with her that might help in determining if the driver may have had too much to drink.

"I've had too much to drink tonight and this thoughtful guy I met in the bar is taking me home," she slurred. The smell of alcohol on her breath confirmed what she had just told me.

"How much farther are you going?" I stopped mid-sentence as my left hand suddenly felt a warm sensation and then a sticky slippery feeling. My mind tried to resolve this initial friendly encounter with that warm sticky substance on my hand. As I moved my hand disturbing the substance on the door, I smelled a strong and nauseating stomach bile. I looked down at my hand and saw what was obviously vomit that had just been deposited on the edge of the car door and my hand by that now not so good looking woman. The stinking bile was running down the side of the car with bits of food stuck in the slimy mass. As I looked at her a little closer, I saw the front of her white dress was drenched in vomit producing a strange mosaic pattern. A pool of the slimy mass was on the floor of the van that ran onto her shoes.

"Are you okay?" I asked the woman.

"Oh, I think so, but my stomach feels a little upset," she mumbled.

I heard my partner telling the driver that he would be getting back to him in a couple of minutes. We met back inside of our patrol car.

"How is the driver?" I asked my partner.

"He has been drinking, but he is okay to drive. I am going to let him go with a warning," he replied. "What is that smell?" he asked.

"The passenger puked all over herself and I got my hand in it," I told him.

"And I thought you were the lucky one talking to that pretty woman," he said as he burst out in uncontrolled laughter. "Man, you stink," he giggled, nearly doubling over in laughter at my expense.

"Cut this guy loose and get me to a bathroom so I can wash this puke off of my hands, pronto," I ordered. My gag reflex almost caused me to mimic the woman's earlier activities, which would only have made matters worse.

My partner hurried back over to the driver and quickly told him to be careful and let him go on his way with his newfound friend. At the restaurant I washed my hands three times before most of that awful smell was finally gone.

35

LUCKY LADY

"21-16, 21," the dispatcher's voice broke the calm afternoon.

"Go ahead 21," I sadly replied. *There goes the peace and solitude*, I thought.

"21-16, copy a report of a two car accident, unknown injuries.

"Copy 21, in route," I said as I performed a power U-turn to get headed in the direction of the accident. The car leapt forward as I punched the accelerator to the floor. Trees and mailboxes zipped past the patrol car. As usual, with an "unknown" injury accident, serious injuries were assumed for the benefit of the victim. I activated the emergency lights, turned on the siren and stomped the accelerator pedal to the floor so I could arrive as quickly as possible. I knew that in many calls of injuries, police officers are the first to arrive and often provide vital initial first aid to victims and today I just might be able to save a life.

The car was at an angle on the right side of the road. A pickup truck was parked near the car with two older men standing around the car. A young woman in her late teens stood next to the car. As we pulled up to the accident scene, I saw the tongue of a boat trailer had gone through the windshield where the driver's head had been. I could not believe the woman had not been killed. I saw the aluminum fishing boat lying on the side of the road. It looked like it had flipped off of the trailer before the trailer hit the young woman's windshield.

"Is anyone injured?" I asked the group standing by their vehicles.

"No, I'm okay," the frightened young woman timidly replied.

"Was anyone else in your car?" I asked her.

"No, I am alone," she said.

"Any of you guys injured?" I asked the two men who were standing by their pickup truck.

"Nope," said the driver.

The young woman was quite shaken up as she told me what happened. As she was driving along the country road she saw the pickup truck coming toward her hit a bump, which caused the boat trailer to detach from the truck. The trailer and boat crossed the road heading directly at her. She had nowhere to go as a large ditch was on her right side and the truck was driving toward her in the left lane preventing her from veering left. When she saw the trailer tongue coming over her hood directly at her head, she quickly bent down onto the right side of the front seat just in time to avoid her certain death. She heard the tremendous crash as her windshield exploded. She felt the glass fragments striking her.

As I looked closely at the damage, I saw that the tongue of the trailer had gone through the windshield of the young woman's car, through the steering wheel, and it continued on through the headrest where the woman's head should have been. A few strands of hair were embedded through the headrest where the trailer tongue nicked her hair as she flung herself out of the way of the oncoming missile.

A chance incident where a life hung in the balance had spared her. Had she not been as attentive and seen the trailer coming and reacted so quickly, she certainly would have died that day.

"Where are you coming from?" I asked the driver as I had seen that his license plate was from Ohio.

"We live in Ohio just across the Michigan border and we came to Michigan to fish," the driver said appearing unconcerned about the near death injury to the other driver.

"Where are the safety chains for your trailer?" I asked him.

"I had safety chains on the trailer, where are they?" he lied.

"Safety chains on trailers are required to prevent accidents just like this one. The young woman could have been killed had she not been so quick to dodge your boat trailer," I strongly told the uncooperative driver.

"I said that I had safety chains on my trailer. You must have missed them because they probably fell off in the accident," he again lied.

"Just a minute, I'll check again," I told them.

I looked the entire accident scene over trying to find the chains from the trailer. After failing to locate any safety chains anywhere near the accident scene, I got down on my hands and knees, and looked at the trailer for bolt holes that might have held chains. None. I looked for weld marks that might have connected safety chains to the trailer tongue. No such welds. The paint on the tongue was smooth and unbroken indicating no chains were ever on that trailer, which would have rubbed off some paint when the trailer detached. I slowly felt my anger rising after I had confirmed that there had not been any safety chains on that trailer whatsoever. The very reason for the safety chains is to prevent a trailer that might become detached striking a vehicle or pedestrian. Not only had these two men failed to ensure the safety of others on the roadway, but they compounded the violation by looking me in the eye and lying about it. The best I could do was to issue a citation for no safety chains that would only result in a small fine by the judge.

"There were no safety chains on your trailer, right?" I accusingly asked the driver.

"I had chains," he repeated, as he looked me in the eye with defiance.

"I will be issuing you a citation for no safety chains. Unfortunately there is nothing more I can charge you with for nearly killing that young woman. Get safety chains on that trailer before you kill someone," I told him.

"There were chains," he muttered still not wanting to admit his wrongdoing as he took the traffic citation and headed back for Ohio.

Fortunately, instead of delivering a death message we delivered the young woman safely to her waiting family. They thanked us and waved at us as we drove away. From that day forward, I no longer saw minor vehicle code violations as insignificant. Had I or some other police officer seen that trailer without safety chains and taken enforcement action, this close call would have been avoided.

36

GOAT RODEO

ummer was slowly fading into fall on the clear cool Saturday morning as I drove by myself along the two-lane Territorial Road in Plymouth Township. An old beat up car with two older gentlemen sped past my patrol car exceeding the speed limit as they turned their heads in unison to look at me. I spun the patrol car around and gave chase. It didn't take long to pull in behind them. When I approached them I saw that they were both wearing warn and dirty bib overalls, and both were very large men in stature and in weight. Neither of them turned back to watch my approach as I walked up to the driver's door, usually a sign that something was amiss. I addressed the driver and they continued to stare straight ahead without looking at me. *Odd behavior once again,* I thought. The hair on the back of my neck started to bristle as those little warning bells began to slowly chime. Probably nothing, these two may just be tired this early morning as the sun was barely showing its smile above the horizon.

"Sir, may I see your driver's license, registration and proof of insurance?" I asked the driver.

"Yes, trooper, my papers are in my glove box," he replied as I closely watched his hands. As I scanned the floor area of the front seat, I noticed four or five fired shotgun shells lying on the passenger's side of the front seat.

Avoiding eye contact, staring straight ahead as I asked for the driver's license and papers, fired shotgun shells, the evidence was adding up and I thought they could be poachers, which made me feel even more wary. The warning bells began to ring louder.

"Do you have any guns in the car?" I asked the driver and passenger.

"There are no guns in my car," the driver replied.

"I don't have any guns," the passenger added.

Both of these two started to shift around in their seats. Movement is a strong sign that the suspects might be preparing to take offensive actions against a police officer, so I was really starting to be concerned. The passenger started to reach down for a shotgun shell when I quickly yelled at him to keep his hands in plain sight so I could watch them. My gun hand instinctively hovered above the grip of my weapon.

I suddenly had a strange feeling that I should look into the back seat of their car, a likely place for hiding a shotgun in the shadows of the floor. As I shifted my eyes from the two potential suspects, I saw a deer lying on the back floor through the dirty side window. These two were definitely poachers, and if they just shot that deer they had a gun somewhere very close to me. If they had a gun I was in immediate danger. Once again the flight or fight self-defense mechanism kicked in, and I instinctively and swiftly drew my weapon in one smooth motion and yelled that they were both under arrest for poaching. Both of the suspects turned at the same time and looked at me like I was some kind of lunatic, and they both babbled something unintelligible but made no offensive movements. That puzzled me.

With all of the noise and movement, the "deer" suddenly raised its head and looked at me. I quickly looked back at the front seat occupants who remained still, and then I looked back at the deer. I was now looking into the eyes of the supposedly dead animal that had just raised its head, but the eyes just were not right. Deer have round pupils in their eyes, but this deer has slit-shaped pupils. My mind was trying to see all potential dangers the driver and passenger in the front seat of the car posed and at the same time I was trying to comprehend why this dead deer's eyes just weren't right, all in that same fraction of a second.

About that same time the deer had fully lifted its head and I saw the horns on the top of its head. My mind finally categorized the animal and I realized that I was exchanging stares with a goat. It was the size and exact color of a small deer, but those eyes were a dead giveaway for a goat. The goat even managed to let out a little blaaaaaaat for me. The driver and his passenger slowly realized what was happening. At the same instant they, as well as I, burst out in laughter so hard that tears ran down my cheeks. The driver and passenger bent over in uncontrolled laughter. When the laughter subsided, I apologized for drawing my weapon and quickly explained to them that I had suspected them of poaching. Being good-natured farmers, they told me that they understood why I did what I did and were glad things ended well for all of us. The driver told me that the goat was their pet and he often took the goat with him in his car, much the same way people take their dogs or cats for rides. I felt a bit stupid, but I knew given what I knew at the time, I had handled the situation properly. In keeping with the mood, I actually asked the goat if he too needed an apology. The goat looked at me with those slit shaped eyes and simply said, "Naaaaaaaaaa!" They were still laughing as they drove away.

37

CATCH ME IF YOU CAN

I was investigating a series of sexual assaults at Northville State Hospital. The patients in that state facility suffered from serious mental conditions so severe that most were unaware of their surroundings. It was difficult to obtain statements from the female victims as they could not grasp the nature of the violations inflicted upon them. After a diligent investigation, a hospital employee became the prime suspect, Mr. Smith. When I ran a computer criminal background check, I determined that he had been arrested in Detroit for two previous sexual assault crimes. Both of the two cases resulted in dismissals.

I had collected vaginal swabs, hair samples, and semen stains from the victim's bedsheets and clothing. I checked logs showing when the suspect worked, what areas of the hospital he worked at on given dates, and other documentary information in an attempt to implicate him of the assaults. No possible evidence went undiscovered. Based on the forensics and other evidence I uncovered during my investigation, I obtained an arrest warrant for the suspect.

Finding an address for this person proved difficult but I finally located an apartment building where it appeared he was living. Since it was during normal working hours I assumed that he would not be present. I went to his apartment building in an effort to determine if he did reside there by talking to the manager and neighbors, showing them a photograph of the suspect. The manager confirmed that the suspect did live in the apartment but she did not think he was there at that time. My plan was to obtain a confirmed address for the suspect so that I could apply for and secure a search warrant for further evidence.

When I knocked on the suspect's door, much to my surprise, he opened it. We both stared at each other for a moment and when he suddenly realized my visit was not a friendly one, he tried to slam the door. Because I was assigned as a trooper investigator, I was wearing a sport coat and tie instead of my standard uniform. I displayed my badge and identification card to the suspect. I wedged my foot in the doorway as he pushed the door, trying to close it. When I finally made entry based on the authority of an arrest warrant, he immediately began throwing claims at me that the only reason he was being arrested was because he was black.

"Why are you hassling me?" he asked.

"Mr. Smith, I am Trooper Investigator Bob," I said.

"What do you want with me?" he asked.

"I have an arrest warrant for you. The charge is criminal sexual conduct," I said.

"Who did I sexually assault?" he asked.

"You are charged with sexually assaulting several women at the Northville State Hospital," I said.

"That's bullshit, I didn't do anything. I bet it's those lying white bitches, right? I'm not going anywhere with you. Besides, if those woman had been black, you wouldn't be here right now, am I right?" he asked.

"That will be worked out in court," I said.

"You are only arresting me because I'm black, right?" he yelled.

"Mr. Smith, you are being arrested because the judge has issued an arrest warrant for you," I said.

I tried to explain to him that race had nothing to do with the allegations, but he would not listen. Until that point in the investigation, race had not been a factor, not until he tried to make it an issue.

He tightened up his shoulders, apparently readying himself to resist arrest. He started to back away from me.

"I'm not going with you, no way," he said.

"You are going with me. You can go the easy way or the hard way, but you are going with me now," I said as I stared into his eyes with a look that conveyed I meant what I said.

After a few tense moments, he relented and I handcuffed him. I escorted him to my car and locked him inside.

"I was arrested twice before for raping women," he said with a smile on his face.

"Really," I feigned, already knowing this from running his criminal history.

"I beat those charges by having my attorney get one adjournment after another until the witnesses finally quit coming to court. I will do the same this on this case," he said.

I asked him if he had sexually assaulted the women at the hospital and he started to laugh hysterically.

"Yep, I have access to as much sex as I want 'cus those women can't remember a damn thing," he said.

He had not counted on forensic evidence to prove his violations. He pled guilty and was sentenced to prison for the vicious harm to his mentally deficient victims.

38

THE PERSONAL INJURY ACCIDENT

After completing my law degree, I wasn't working the road any longer. I had been promoted to sergeant and assigned to instruct legal courses at the state police academy. On the way back to my office from a meeting at the state police headquarters in East Lansing I was driving an unmarked state police car. Nearing the academy I saw two crushed cars on the shoulder of the road. Smoke rolled out from under the hood of the nearest car. Glass and pieces of plastic that had once been part of the two shiny cars, now bent and twisted, lay on the road. I was the first car on the scene. Experience instantly told me there would be injuries given the degree of damage to the two cars.

Out of habit I immediately started to mentally prepare for what I was about to see and what I would need to do. Gasoline ran onto the road from the ruptured gas tank of the young woman's car farthest from me. The odor of gasoline was strong, suggesting to me that a lot of the gasoline had already spilled onto the road presenting a life-threatening fire danger. I radioed the Lansing Post and asked them to send an ambulance, fire trucks and uniformed officers. The hair on the back of my neck stood up as

I ran through the gasoline that had puddled next to the driver's door. I prayed no sparks would transform the pool of gasoline into a funeral pyre for the driver and me. A quick check with the first car revealed the driver had somehow avoided any serious injuries, though he was a bit dazed.

As I ran to the second car I heard the young woman's hysterical screaming. I knew I was about to see severe body trauma on that driver. The blood I saw running from the wound was darker red and oozed out from the fractured femur that had torn through the flesh of her right thigh. I saw that no arteries appeared to have been severed. A severed artery, indicated by spurting bright red blood, would signal that her life's blood was draining onto the ground. With a severed artery this young woman would have likely been dead in less than a minute. *A compound fracture*, I thought, serious enough that she needed to remain still. The blood flowed onto the floor of her new car and pooled around her feet.

As I leaned into her car to further assess her injuries, I saw a beautiful blond-haired young woman of some 18 years of age, screaming uncontrollably. Her white dress was painted with hot, sticky red blood that flooded from her right thigh. I pulled her skirt up above the wound on her leg and saw the jagged, splintered, pure white end of her femur sticking out of her smooth, tanned skin with the red muscle visible below. I quickly retrieved the first aid kit from the trunk of my car and ripped open a gauze bandage and applied direct pressure on her torn skin to hold back most of the blood flow. The blood was hot as it ran across the backs of my hands, which held the gauze bandage on the ragged opening over the torn flesh of her thigh. There were no rubber gloves in our first-aid kits back in those days. Her right thigh was a half foot shorter than her left thigh. The two pieces of broken bone no longer prevented the contracting muscles from pulling the leg shorter since her broken femur overlapped. One end stuck out of her muscles and the other sharp end had retracted back inside of her leg amongst her vulnerable veins and arteries.

"Miss, please keep as still as possible so you don't cause any further injuries," I told her.

"Oh my god, it hurts so bad, please make the pain stop," she pleaded with me.

"An ambulance is almost here. Just relax and keep very still," I said trying to calm her as much as possible.

I feared that if she moved too much she would cause the end of her jagged femur inside of her thigh to slice through an artery and kill her in less than a minute from blood loss. She screamed when she saw the bone protruding from her thigh. Her screaming mouth was only six inches from my ear as I leaned into her car to keep pressure on the wound. I knew my hearing would be reduced for days after this as her uncontrolled wailing continued unabated. I told her not to look at the wound and her leg bone and to stay still as I laid a gauze bandage over the bone to prevent her from seeing it again. She knew I was helping her, and she did her best to stay still but the pain played with her head.

Then the uncontrollable shaking of a person going into shock set in, and her leg and the rest of her body quivered uncontrollably. With that shock setting in, she was now getting cold even though it was a warm summer day. I placed an emergency blanket on her to help her retain her body heat, which would minimize her going into shock. She tightened her grip on my wrist, which seemed to soothe her a little bit, and her eyes pleaded with mine to help her.

"The ambulance is almost here, do you hear it?" I asked her to help keep her mind off of her injuries.

"Yessss," she said as her voice and her body quivered with pain.

The siren of the approaching ambulance wailed loudly as it stopped near us. Firefighters also arrived and were now washing the spilled gasoline away, removing the fear of a deadly fire erupting around us. I breathed a sigh of relief. Not all accident victims can be helped, but I felt good at being able to help the woman in some small way. I wasn't disappointed when the ambulance crew relieved me of holding the direct pressure that I had been applying to her thigh.

"Thank you, trooper, we'll take it from here," the EMT told me. "Thanks for holding this down until we arrived," he said.

"Glad I could help," I replied as I walked back to my car.

Though I was not working the road as a trooper any more, I realized that police officers never leave the duties of the road, ever, on duty or off, working or having retired. When the need arises, training and experience kick in and you deal with the situation. The most pressing issues become the focus and the officer's mind, blotting out other lesser important things, so they must make a conscious effort to constantly look for other dangers like fire, vehicles about to hit the victim's car, and more. That's what officers have been trained to do and that is what they instinctively do when confronted with emergencies.

Back at the state police academy I cleaned the young woman's blood from my hands and uniform. It was lunchtime and I was hungry. I was drawing little designs in the catsup with my French fries eating them slowly thinking of the young woman and the pain she had to endure. I was happy to have been able to help that woman in need; it made me feel good once again. I realized that in many ways I missed working the road in spite of all the negatives that come with those duties because of all of the rewards, excitement, unknowns and opportunities to help those in need. I had heard so many MSP officers of ranks above trooper say that the best job they ever had was working the road as a trooper. This experience affirmed that I had been right in choosing police work as my career... or had it chosen me? I felt that warm comfort of a job well done. Then I looked down at the pool of bright red catsup on my plate and I imagined a jagged white femur sticking out of it.

39

BROTHER IN BLUE

It was eight years after I left the Northville Post as a road trooper working as a lieutenant in the Executive Division at headquarters in East Lansing when I called the District Commander in Michigan's Upper Peninsula, otherwise known simply as the U.P. He commanded the Eighth District located in Negaunee, the heart of the U.P. I had called him regarding a legal issue I had been working on for him.

"Are you sitting down?" he abruptly asked.

"Well no," I replied, puzzled by his unusual business-like tone.

"You better sit down," the captain directed.

"Your brother has been in a shooting. He was wounded, but he's okay." I instantly felt the dread envelop me as I mentally kicked myself for having talked my brother into joining the state police. Now he was hurt and I felt that it was at least in part my fault. Would he ever be able to return to work? He had a wife and three small children with whom I was very close. My stomach ached and I suddenly had a very bad headache.

My mind quickly replayed my involvement in steering my little brother toward a career with the MSP. Brian had knocked around in various jobs before he attended an American Legion-sponsored Student Trooper School at the State Police Academy for young adults with an interest in possibly becoming a trooper someday. Several years later he trained for and became an EMT working on an ambulance. He was ten years old when I entered the state police recruit school and over the years I had talked to him about my experiences working the road as a trooper. While I was a sergeant teaching law classes at the State Police Academy I suggested he consider becoming a State Trooper as well. Several years later, and much to my surprise, he applied for and was accepted to attend the State Police Trooper Recruit School. I was a very proud brother watching him march down the aisle during his trooper graduation.

Over the years, it was gratifying to hear his stories of bad guys arrested, excellent investigations conducted, accidents investigated, and citizens helped while he worked first at the Ypsilanti Post, and then when he transferred to the Manistique Post. His stories helped me relive some of my experiences as a road trooper. I was happy and proud to have helped steer him into the State Police.

Thousands of scenarios ripped through my brain about what his injuries might be and how it might have happened. Was it a car stop where the suspect came out shooting just as he was being stopped? Did the assailant shoot my brother as he responded to a domestic violence call? Maybe he was responding to a bank alarm when he was shot.

The captain stopped my thought process explaining, "The suspect, a local guy by the name of Mack Schmid, had gotten into an argument the night before the shootings over the three hunters who were hunting bear in the same area as he was hunting even though it was on state-owned land. Schmid confronted the victims who were seated in their car. He shot the driver at point-blank range with a high-powered rifle instantly killing him while he sat behind the wheel of his car. Schmid shot and killed the front seat passenger seconds later. The third potential victim bolted from the car and ran into the woods before Schmid could shoot him. As the back seat passenger ran into the woods, Schmid shot at him but the shots missed him and he escaped unharmed."

"But Captain, how did my brother get shot?" I asked.

"Your brother and another trooper were dispatched to try to intercept a vehicle that was stolen by Schmid this morning. They found him, stopped him, and a shoot-out occurred. Your brother was shot in the head and left forearm." I was still worried. When not fatal, head wounds are very often quite serious and permanent. My mind was overwhelmed with all of the possibilities. I imagined blood running from some unknown wound inflicted by a high-powered rifle covering my brother's head and face.

Following a series of telephone calls to his post and talking with troopers, sergeants and the post commander, I quickly learned that my brother had been hit in the side of his head by broken windshield glass, bullet fragments and metal car fragments. The wounds bled heavily but no serious damage had occurred. The left arm wound was also a car fragment or bullet fragment that had induced minor damage. Relief enveloped me and I felt totally drained. It was late in the day, so I went home and packed my bags. Early the next morning I headed to the U.P. some seven hours away. I don't remember much of the drive, as my mind was preoccupied with all of the questions swirling in my head. How did the suspect get the drop on my brother? Knowing how well trained troopers are I would have expected my brother and his partner would have neutralized the suspect before he shot my brother. Was my brother's partner also injured?

My brother was assigned to the Manistique Post, some 350 miles north of Lansing. I drove directly to the post. When I opened the front door of the post I saw my brother with a bandage on the side of his head and another on his elbow. He gave me a silly grin.

"Are you okay?" I asked him.

"Yes," he simply replied. "Let me show you the suspect's car."

"Where is it? I asked.

"In the post garage," he replied over his shoulder as we entered the attached garage.

As I looked at the forest green Ford Explorer that Schmid had stolen at gunpoint from the owner in Seney, Michigan, I immediately saw many bullet holes in the doors and windows. The back window glass was adorned with many copper colored streaks.

"Last night after the murders of the hunters, Schmid was located and surrounded by law enforcement from around the county. They had Schmid cornered in a large wooded area. The state police Emergency Services Team (Michigan State Police's equivalent of a Swat Team) searched for him using their night vision equipment. Schmid was previously some sort of a military weapons expert and he had been wearing night vision goggles when confronted by law enforcement. One trooper had a chance to take a shot at Schmid but passed it up as too risky. Later that night Schmid also had a shot at a trooper but didn't take it, possibly because one of the troopers had not shot at him."

"How did Schmid escape with him being surrounded?" I asked.

"He must have slipped between officers in the darkness. Schmid stole the Ford Explorer at gunpoint in Seney the following morning and my partner and I got the BOL for the stolen Explorer with Schmid driving it," he continued. "We were in separate cars going up toward Seney when a green Explorer passed us going south. Following the BOL, I wrote the license plate number on the palm of my hand, and looking at the Explorer that passed me I saw that it matched the plate on the vehicle. I turned around and got behind him. He turned onto a dirt two-track road but he must not have known it was a dead end. When he stopped, I slid to a stop close to him. I saw him jumping out of the stolen car with a rifle, so I jammed the patrol car into reverse and backed away from the suspect. As I was getting out of the patrol car and ducking down behind the door pillar I suddenly saw a blinding flash of white light and thoughts of my wife and my three kids flashed across my mind. I knew I was dead and I was going to that bright light people talk about in near-death experiences. I opened my eyes and I was surprised I was still alive. My next thought was, that son of a bitch! My training kicked in and my will to survive took over, so I popped up with my rifle and saw him by the rear of his vehicle and I shot at him. He ran behind the side of his vehicle. I saw him through the glass and I put the sights on his head and squeezed the trigger shooting through the glass window. I saw him drop down out of sight. He came back up and I shot again several times through the glass and door. My partner was shooting at him also with his shotgun. The suspect came out from behind the vehicle and I shot at him again knocking him down."

The autopsy of Schmid revealed that he had been shot in the face, neck, and several times in the upper chest. A rifle bullet had passed through his left hand while it held the rifle pointed at my brother. My brother's bullet shattered the bones in his right elbow causing him to drop his rifle. My brother and the suspect had been aiming at each other at the same time and my brother had shot only an instant quicker than the suspect. Had the suspect shot first, things may not have turned out well for my brother. Once the suspect was on the ground he shot himself in the chest, taking his own life and ending the shoot-out.

The departmental psychologist asked to see my brother. My brother didn't think he needed to talk to him as he felt the shooting was fully justified and he was mentally reconciled with the shooting. After all, it was the suspect who shot at him and his partner first after already killing two innocent civilians and trying to kill a third. He just responded the way he was taught. That is how my brother thinks. He is the most feisty and tough person that I know. The psychologist concluded the same thing and cleared him for a full return to duty.

Later that same day my brother and I went duck hunting at my urging. Ducks were flying and we shot a few. My goal was not to shoot ducks, but rather to see if my brother would react to a firearm following his close encounter with death. I had concern for my brother, as well as his wife and his three children. I knew the outcome of officers who had been in very similar shooting situations and were not as fortunate as my brother. I was constantly aware that I had been a strong influence in him becoming a trooper which put him in that gun battle, and the responsibility weighed heavily on me. I don't know how I would have been able to deal with the situation had he been seriously injured or worse. I needed to make sure in my mind he was able to put this near tragic incident behind him and feel comfortable with guns to be at full capacity to continue to work the road. He passed my test. In my mind, I cleared him for a full return to duty too.

This story made national news and was picked up by a television program airing at that time called "Real Stories of the

Highway Patrol." My brother had been selected for a transfer into undercover narcotics just before this shooting. When the story was being filmed my brother could not appear in the television episode as it would have jeopardized his identity in his undercover role. I was asked to portray my brother with my brother's partner acting as himself. My brother served as an advisor to keep the script as close to the actual events as the producer would allow, though the producer couldn't resist adding some Hollywood-type excitement.

The filming lasted for 16 hours on a single hot day where temperatures exceeded 100 degrees. When it finally aired, the episode lasted for only four and a half minutes, pared down from those long 16 hours of filming. Other than a few unrealistic scenes, the story captured the true events of that fateful day. That was my debut as an actor on national television and I found it quite interesting to watch how a television episode was put together. It was even more gratifying to see that the producer was generally willing to listen to the officers who were actually involved to make a realistic episode from the actual events.

Although everything worked out that time, like all troopers, my brother still faced danger every day, and I nearly lost him again. Within a few weeks after getting shot, my brother transferred into narcotics as an undercover officer. Almost three years to the day after the shooting and on the last day before he transferred back to the uniform division resuming road patrol duties, he jumped into a Michigan National Guard helicopter to go on his last HEMP mission. A HEMP mission involved flying over vast miles of desolate woods looking for marijuana plots planted by drug dealers. Other officers told him they would cover the flight for him but being the dedicated sort that he is, he handled his last assigned flight himself.

As the helicopter started to lift off, it unexpectedly pivoted to one side. When the rotors struck the ground and disintegrated, large pieces of rotor flew into the helicopter like a barrage of missiles. The helicopter crashed hard onto the ground from some eight feet up, causing him to believe that he had broken his arm. Dense smoke erupted inside of the helicopter.

After a few seconds he unstrapped his safety harness and saw the pilots were not getting out. With the dense smoke continuing to fill the helicopter, my brother feared it was about to burst into flames, which would kill all aboard. He crawled to the pilots and started to pull them out of the helicopter. Soon the other narcotics officers who had been waiting for the helicopter to take off ran up and helped to pull the dazed pilots out of harm's way.

Fortunately everyone was able to safely escape the fiery crash. Later state and federal investigators told my brother that he could now say that he is one of a very few people that had walked away from a helicopter crash. Once again, I regretted talking him into joining the State Police. It's one thing to take risks yourself, but it is quite another thing to be responsible for someone else, especially a family member that you put into harm's way by encouraging him to take up a dangerous career. I wrestle with that every day, even long after I have retired, as he still works as a trooper and danger is only a moment away.

40

THE PRESIDENTS

Police agencies and their officers are often asked to provide additional assistance to the Secret Service during presidential visits. The tasks are varied and range from distant assignments providing traffic control to close-in support of varying roles. For the average officer, these assignments are sought after because they are extremely rare and prestigious, not to mention exciting. They instill a renewed sense of duty and patriotism and give bragging rights to fellow officers and family. On the other hand, with them comes the very real potential of danger that can never be disregarded. My three assignments were very different but very exciting in their own ways.

My first presidential protection assignment came when Ronald Reagan first ran for president. He was attending a large convention held at Cobo Hall in Detroit. My partner and I were assigned a lonely stretch of highway far from Detroit. We knew we were clearly out of the picture but we realized if something bad was coming to Detroit from our direction, we just might be able to stop it or at least provide a warning. It was an uneventful late evening until we were asked to pick up our post commander at Cobo Hall. Since we had to drive down to Detroit to pick him up, we would be able to at least get close to the festivities and see something. When we arrived, we were invited into the Hall. It was very interesting to see the people who gather for presidential election events. Food and alcohol flowed and the attendees were clearly dressed for the occasion in expensive dresses and tuxedos. Those folks were very friendly to the officers, engaging us in conversations and asking many questions about our state, our department and us as individuals. They in turn readily answered our many questions regarding the inner workings of politics, where they were from and other questions of a general nature. It was truly a special experience being personally involved at our level in a presidential election event.

When it grew late my partner and I felt compelled to return to our assigned lonely stretch of freeway far from the City of Detroit. Very few cars were on the road in those early morning hours sometime around 4 a.m. A speeding car approaching promised to break the boredom of that quiet early morning. With years of experience behind us, we became suspicious when the car took too long to pull over after we turned on our emergency lights. We tapped the siren.

Five males sat in the car and not one turned to look back at us as we walked up to them. That was a little unusual and we started to hear the warning bells ringing loudly in our heads. All of them were of the approximate same age. Each was in casual clothes but very neatly dressed. I asked the driver for his driver's license.

"I don't have it on me, it's in the trunk," he said. He was not antagonistic in any way, but the cold precision with which he spoke and the suspicious claim that his driver's license would be in the trunk were clear warnings.

I signaled my immediate concern to my partner by flashing a questioning look at him; he nodded ever so slightly in return. I saw that my partner was also on edge as he positioned himself so he could take in the full view of all occupants in the car. His face tightened and he placed his hand on the grip of his weapon though keeping it in its holster. I positioned myself behind and to the side of the driver who was behind his car putting his key in the trunk lock. I wanted to watch him and the occupants of the vehicle at the same time. If something was going to happen it would happen very quickly, so we had to be prepared for whatever was about to happen. I watched his hands intently when he lifted the trunk lid. In one simultaneous and swift motion, my partner and I drew our weapons with me pointing my gun at the driver's chest and my partner pointing his weapon at the passengers.

"Freeze, don't move," we both shouted in unison. The trunk was full, and I mean full, of automatic rifles lying lose in full view of two nervous troopers. Was this carload of men part of a threat to Ronald Reagan? The driver and passengers were so clean cut that I thought they might be police or Secret Service but I had no way of knowing. If they were, they should have identified themselves the moment I approached the driver.

The driver looked at me and said simply, "Secret Service." I asked for identification, and the driver, at my directive, slowly pulled out his identification from a duffle bag in the trunk of the car. My partner asked the passengers for their badges, which they slowly produced. I asked the driver why he had not identified himself before getting out of his car. He said he was dog tired after working long hours and he just did not think of it. I told him he was close to getting himself shot and suggested that the next time he was stopped he might think of identifying himself immediately so no one would be hurt. That was a very close call that happily ended well for all involved. We all said our good-byes and they drove off down the freeway. So much for a quiet night on a lonely stretch of road seemingly far out of harm's way!

My second dignitary protection assignment was less exciting but just as important and took me to Metro Airport in Detroit. Vice President George H. W. Bush was flying in for an event in the City of Detroit. A great deal of planning had been done, and all of the officers assigned were thoroughly briefed on the plan and on our individual roles. My assignment was to guard a railroad overpass on the road leaving the Detroit Metro Airport under which Vice President Bush would pass in his motorcade. With my high-powered rifle I guarded that spot for several hours to ensure that no one who might have a firearm or explosives came anywhere near that overpass.

I saw two men in white overalls working on putting up a new advertisement on a billboard sixty yards away from my location. The only problem was that they never accomplished much during my several hours watching them. I thought that either they were bad guys who I could have shot easily had they tried something, or that they were Secret Service providing yet another layer of security for the vice president or possibly people getting paid for a job that they were really bad at. I never found out who they were. I was beginning to think that maybe the plan had changed, which sometimes happens even with little notice, when suddenly my radio announced that the motorcade was coming.

The motorcade roared past my location and in seconds they was gone. I was then given the order to return to my normal duties. I knew that I had not done much during my time on that assignment, but at least nothing bad happened. I was gratified for the opportunity to provide a part in protecting a visiting vice president.

Though the role appeared small, I knew it was an integral part in ensuring the safety on that visit and I realized the importance of my vigilance during my time on that overpass.

I was fortunate to be assigned to my third presidential protection detail when President George H. W. Bush was running for re-election and a presidential debate was scheduled at the Wharton Center located on the Michigan State University campus, in East Lansing, Michigan. The two contenders were William Jefferson Clinton and Ross Perot. I had been selected to assist with close-in duties in plain clothes (coat and tie rather than a uniform). Some of those duties consisted of helping at the hotel where President Bush and Barbara Bush were staying. Other duties involved assisting with work at the Wharton Center where the debates were held. However my primary duty was to assist the bodyguard of Wisconsin Governor Tommy Thompson.

The activities of the participants were frenzied and fast-paced to say the least. These activities included the debates themselves, interviews with numerous television and radio stations all located at or near the Wharton Center, and related political events. Needless to say, many duties arise while moving the participants from one spot to another. The utmost duty involves the safety of the protectee from every type of potential hazard while ensuring the protectee arrived where he was supposed to be at the appointed time. There were many political supporters at the event we had to watch. Who looked out of place? Why was the person moving through the crowd toward the protectee? Who seemed not to be participating in the festivities and was simply watching? The food was abundant and in numerous varieties guaranteed to appease all attendees who milled around necessitating me to keep my eyes moving to watch for possible threats. It was gratifying to see nothing even remotely out of the ordinary occurred to cause any stir and the event went as planned. In this business I quickly learned, nothing happening is a very good thing.

My last experience occurred after I had retired, but it's still added to my memories with U.S. Presidents. It was when I attended a visit by President Barack Obama during a speech at Northern Michigan University in Marquette, Michigan. I was retired at that time but I was in the room where the president gave his speech. To simply be in the same room in person with POTUS (President of the United States) is quite an experience. While I was only an observer, my younger brother Brian, who is a trooper assigned to a post in the Upper Peninsula, was serving on that protective detail. I watched with pride knowing how proud he was to help in some small way guarding a president during an official visit.

It was truly an honor to have been able to contribute in some small way to help ensure the safety during three presidential visits. It is something I wish all police officers could experience in their careers but which most police officers never will. I will cherish those assignments and memories for the remainder of my time here on earth. Even with many negative experiences occurring on a regular basis, the good experiences balance out the bad ones and they should be remembered and enjoyed over and over again.

PART

5

41

THREATS, APPARITIONS AND WAITING

Often during my years with the MSP and even in retirement, I would see a person and comment to my wife that the person looked familiar. She said that I think I know everybody I see. She either laughed or scoffed depending on whether I think the person is someone I had a positive encounter with or someone I arrested and who may have made a threat against my family or me. Not only is this a problem with actual people I meet, but with people in my dreams, leading to many sleepless nights. These recurring dreams seemed so real that I have awakened on a number of nights covered with sweat. Sometimes I wonder if the people I see on the street are people I have only dreamed of late at night.

I could see the glare in his eyes as he glared into my eyes, his jaw set. The gun in his hand was steady and pointed directly at my chest. I knew I had less than a second to stop the assailant who was intent on killing me. I drew my service weapon, centered the sights on his chest, and pulled the trigger. My weapon did not fire. The suspect starting shooting at me and I heard the crack of his gunfire. I frantically pulled the trigger multiple times with no response from that cold chunk of steel in my hand. Sweat poured from me. What else could I do? Was I going to die?

I could see the fire in his eyes as he glared into my eyes, his jaw set, the gun in his hand was steady and pointed directly at my chest. I knew I had less than a second to stop the assailant who was intent on killing me. I drew my service weapon, centered the sights on his chest, and pulled the trigger. The bullet left the barrel of my gun and dropped only a foot from the end of the barrel. I could not believe my eyes. I pulled the trigger again several times and watched the bullets lazily fall onto the ground just in front of me. I heard the crack of gunfire as the suspect starting shooting at me as I heard the crack of his gunfire. I frantically pulled the trigger multiple times and I hopelessly watched my bullets fall onto the ground inches from the barrel of my gun. Sweat poured from me. What else could I do? Was I going to die?

I could see the fire in his eyes as he glared into my eyes, his jaw set. The gun in his hand was steady and pointed directly at my chest. I knew I had less than a second to stop the assailant who was intent on killing me. I drew my service weapon, centered the sights on his chest, and pulled the trigger. My bullets left the barrel of my gun and appeared to strike the suspect squarely in his chest. The suspect did not react. I pulled the trigger several more times and watched the bullets seemingly strike the suspect in the chest again and again. The suspect was not affected by my bullets. I heard the crack of gunfire as the suspect started shooting at me. I frantically pulled the trigger multiple times but my bullets had no effect on the suspect who was bent on killing me. Sweat poured from me. What else could I do? Was I going to die?

These events, and other variations, crept into my dreams on many quiet nights. I often awoke out of breath with my shirt wet with sweat while I struggled to figure out if the event was real or just another nightmare drawn from years of close calls. Having talked to many other police officers I have come to learn that these dreams are a common occurrence among us who have been lucky to avoid death ourselves too many times. As hard as I tried to put these events in some tightly sealed box and lock it way back in the corner of my brain, I could not. It was as though someone kept sneaking into my brain unlocking these securely locked boxes. These thoughts kept on coming and they seemed as real as if they were happening once again for the first time. I recall some of the events that spawned these dreams as though they just happened; others are thankfully fading away into the mist, finally.

One incident that recurs in my nightmares happened during my first year as a trooper. My partner and I were sent to handle a home invasion that had just occurred. The young son of the homeowner was getting off of his school bus when he was approached by two men coming from around the back of his house carrying rifles and shotguns. They told the young man that they were undercover police and they had seized guns from his house as evidence. The suspects jumped into their car and sped off. Given their appearance, unprofessional behavior and no offer of a search warrant, the young man knew that these two had just broken into his parents' house.

We arrived on the scene and obtained a description of the suspects and their getaway car. We had a partial license plate number from the victim. After some intense investigation and computer work we determined the owner of the car who hesitatingly told us that he had lent his car to acquaintances but he did not know they were going to commit any crimes. Following a series of interviews we had enough evidence to compel two suspects to stand in a police line-up. The victim was able to identify one of the suspects but not the second suspect.

As part of our investigation we became aware of information from other police agencies suggesting that the suspects had committed other serious crimes, including at least three murders that they were never brought to trial for due to a lack of evidence. These guys were very dangerous with lengthy criminal records. At trial, the jury took little time in convicting the suspect identified in the line-up. Immediately following the jury announcing the suspect guilty, he looked me straight in my eyes with his steely gray eyes and said, "I will kill you, and then I'll kill your entire family. I promise. Don't ever stop looking over your shoulder because someday I will be there and I will kill all of you." He was then pulled away by the deputies and taken to the lock-up. That was the first death threat I had received and I started keeping a careful eye out both on-duty as well as off-duty.

Another time my partner and I had arrested a local criminal in a small town. Although he did have a long criminal record with violent crimes, this was a minor crime, which I can't even recall. Later in the week another small town criminal, who we had recently given a break on some petty violation, told us the suspect we had arrested earlier in the week was looking for us. He had a rifle and a pistol in his car and he swore that he would kill both of us when he found us. Our informant told us to be careful as the suspect was very serious. If it was a fight he wanted, we were willing to oblige him. For days my partner and I both carried either a rifle or shotgun within arm's reach. We looked for the suspect for over a week but we failed to locate him. Never knowing when he might find us, we kept a sharp lookout for him. Even off-duty I tried to remember that face, so if the day arrived when he found me I would be ready to take all appropriate action. We never found out what became of him.

I recall another incident where I had made an arrest for a crime that resulted in yet another potential death threat. I can no longer recall the nature of the arrest, but I don't believe the arrest was for anything too serious. But it must have struck the suspect the wrong way. Shortly after the arrest I heard from a local business owner that the suspect had been in their establishments asking questions about me, my whereabouts, and how to contact me. He made a number of statements that when he found me he would kill me for arresting him. This went on for weeks. The weeks turned into months, then into years. I still keep a sharp vigil though I have forgotten his name and what he looks like. Now I simply look for people watching me.

In another case, I was working undercover in narcotics when I bought a large amount of marijuana. The suspect had a detached aura about him. He didn't look me in the eyes when we made the drug deal; he looked through me. His eyes had a stare that I knew from years of experience meant business. All throughout the drug deal he tapped the automatic stuffed in his belt while he looked through my eyes. No smile, no sense of humanity, just a cold presence. The simple parting words from him sent a stone cold chill through me, "Don't fuck with me, man." He turned to leave and was quickly arrested in this buy-bust investigation. His words stuck with me for many years as I never knew if I would see him coming around a corner some day when I least expected it.

One incident reminded me never to assume someone is harmless because they initially appear innocent. I had just gotten off duty but had not changed out of my uniform yet when I heard the radio traffic at the post. A high-speed pursuit from a local police agency south of our post was headed our way. Shots had been fired by the suspects and by the pursuing officers. One of the other Northville Post troopers had tried to ram the car but unfortunately only succeeded in disabling his own patrol car. I grabbed a shotgun and jumped into my patrol car and headed down the road. Within the first minute that I had been on the road the suspect vehicle passed me going in the opposite direction at high speed then turned into the lawn of the Northville State Hospital near some buildings.

I spun my car around and saw the suspects erupt from the car and run into the state buildings. As I slid to a stop I opened my door and grabbed my shotgun, racking in a round as I bolted from the patrol car. The head of a woman popped up from the far side of the suspect's car only 15 feet away from me. I put the front sight of my shotgun on her head and ordered her to raise her hands. She would not move or put up her hands. I ordered her hands up a second time telling her I would blow her head off if she didn't put her hands up.

Slowly she raised her hands and stepped out from around the car. I handcuffed her and saw a pistol lying on the ground at the exact spot where she had been standing. She clearly would have shot me had she been given the opportunity. Her curt directive to me when she stared into my eyes as I was putting her into my police car was, "Fuck yourself." That confirmed to me that she would have carried out her fatal intentions had I taken my eyes off of her for only a second. The prosecutor declined to file any charges against her and she was released. Some nights I dream that I had looked away for only a moment and that woman shot me dead.

There have been many other similar situations. Although many I suspect are finally starting to fade away in the fog of advancing age, it has been difficult to completely erase these faces, the threats, the fears. These death threats came in clearly worded warnings, and they came in wordless actions and icy stares from the suspects. Unlike military experiences where the enemy lives thousands of miles away with oceans separating the soldier and his enemy, my enemy lives in the same state as my family and I do. One of them could be expected to cross my path in the future, if not by intentional actions then by mere happenstance. These threats continue to haunt the quiet dark of my nights and force me to always be vigilant, always look for anything out of the ordinary and for people watching me.

42

WHAT IS IT REALLY LIKE?

I am frequently asked what it is really like working as a police officer from many different people I meet. While I have had a wide range of experiences, no two officers experience all of the same types of situations. The type of policing model employed by different police agencies, to some degree, affect the type of experiences an officer may become involved in. A few examples and a generalization might help understand the nature one might expect in a career as a police officer.

Recalling an incident early in my career, I remember the day I left for work and my wife was preparing to head to work at an insurance company. I had an uneasy feeling, a premonition, that this might be the day that I would never again return home to her. I was working as the sole Bridgeport Township patrol officer and was startled out of that premonition by the excited dispatcher announcing on the police radio that a man in Buena Vista Township, which adjoined Bridgeport Township, was shooting at his wife. The couple had an argument while she was sitting in her car in their driveway. The radio blared that the older man had just run into his house and had barricaded himself in.

As I neared the address to back up the officers, I heard the report that one of the officers who had knocked on the suspect's door had been shot by the suspect through the front door, and the officer had fallen off the porch. Later I learned that the bullets ripped through the front door forced the officer to back up hastily where he fell off of the porch, landing on his back, knocking the wind out of him. Since the officer wasn't moving, his partner thought he had been killed and reported that his partner had been hit with gunfire. All available backup was requested. I realized at that early stage in my police career; that I would never know when I said good-bye to my family and left for work that it might be the last time. Such has been the fate of all too many officers.

Contrary to some opinions, police officers are people who also laugh, cry, love, hate, bleed and die. A good police officer is much more than a law enforcement officer. The police officer helps solve the root cause of problems they encounter with compassion and understanding, thereby reducing the incident of crime. This is the essence of the concept of community policing. Although the terms police officer and law enforcement officer are often used interchangeably, upon a closer look there are significant differences. A law enforcement officer enforces the law by writing the traffic ticket, making the arrest, investigating the crime, and then moves on to the next call for service. The experienced police officer does all that the law enforcement officer does, but also looks deeper into the traffic violation to understand why the violation occurred and attempts to figure out if there was an improper causation. The cause of the violation may be faulty signage such as a tree blocking the speed limit sign or a sign that has been knocked down and not the fault of the alleged violator. In a theft investigation, the officer, upon looking deeper into the reason for the larceny, might find that the family has no income and would benefit from being provided information on how to obtain assistance which would prevent further criminal conduct.

Police officers are people trained to perform a certain type of activity, police work. Police work is every type of activity one might imagine, from the mundane to violent and life threatening. The majority who choose a career in policing are conscientious, wise, sensible, well-trained, capable, caring and fair. They perform their duties believing that justice is blind regarding gender, race, religion and national origin. Often they live in your neighborhood and their children go to school with yours. The National Law Enforcement Officer Memorial Fund estimates that there are more than 900,000 sworn enforcement officers in the United States. Given that large number, it is reasonable to expect a few will not meet the standards demanded by those they serve.

Recently, some seven or so high profile incidents have made national headlines for alleged abuse by police officers. Unfortunately, many people will judge all officers negatively, even those who had no involvement in the cases and who would condemn the serious offenses of errant officers. While a criminal accused of a criminal violation is presumed innocent until proven guilty, often a police office does not enjoy the same presumption in the media.

I am often asked how ethnicity played a part in my interactions on traffic stops and investigations during my years with the MSP, given the recent high-profile incidents on national news. In the Northville Post area, large populations of many ethnic groups abounded. Detroit had many Polish, Hispanic and African American residents. Dearborn had many Middle Eastern residents. Mixed in were the German, Irish, Native American, and the list goes on. I can say that I was only involved in one single incident that race became an issue.

I was dispatched to Schoolcraft Community College regarding a report that an approximately 5'10" black male in his early 20s was selling drugs from his blue Chevrolet parked in the rear parking lot. When I arrived, the parking lot where I was stopped by a school security guard who pointed out the suspect. I approached the suspect and advised why I was contacting him. Immediately, the suspect accused me of contacting him due to his race. He became highly agitated and began calling me names. A large crowd gathered and I called for backup officers. Ultimately, the suspect and his car was searched and failed to turn up any evidence of drug dealing. I told the suspect that since no evidence of any crime was found, he was free to leave. Several weeks after that incident, I was told by the post detective that he had been assigned a complaint from the suspect that I had violated his civil rights. Initially when the post detective interviewed the school security guard, the guard denied telling me the suspect had been selling drugs. That caused an appearance that I had somehow violated the suspect's civil rights. Finally, the security guard recanted and truthfully told the detective that he had told me the suspect had been selling drugs. When asked why he initially was untruthful, the guard said that he was afraid he might lose his job if he admitted to reporting what he thought the suspect was doing on school property. It was the complainant and not the police officer that caused the issue.

Of the hundreds of police officers with many police departments in my post area, no high profile incidents of police abuse came to my attention. The recent high profile incidents are difficult to assess as I do not know all of the underlying facts of those incidents. It is easy to make assumptions on a few bare facts, however that is almost always a mistake and often inaccurate. However, some of these incidents appeared to me to be obviously outside of the lawful authority of officers, while others appear justified.

All people matter, young and old, male and female, one ethnic group or another. To a good police officer, it should be simple: all people matter and all people should be treated as the facts dictate.

Unfortunately, as in all other professions, some officers abuse their power, don't keep up with the law (if they ever knew it), are grossly out of shape, exhibit prejudices, shirk their duties, sleep on the job, belittle or mistreat others in an effort to make themselves feel important, focus on activities to get them the next promotion rather than taking care of those under their supervision, and ignore the law in their personal lives and make attitude arrests. The rest of the police officers seem to fall on a spectrum somewhere between this extreme and being perfect officers. Every day when I put on my uniform I knew that I labored under the suspicion of the people I met as the result of a few bad apples even though I never abused anyone, nor had the majority of dedicated officers.

Police departments also vary in their policing model depending on their leadership. Some departments want their officers to cause as little controversy as possible. Few arrests or traffic citations are encouraged. Prominent people in these communities are often exempt from enforcement of the laws if they have high standing in the community or have made financial contributions to those in power. Low profile making no waves is the name of the game for the officers in those agencies. This was the direction I was told to follow when I worked for Bridgeport Township Police Department. I was told to be visible but not to make many arrests because to do so would require me to attend court and take me from the township. It was understood that local business owners were supportive of the township and should be left alone. In my experience, I knew of other police departments and sheriff's offices who followed similar practices, especially around election time.

On the other extreme, some police departments strongly encourage aggressively pursuing crime. They believe that if they stop minor violators, they can, and often do, find evidence of serious and violent criminal activity. The goal of enforcement action is to nip crime in the bud sparing future victims whenever possible. A simple traffic stop for a minor offense frequently leads to the solving of a major crime, thus removing a very real and dangerous person from society. Often just checking a little further on questions that don't seem to add up will reveal a serious offense being committed right in front of the officer. This model is suggestive of my career with the state police as well as other police agencies that I have known during my career.

When I was assigned to patrol a freeway within the Northville Post area, I overheard radio traffic dispatching an officer to an unwanted visitor complaint. This would generally be considered a minor call for service. The officer soon cleared that complaint advising no crime had been committed. With only a little information I gleaned from the radio traffic, my experience told me that there was more to this call than the original officer had discovered. I left my freeway patrol and contacted the complainant without an order to do so. As the result of answers I received to my specific questions I opened a criminal investigation that spanned more than two years resulting in solving 13 Uttering and Publishing (felon stolen check) cases, 15 Breaking and Entering cases, and 1 Armed Robbery case, solving crimes for other police agencies across the lower peninsula of Michigan. Two suspects also received lengthy prison sentences from this seemingly minor call for service, preventing future victims at the hands of these two. I received a meritorious service award for my efforts in that investigation.

Above all, police work has days filled with boredom when nothing more than minor traffic violators attract the officer's attention. Other days deliver satisfaction and pride when a difficult case is finally solved giving closure to the victims. Some days provide grief upon handling a traffic crash where I pulled deceased family members from their mangled car along with a deep feeling of disgust when the drunk driver expressed ambivalence at having caused such carnage. Then there are days when I experienced numbing fear wondering if the gasoline from the ruptured gas tank of the car involved in a traffic crash would ignite while I worked to extricate trapped passengers. I have felt many other emotions depending on the minute of a given day or night, like nausea as the acidic smell permeated the air when a drunk driver who I had placed under arrest vomited stomach bile on the back seat of the patrol car. Work can be slow or coming at break-neck speed. Life can be snatched away in a moment from someone asking for help or maybe even the officers trying to assist. One thing is certain, no matter what type of police officer or type of department an officer may work for, a career police officer will have seen far more than the average citizen could ever imagine. Sights, sounds, smells and even tastes are embedded in an officer's mind. Those sensory experiences are never forgotten, the wounds are ever present and those experiences can suddenly and without warning become as real as if they were happening again years after they originally occurred, given the right stimulus. But it seems like the bad situations are the ones stuck in my mind. The faces of terrified people, the smell of burned or rotting human bodies, and the screams of injured victims, just keep on coming back to be relived over and over again even though I tried to bury them deep into the most remote recesses of my brain seeking much needed sleep.

Police officers deal with people with a wide array of issues. Not all of them are bad people, though. Often, generally good people make mistakes or are driven by pressures that have built up over time. Some people have called upon the police to save them from a host of dangers real or imagined. Others call asking for assistance with a spouse, neighbors or those that would victimize them. Yet others are the focus of the police officer's enforcement actions. Officers write traffic citations to errant drivers, they arrest perpetrators who often show little or no remorse for their criminal offenses, and they put the worst offenders in prison for the unimaginable acts they have intentionally committed.

Some offenders are very bad people with no heart, no conscience, and no soul. These are truly dangerous people that steal, rape, brutalize and kill other human beings with absolutely no remorse. Attempts to arrest these hardened criminals can often put an officer's safety and life in jeopardy. Often a fight for the officer's very life occurs in making these arrests.

Going into a situation, officers don't know which type of person they are dealing with, and figuring that out before it is too late can be the difference between living and dying. This is the "walking through a mine field" analogy officers talk about and deal with on a daily basis. Officers never know when they are going to step into an explosive situation until it suddenly and without warning it explodes. The seasoned officers are always looking for small clues in every situation to alert them to impending danger that may give them that slight advantage. Sometimes inexperienced officers miss the clues of impending danger until their worst fears are realized. In a nutshell, this is police work.

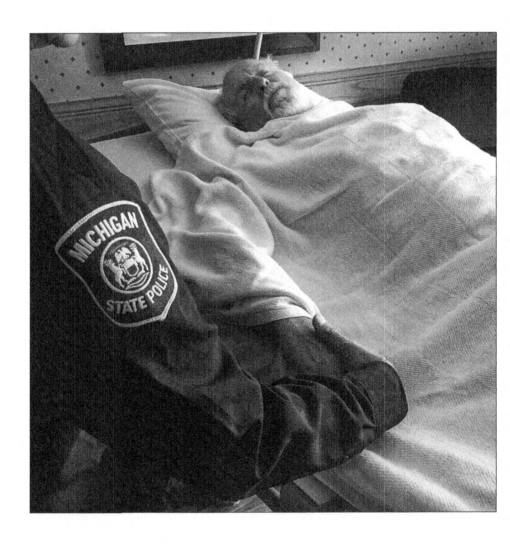

43

LIFE'S LESSONS

New police officers enter the profession believing that they can fix the crime problem. They steadfastly follow orders with the belief that they can and will make a difference. What they really do is stem the tide, but stem the tide they must for the safety of others. The same crimes keep being committed by the same types of people for the same reasons in the same way with the same results. Perpetrators continue to hold the false belief that they can commit the perfect crimes and get away with them. Nothing changes. Only the names of the perpetrators, the names of the victims and the dates change. However, as the Irish orator, philosopher and politician Edmund Burke stated "All that is necessary for the triumph of evil is that good men do nothing." Police officers must take a stand and make the difference to the best of their ability. They cannot be asked to do more, but that much they must do.

Only a select few are chosen for police work. Most of them shoulder the responsibility, growing to know patience, tolerance, perseverance, and dedication. Blessed truly are those who have chosen to do the job for the right reasons and stem the tide of violence, abuse, neglect, greed, and indifference. They do what they can, when they can and for whom they can. It was always hard work but for these officers, it was always rewarding work. To say it was an honor to be part of their profession would be a gross understatement. Good officers intuitively know that in difficult situations they must do what Winston Churchill professed:

It's not enough that we do our best,
Sometimes we have to do what's required.

During my career with the MSP I was fortunate to help to accomplish some things for the State Police that had eluded others in the department before me for many years. Among a number of significant accomplishments one that stood out was when I was assigned the role as the project manager for the planning and construction of the precision driving facility at the State Police Academy (or simply the driving track). Many other State Police Officers and members of other state agencies contributed to this much-needed project to instruct new troopers, as well as police officers from across the United States, including officers from other countries, with precision and high speed driving skills. The project had been previously attempted for some 23 years without success. The barriers to completing the project are far too numerous and too detailed to bore the reader with. Suffice it to say, many seemingly impossible issues arose during the planning and construction of that wonderful facility. So numerous and seemingly impossible were the challenges, that during that project I wrote these words in my daily planner one day to remind me each day of the importance of that project, and long afterwards, that anything is truly possible:

My job is not to recognize the impossible, but simply to
accomplish it.

What I learned is that many seemingly impossible tasks are only mental barriers resulting from never having tackled such a daunting challenge. Most of the time, training, knowledge, and perseverance are more than adequate to overcome and accomplish the task at hand. I learned that I simply needed to believe in myself and my abilities to be successful. Handling situations in which I had no knowledge or experience is how I grew in knowledge and experience. I learned that I could not simply follow the same old game plan of those before me, or as Albert Einstein so aptly stated, "Insanity is doing the same thing over and over again and expecting different results." The fine line is to recognize those rare situations where the obstacle is just too much to handle by yourself and know you must seek out additional resources to avoid harm or failure. For my efforts I was recognized with a Director's Commendation which was a very humbling honor.

There are things I saw, experienced, and read about that helped shape the way I handled my calls for service. Otherwise it might have been easy for me to become callous, indifferent, and impersonal. Hard lessons can induce change for the worse. For the truly professional police officer, the years of experience are culled, and the positives are collected and used to benefit the officer. The bad experiences are remembered so as not to repeat them. Indeed, Edmund Burke also stated, "He who wrestles with us strengthens our nerves and sharpens our skill. Our antagonist is our helper." Even bad experiences helped make me better and often they were my best teachers. When I looked past the pain, I often found the helpful and valuable lessons hidden in those experiences.

Sometimes those who cause us the most grief, sorrow and pain end up helping us grow into what we never would have been but for that traumatic experience. It takes a continuing conscious effort on the officers' part to guard against becoming hardened and indifferent in spite of all of the misery and hate they encounter. Only by continuously trying to be better than yesterday will officers stave off the laziness, indifference, and the "retired in place" attitude. I've seen whole police departments filled with glory-seeking, boisterous, big-mouthed officers. I've seen polite, caring, empathic souls that epitomize the police service. And of course, I've seen all sorts of police officers between these two extremes.

I remember the telephone call my mother made to have her family saved from the bat. I remember all of those flat tires that I changed for stranded motorists who needed help. I can't remember the number of telephone calls that I answered at the post asking if weather conditions would allow the caller to make it to their anticipated destination; even when I recommended that they delay their trips, many still said they were going anyway. Over the years I still remember that these calls are not to be seen from my eyes or the eyes of other police officers, but must be seen from the eyes of those requesting assistance. The calls are serious to the callers, so they should be handled by officers as serious calls for help. A police officer does not represent himself on the job, rather they represent the agency they work for. That must never be forgotten.

Even the best officers can get a little down when a shift or an assignment prevents them from attending a family function or when they draw a less desirable detail no one else wanted. It was often during a holiday when most people were home enjoying their families that we were called upon to take an undesirable assignment. One story I had the privilege of coming across and keeping close to me during my years in policing that had a profound impact on me is entitled "A Christmas Cop Story." Whether this story is true, I do not know, but is has given me renewed perseverance and humility.

In 1974 when I first joined the police department, I knew there would be special occasions my family would spend without me. Knowing that fact didn't make the task any easier. The celebrations I missed those first years depressed me and sometimes made me feel bitter. Working on Christmas Eve was always the worst. On Christmas Eve in 1977, I learned that blessing can come disguised as misfortune, and honor is more than just a word.

I was riding one-man patrol on the 4 p.m. to 12 midnight shift. The night was cold. Everywhere I looked I saw reminders of the holiday: families packing their cars with presents, beautifully decorated trees in living room windows and roofs adorned with tiny sleighs. It all added to my holiday funk.

The evening had been relatively quiet; there were calls for barking dogs and a residential false burglar alarm. There was nothing to make the night pass any quicker. I thought of my own family and sunk further into depression.

Shortly after 2200 hours I got a radio call to the home of an elderly, terminally ill, man. I parked my patrol car in front of a simple Cape Cod style home. First aid kit in hand, I walked up the short path to the front door. As I approached, a woman who seemed to be about 80 years old opened the door. "He's in here," she said, leading me to a back bedroom.

We passed through a living room that was furnished in a style I had come to associate with older people. The sofa had an afghan blanket draped over its back and a dark, solid Queen

Anne chair sat next to an unused fireplace. The mantle was cluttered with an eccentric mix of several photos, some ceramic figurines and an antique clock. A floor lamp provided soft lighting.

We entered a small bedroom where a frail looking man lay in bed with a blanket pulled up to his chin. He wore a blank stare on his ashen, skeletal face. His breathing was shallow and labored. He was barely alive. The trappings of illness were all around his bed.

The nightstand was littered with a large number of pill vials. An oxygen bottle stood nearby. Its plastic hose, with facemask attached, rested on the blanket.

I asked the old woman why she called the police. She simply shrugged and nodded sadly toward her husband, indicating it was his request. I looked at him and he stared intently into my eyes. He seemed relaxed now. I didn't understand the suddenly calm expression on his face.

I looked around the room again. A dresser stood along the wall to the left of the bed. On it was the usual memorabilia: ornate perfume bottles, a white porcelain pin case, and a wooden jewelry case.

There were also several photos in simple frames. One caught my eye and I walked closer to the dresser for a closer look. The picture showed a young man dressed in a police uniform. It was unmistakably a photo of the man in bed. I knew then why I was there.

I looked at the old man and he motioned with his hand toward the side of the bed. I walked over and stood beside him. He slid a thin arm from under the covers and took my hand.

Soon, I felt his hand go limp, I looked at his face. There was no fear there. I saw only peace.

He knew he was dying; he was aware his time was very near. I know now that he was afraid of what was about to happen and he wanted the protection of a fellow cop on his journey.

A caring God had seen to it that his child would be delivered safely to him. The honor of being his escort fell to me.

When I left at the end of my tour that night, the temperature seemed to have risen considerably, and all the holiday displays I saw on the way home made me smile. I no longer felt sorry for myself for having to work on Christmas Eve.

I have chosen an honorable profession. I pray that when it's my turn to leave this world there will be a cop there to hold my hand and remind me that I have nothing to fear.

I wish all my brothers and sisters who have to work this Christmas Eve all the Joy and warmth of the Season.

On the article was this credit line: janal879r@msn.com.

After leaving the road and having earned my law degree, I had the good fortune to be assigned to the Training Academy. This is the place where applicants are transformed from whatever life they previously lived into troopers. That transition is difficult, long and life-changing. The reason for this dramatic change can be credited to the permanent and temporary staff members that give all of their knowledge, experience, dedication, and an almost super-human focus to the minutest detail in the development of each and every recruit and soon-to-be trooper. The staff deeply cares about the outcome that will be produced at the end of the trooper recruit school. They know the future troopers' very lives may depend on how well they are trained and the reputation of the department, much revered, will be protected and advanced. Even those professional trainers must always remember the goal is not to turn applicants into robots, but into the best police officer the applicant can become. They also know that the new trooper may someday be their partner, charged with overseeing their own safety.

I had the honor of training many of the past and current members of the MSP. I taught legal classes in addition to precision driving and legal scenarios for many years, while assigned to the academy or as a guest lecturer. I always interspersed my real-life experiences from working the road with the required class material. I always felt that just instructing the course material was not enough for the soon-to-be troopers. I needed to share those experiences that just might save a new officer's life. I owed each new officer that much.

Caring so deeply for the safety of the troopers-to-be, I always interspersed my knowledge and experience in survivability based on my personal experiences, adding, "In every fight there is the loser and the trooper." That always evoked laughs, glances at their fellow recruits, and odd looks from a few recruits. My goal was to lighten the mood a little bit in an atmosphere that was charged with intense pressure and fear. I explained to them my light switch theory. "When the *stuff* hits the fan, you immediately flip that inner switch and become the suspect's worst nightmare and take care of business, but when they are subdued, you immediately turn it off." Another favorite I had was to tell them, after looking them straight in the eyes, "If any of you gets hurt, I will find you and kick your ass." I also told them, "If any of you get killed, I will haunt you!"

Every time I passed along that knowledge I supplemented it with actual examples that I had personally experienced, along with options they too might employ to always prevail. As their knowledge and experience grew, they began to understand these words were not only intended as humor to lighten the mood (though at times it did). They grew to realize the lifesaving lessons that were subtly, but permanently, etched into their minds. I still hear troopers tell how those words helped them during their careers in various ways. What a humbling feeling it is to hear those words of appreciation and to know that I may have just helped some of them avoid injury or worse and helped them conduct an excellent investigation helping the victims of those crimes they investigated. The good officers do what's right, simply because it is the right thing to do. I can think of no more reward than knowing I may have helped others. It was my job, and the job of all other troopers, to pass on the knowledge, the work ethic, and the reputation of the agency to the new troopers to always do their best. I may just have accomplished that goal in some small way.

My son applied to the MSP. After several years of trying to be selected for the academy, and after enlisting in the United States Marine Corps, he was finally accepted to help in carrying on the department's motto of "Preserve, Protect and Defend." The records state that of some 3,000 plus applicants only 92 were selected to start the training. The MSP planned to start 130 applicants but only 92 met the rigorous screening requirements to be offered a seat on day one in that Michigan State Police Academy class for the 123rd Trooper Recruit School. By the end of the 19-week academy, 78 remained to accept their badges and enter into a sacred profession. My son was given badge number 248, my old trooper badge number.

He was assigned to work in the City of Detroit upon graduation. I listen intently to his almost daily and excited stories, similar to what I previously experienced, and as I have listened to the stories of my brother. I know the dangers my son faces and I rest uneasy knowing what he has yet to learn and the future dangers he will undoubtedly face.

Those staring faces that continue to visit me on many quiet nights that I encountered so many years ago no longer haunt me. The faces have each taken on a friendly persona since I have come to realize that they had been sent to teach me the lessons that I needed at that time in my life. Those faces now console me rather than torment me. I actually thank them when they visit me for what they have shared with me in spite of the shocking circumstances I experienced as a new police officer when I first met them and failed to understand them and at times feared them. Hopefully my fellow officers are able to see the lessons they are presented during their duties and can find the wisdom to make themselves better people both on and off the job. Each of these lessons presented have been paid for with someone else's pain and suffering and must not be wasted.

44

RETIREMENT

"**D**ouble dipper," drawing a pension from the state police while drawing a salary from employment with another state department. I have been called much worse but double dipper really grated on me. I had faced it all and I had survived. I lost count of the times I cheated death by guns, knives, chemical spills, police car accidents, ice-coated roads, electrical wires knocked down in car accidents, fists, saliva tainted with hepatitis and HIV, and a host of other deadly diseases that had been spat on my face, neck and head by pissed off arrestees. Some of my fellow brothers and sisters had not been so lucky.

I was a certified police officer for over 38 years. During that time 6,383 brothers and sisters in the United States gave their lives doing their jobs as police officers, which included 52 Michigan State Police, who lost their lives protecting citizens and visitors. Police work is a dangerous job.

Another poem that appeared in the *Michigan Trooper Magazine* that helped me along the way in difficult times goes like this:

The Judgment

The Trooper stood and faced his maker, which must always come to pass.
He hoped his shoes were polished and shining, just as brightly as his brass.

"Step forward now, Trooper, how shall I deal with you?
Have you always turned the other cheek? To your Master have
you been true?"

The Trooper, with squared shoulders, said, "No sir, I guess I ain't.
Because those of us who wear a badge can't always be a saint.

I've had to work most Sundays and at times my talk was rough,
And sometimes I've been violent, because the streets are tough.

But I never took a penny that wasn't mine to keep.
Though I worked a lot of overtime, when the bills just got too steep.

And I never passed by a cry for help though at times I shook
with fear,
and sometimes, please forgive me, Lord, I've wept unmanly tears.

I know I don't deserve a place among the people here.
They never wanted me around except to calm their fears.

But if you have a place for me here, well…it need not be too grand.
I never expected or had too much, so if you don't …I'll
understand.

There was silence all around the room where the saints
respectively stood.
As the Trooper waited quietly for the judgment…bad or good.

"Step forward now, Trooper, you've borne your burdens well.
Come patrol a while on Heaven's streets, you've done your time
in Hell."

I still see the faces staring, just staring into my eyes. I see those thousand mile stares that look right through me. I still see the faces that plead for me to help them and the faces that want to grind the very life out of my body with that steely look of hatred. Little faces scared out of their wits, begging me to help mommy because daddy or her boyfriend was beating her again. Faces not believing someone violated the sanctity of their home to steal the few belongings they had accumulated, then as the ultimate act of cruelty and contempt, would defecate on their kitchen floor. The faces, knowing they are about to hear their worst nightmare come true, but wanting to change the past so they don't have to see me standing at their door with my look of despair. Their silent scream won't fix what they know is coming. Nothing changed in my 38 years of police work except the names, the places and the sadness. I often experienced complete sadness at the depraved human condition that would allow someone to perpetrate such acts of contempt on hardworking decent people. Have they never been taught right from wrong?

Happy times finally came when the gun belt was hung up for the last time. No longer must I as an officer distrust and watch everyone everywhere, always. Those habits drilled into me to always question who those suspicious people are and why are they doing something suspicious are beginning to be less of a concern, yet I remain vigilant. I still wonder what that bulge under a stranger's coat might be. I still watch their hands, which experience has proven is where the weapon will be. In retirement I still never sit with my back to the door in a restaurant or a bar. As hard as I try, I still don't hold many things in my right hand, my old gun hand, as it would have slowed down my drawing of my service weapon. Though I no longer have to remember that I should never, ever turn my back on the driver when I walk back to my patrol car as I no longer drive one, I am careful when rendering assistance to other motorists to avoid being hit by passing traffic.

I enjoy retirement but I can't help wondering if some of those that I arrested might come around the next corner while shopping or at some public event. I find myself still assuming everyone is bad and dangerous until proven otherwise, a habit I try to put behind me. I no longer have to pretend nothing happened during my shift and put daily carnage behind me when I go home. Now I can talk of important things like whether the flowers need watering, when the garbage needs to be taken out, and if I heard what happened to the Smiths yesterday. My family is very important, it is the reason I live. My wife and I enjoy a meal out at a local restaurant without hoping I can finish before I get a call to respond to an emergency. My sleep now comes easy and is restful. I visit my children and play with the grandchildren without having to worry about pending cases and what evidence I might be able to uncover to help put criminals away so they cannot hurt anyone again. When I hear sirens passing by I know I don't need to drop everything and race to the scene. But those hard-learned lessons on survival never leave my mind. I realize, even in retirement, forgetting those lessons can cost police officers their lives. This happened to a retired state police officer in the town where I live only a couple of years ago when he and his wife encountered an intruder entering their house, shooting both of them to death.

Another text that I saved for inspiration while working as a road trooper and beyond is entitled "Always A Cop." The author, wishing to remain anonymous simply signed it, *From a Retired Michigan State Police Emergency Support (E.S.) Team Member.* The

Emergency Support Team is the Michigan State Police equivalent of what is commonly known as SWAT members. The wisdom goes like this:

Once the badge goes on it never comes off, whether they can see it or not. It fuses to the soul through adversity, fear and adrenaline and no one who has ever worn it with pride, integrity and guts can ever sleep through the "call of the wild" that wafts through bedroom windows in the deep of the night.

When Cops Retire

When a good cop leaves the 'job' and retires to a better life, many are jealous, some are pleased and yet others, who may have already retired, wonder. We wonder if he knows what he is leaving behind because we already know. We know for example, that after a lifetime of camaraderie that few experience, it will remain as a longing for those past times. We know in the law enforcement life there is a fellowship, which lasts long after the uniforms are hung up in the back of the closet. We know even if he throws them away they will be on him with every step and breath that remains in his life. We also know how the very bearing of the man speaks of what he was and in his heart still is.

These are the burdens of the job. You will still look at people suspiciously, still see what others do not see or choose to ignore and always will look at the rest of the law enforcement world with a respect for what they do, only grown in a lifetime of knowing. Never think for one moment you are escaping from that life. You are only escaping the "job" and merely being allowed to leave "active" duty.

So what I wish for you is that whenever you ease into retirement, in your heart you never forget for one moment that "Blessed are the Peacemakers for they shall be called children of God," and you are still a member of the greatest fraternity the world has ever known.

Many police officers tend to associate off-duty with other police officers. This seems to be due to a general understanding of the demands and dangers of the job. I often hear non-police officers, termed civilians by police officers, ask uncomfortable questions like, "Have you ever shot anyone?" Another common conversation is, "Let me tell you about the time that cop wrote me that bullshit ticket." A real grating discussion comes when you are asked, "Do you get a pension?" Officers don't want to openly discuss such topics. There is a degree of safety talking to another police officer built on common trust. A writing I found many years ago sums up this common understanding between police officers.

Civilian Friends vs Police Friends

CIVILIAN FRIENDS: Get upset if you're too busy to talk to them for a week.

POLICE FRIENDS: Are glad to see you after 20 years, and will happily carry on the same conversation you were having the last time you met.

CIVILIAN FRIENDS: Have never seen you cry.

POLICE FRIENDS: Have cried with you.

CIVILIAN FRIENDS: Borrow your stuff for a few days then give it back.

POLICE FRIENDS: Keep your stuff so long they forget it's yours.

CIVILIAN FRIENDS: *Know a few things about you.*

POLICE FRIENDS: *Could write a book with direct quotes from you.*

CIVILIAN FRIENDS: *Will leave you behind if that's what the crowd is doing.*

POLICE FRIENDS: *Will kick the crowds' ass that left you behind.*

CIVILIAN FRIENDS: *Have shared a few experiences.*

POLICE FRIENDS: *Have shared a lifetime of experiences no citizen could ever dream of.*

CIVILIAN FRIENDS: *Will take your drink away when they think you've had enough.*

POLICE FRIENDS: *Will look at you stumbling all over the place and say, "You better drink the rest of that before you spill it!" Then carry you home safely and put you to bed.*

CIVILIAN FRIENDS: *Will talk crap to the person who talks crap about you.*

POLICE FRIENDS: *Will knock the hell out them for using your name in vain.*

There are those that think they understand. And then, there are cops.

Good cops don't think they are better than non-cops because of the experiences they have encountered. It is just that non-cops have not been exposed to what officers have been exposed to so they don't understand some things cops do or say.

Recently my wife and I were shopping in a sporting goods store. I saw a face that looked vaguely familiar (again). My wife laughed and said, "You always think everyone looks familiar." But in this case, he looked at me with a faint look of recognition of me as well. We both looked away from each other for a moment, but for only a second, when we locked eyes again.

"Bob," he said, remembering my name.

"Harry," I said. We literally rushed each other with hands outstretched and shook hands, but only briefly. We were overtaken by emotions as we hugged, neither of us uttering a single word because none were needed.

You see, Harry and I worked as troopers at the Northville Post but in different squads many years ago. We saw each other often as his shift went on duty and mine went off duty. He lived in Detroit with his family and one evening while off duty he walked to the corner market to buy milk for his daughter. He walked into an armed robbery in progress. After a struggle he was shot three times, quite seriously. While he was in the hospital recovering the suspects had not yet been caught. I had the honor of being one of several of the post troopers to stand guard over him while he was awake and while he slept safely under my watchful eye. That was a tense time at the hospital and at our post until the suspects were finally arrested and sentenced to prison.

This is the same trooper who reached into a burning car to pull two terrified young children out of a certain death accident. He burned his hair and scalp along with his arm saving them. He later said their screams compelled him to not give up until he got them to safety. You see, he also had young children at home and knew of the loss if he failed. He could easily have died trying to save the two youngsters, but he did pull both to safety so they could live on. If he ever read this, he would probably find me and chastise me for making a big deal out of his efforts. That is his level of humility. Good officers don't do their job for self-aggrandizement; they do it because it is necessary to help others. It is as simple as that.

Those emotions at that time of Harry's shooting are impossible to describe. It was as though my brother had been shot, and all of the troopers at the post had their brothers and sisters shot, all in one millisecond. And yet, some 30 years later without ever seeing each other once in that time, when we looked into each other's eyes, volumes were spoken in a split-second. It was as though we had just seen each other only days before. That close call of almost losing one of our post troopers affected each one of us beyond words. That is the camaraderie of good police officers. Meeting troopers who I have been close to in the past helps ease the difficult memories as do visits to a special place in the U.P.

In retirement I found a safe place, that place where I could go to find total peace from flashbacks of faces and events, smells and sounds, fears, some too far removed to remember but only in a vague sense, yet others as vivid as if they happened only hours ago. Some become real enough once again to be relived with all of the fear and pain and sleepless nights. For me, that place is on the northern edge of Presque Isle, in Marquette, Michigan. The isle consists of black rock that has existed for thousands of years, carefully sculpted by the endless waves of Lake Superior, the largest body of fresh water by volume in the United States. When I park my car and walk the sort distance through the fragrant cedar trees and emerge on the ancient rock, I at once feel total peace as my problems vaporize and leave my mind and body feeling completely refreshed.

Little wonder this place is magical. Charlie Kawbawgam, one of the last chiefs of the Chippewa Indian tribe of the Upper Peninsula of Michigan, spent his final years here with his wife Charlotte. His story is captured in Robert Traver's *Laughing Whitefish*. Some say the isle was a spiritual place for the Chippewa, for me it certainly is. I visit as often as I can, especially when past experiences from cases I was involved in come rushing back in jumbled fashion. On a brilliant day, while on the black rock, memories come flooding back like a waterfall pouring through my head.

On a warm sunny day, the cool breeze enveloped me, as I continued to enjoy the peace on Presque Isle. Sitting on the rocks, I saw a gaggle of young college students who looked at me obviously wondering who I might be, what I might have done in years gone by. They undoubtedly saw my glasses, now necessary from years of paperwork and computer use. My hearing aids, now necessary from years of shooting thousands of rounds of ammunition, are obvious. For me, both served as badges of the job I had done, but when a young couple with two small children walked by suddenly noticing me and briskly pulling their children past me, I realized maybe they thought I was a threat to be feared. When an older gentleman walked past smiling at me with a quick nod, I could tell that with his life of experience he knew I posed no threat.

Everyone has a past. I wondered what each of those who had noticed me had done in their lives. They knew nothing of mine. This questioning of all that I saw was consistent with my training and experience as a police officer. Curiosity and the ability to see what most people never notice is what every good police officer develops and by following that curiosity crimes are solved and at other times lives are salvaged. I had learned that everyone has a story and everyone has dreams, many times never to be realized.

On this same day I spotted a beautiful majestic bald eagle holding aloft directly above me on the winds that caressed the pure blue water of Lake Superior. The eagle was also watching me. It sized me up, wondering and considering its next move. I knew that it had seen too much in its short lifespan of hope, despair, life and death. I was no threat so it held aloft testing the breeze. A deer mouse scurried around the rock outcropping searching for food but the eagle showed no interest in that potential meal. The tiny white flower growing tenaciously out of a small crack in the barren rock held steadfast, ever waving in the relentless breeze but bending when it must to avoid being broken. The smell of northern white cedar, white pine, fresh water and a mix of wild flowers assailed me.

The symphony of the wind swirled around me mixed with the squawk of the sea gulls and the lapping waves on the rock. Fresh water spray from the rhythmic series of white caps cleansed all within its reach. The world here was in balance with its splendor. Each creature knew it was connected to each of the others and only pure motives existed at this time, on this day, in this place. None sought to injure the others nor take more than they needed, especially at the expense of others. God had carefully taught each of us mutual respect, but those lessons were hard earned and paid for; little in this world that is good is free. While I had learned through my years as a police officer that there are many good people, my experience also taught me that far too many had lost any sense of balance and respect so obvious in nature.

I'm not sure who moved first, but suddenly the eagle and mouse were gone, vanished in an instant. The wind remained, the spray still felt so refreshing, and the little flower still clung to the black rock against the relentless wind. The thoughts had left my head, my body felt weak, but I was at ease. The violent memories of my past years faded from my consciousness, the loud pounding in my head silenced, the smells of decaying bodies carried away seemingly by the wind, and those piercing stares from faces begging for help that would never come faded quietly away at last. All was at peace. The warmth of the sun invigorated me. The gentle rhythmic sound of the waves breaking on that eternal black rock eased the pain in my head.

I slowly, painfully, arose and walked back into the welcoming forest where I had left my car. As I sat down in my car, I once again felt the comfort and the safety in what used to be my Blue Goose. I was back in my protective sanctuary of endless years. The confidence slowly pumped back into my body and I drank it in. I wondered how soon it would be before the next episode would return. Would they never leave me in peace? No one ever retires from this job, even long after they hang up their uniform. I drove away without looking back at the serene waters of Lake Superior wondering when those apparitions would once again pay me a visit.

The police cycle starts anew with new names, new faces, but with the same experiences to be encountered, and sadly with the same results. This is their chosen profession, a dangerous one, and they will carry out their duties nonetheless. My experience has shown me that nearly every police officer who reaches retirement has had at least one experience in which they cheated death by a hair's width, and many have been lucky on a number of occasions. Each officer who finally takes their retirement has truly earned it more times than most people, including their families, will ever know. I believe that good police officers will always do what they can, when they can, for whom they can, both on and off-duty. When they finally turn in their badges, I pray that they can rest knowing that they always did their best, did what was right, respected everyone they encountered and kept their family dear to them. Little else truly matters. And I pray their nightly dreams are pleasant or at least short in duration. *Tuebor.*

AFTERWORD: TUEBOR

It should be obvious that the people described in the experiences that I have shared in *Tuebor are generally devoid of racial identifiers, and that is intentional. The purpose was not to attempt to avoid characterizing any particular racial or gender group, as my thousands of experiences have involved people of most, if not all, ethnic backgrounds. Further, society continues to become more mixed,* so characterizing someone by ethnicity may not be accurate or prudent. My own ethnicity consists of Irish, German, English, and many other groups I have yet to discover. My wife's background includes French, Irish, German, English, Native American, and, I am sure, many others as well. My experience has taught me that no one of any pure or mixed ethnic group, socio-economic class, gender classification, educational level, or other grouping is above becoming involved in deviant behavior. It is the person who does wrong, not the ethnic background of that person. That is the lesson that I hope readers of *Tuebor will take from the experiences that I have tried to present.*

I completed this book from my personal experiences along with the experiences of other police officers that I observed following my retirement. Many of my experiences shared in *Tuebor have been with the Michigan State Police, but also include* interactions with federal, county, city, township and tribal police officers. The Michigan State Police values strict selection criteria and thorough initial and ongoing training of their officers. In addition to rigorous oversight of all department personnel, enlisted and civilian, Michigan State Police employees are the recipients of an ongoing process to ensure professional and legal behavior. When officers have committed wrongdoings in the Michigan State Police, they have been promptly investigated and adjudicated internally and also in the court system when the facts justified, to ensure legal, just, and fair treatment of all persons coming into contact with this agency and its personnel.

Much has changed in the world of policing since I retired, including scientific advancements in the area of DNA testing, cell phone tracing and computer data searching, GPS location methods. These and other valuable enhancements have enabled officers to solve many inactive cases, some twenty or more years old, bringing closure to those affected. Science has also allowed the positive identification of human remains, resolving many missing persons' cases, bringing some level of closure and relief to grieving family members who now know the fate of their loved ones.

Along with these positive scientific changes, there has also been an increase on the part of some officer's use of illegal fatal force as evidenced by recently reported killings of unarmed suspects by police officers. These high-profile cases involve illegal use of force against citizens in an effort to affect an arrest sanctioned under the U.S. Constitution Fourth Amendment. Recent indisputable incidents, captured on video, substantiate these acts, like the 2014 Cleveland, Ohio shooting of Tamir Rice, a 12-year-old who was holding an airsoft pistol. The officers pulled up in their car to within a few feet of where the suspect was standing placing themselves in harm's way rather than stopping a safe distance from him and using their car as cover where they might have safely resolved the situation without resorting to violence. Other incidents have shown officers shooting unarmed suspects who posed no immediate threat to the officers or any citizen, killing the suspects depriving the suspects of their constitutional rights..

Other tragic events such as those that occurred in Ferguson, Missouri, were looked at by some political leaders as simply a killing of an unarmed African-American male by a Caucasian police officer. On those facts alone, many conclusions could, and were, drawn from those isolated facts. A closer look at all of the facts disclose that Michael Brown had committed a strong-armed robbery of a local market and the store clerk was threatened with physical harm by Brown as shown by store surveillance footage. Brown then assaulted Officer Darren Wilson as Wilson sat in his marked police vehicle. These are all relevant facts necessary to draw potential mistreatment conclusions regarding this incident. Was the shooting and killing of Brown ultimately legally justified? That is where the criminal justice system comes into play to make that determination, not people who took the law into their own hands. The rioters in Ferguson burned many local businesses that were owned by hardworking African-American families, effectively putting them out of business and destroying their lives. The local business owners did nothing to deserve the lawless actions of the people who chose to commit serious crimes. In another case, North Charleston, S.C., police officer Michael Slager shot and killed Walter Scott, an unarmed suspect who ran away from the officer during a routine traffic stop. Prior to Scott running away from Slager, a physical struggle between Slager and Scott lasted for nearly two minutes with the officer's Taser striking Slager rather than the suspect. Video shows one dart struck Slager's shirt and the second dart hit his leg area (both darts need to be in contact to deliver the 50,000 volt charge disabling the person). Within seconds after Scott broke away from Slager, Slager fired eight shots and hit Scott in the back killing him. Slager was indicted for murder in that incident. At the time Slager's Taser was deployed against him by Scott, Slager's use of fatal force would likely have been justified. In 1985 the United State Supreme Court decided Tennessee v. Garner stating that the use of deadly force is not justifiable simply to prevent a fleeing suspect's escape if the suspect does not pose a significant threat of death or serious harm to the officer or others. Therefore, once the unarmed Scott began running away from Slager, he was no longer an immediate threat to Slager or anyone else and the use of fatal force was no longer justified to effectuate the Fourth Amendment seizure.

Very recently, in Dallas, Texas, Micah Xavier Johnson, an African-American, fatally shot five police officers and wounded seven other officers in retaliation for past instances of what Johnson perceived as racial injustice. There was no evidence that the officers killed by Johnson ever engaged in any illegal actions against anyone, but they were randomly killed nevertheless. Johnson's actions were simply devoid of any legal or moral justification. What right did Johnson have to target police officers who were not involved in the injustices viewed by Johnson? Again, it is up to the justice system to resolve these events, not people taking the law into their own hand.

As stated by John Adams, the second president of the United States, this nation is country of laws, not of men. Everyone is to be governed by the same laws, regardless of their station in life, ethnic background, whether it be the most common citizen or politician, high-ranking bureaucrats or even the president of the

United States; all must be held to the just laws of America whereby the court system determines guilt, not the person on the street.

With my many years of experience in instructing the gamut of required criminal law classes, I am unable to find any scintilla of justification for these outrageous incidents, legally or morally. I have been crystal clear in instructing the legal mandates that fatal force can only be justified as a last resort, that is, after all other efforts have failed or would likely fail and which are necessary to protect citizens or the officers themselves from serious harm or death. Certainly in the case of an unarmed suspect, fatal force is almost never justified. In these situations involving unarmed suspects, officers are, or should be, trained to make a physical arrest, calling for backup when necessary, if it is available.

There are exceptions to using fatal force against an unarmed person. One example would be if the suspect is overpowering the officer and putting the officer in fear of imminent death by physical force such as choking or beating the officer with his fists. Another situation that happened to me during my career over a dozen times involved suspects attempting to take my gun from me. In these situations, I could not wait for the suspect to take my gun from me to find out what the suspect's intentions might have been. Though ultimately I did not need to take any of these suspect's lives, I did inflict quick and effective harm to the suspects to prevent my weapon from being taken. If a suspect is able to disarm an officer, the result can be deadly.

An example of the danger officers face following being disarmed involved an officer having his weapon taken incident occurred in July 2016 where an incarcerated suspect was being taken from a court room to a holding cell in the Berrien County,

Michigan, courthouse. The suspect overpowered an officer and took his gun. The suspect then fatally shot two bailiffs and wounded a sheriff's deputy and a civilian. The murdered head bailiff was a retired Michigan State Police officer who I personally knew. The second bailiff killed was a retired Benton Charter Township Police Department officer. What should have been a seemingly safe retirement job for these two police officers turned deadly. The suspect's wife felt that her husband was not a monster but had acted out of fear that he would not be able to see his family before being sent to jail. As a result, two officers who had survived police careers protecting citizens are now dead and their families must live the rest of their lives with their unbearable loss.

Not to be left out of the equation are the self-proclaimed spokespersons who take it upon themselves to speak on behalf of African-Americans. They have the benefit of high profile names that command media attention and are given media access to provide their slanted version of the facts to the masses of citizens watching them on the nightly news. This too only inflames people to commit additional crimes in a misguided effort to resolve real or perceived past wrongdoing. If those in these leadership roles gave a balanced message instead of inflaming the public for political advancement, then we as a society could work together to solve issues of racism. In Ferguson, Missouri, the rioters looted, destroyed and burned property. The millions of tax dollars spent quelling these riots, with injuries and deaths, could have been avoided if the media and spokespersons had disseminated a message condemning further violence to the people rioting in Ferguson. These high-profile spokespersons have a chance to make a positive difference if they will only rise above the passion and self-serving efforts and allow logic and common sense to guide their actions to the benefit of all citizens and not just the ethnic group they profess to represent. They were right to condemn wrongs committed against members of their ethnic group, but at the same time they were wrong to fail to condemn criminal actions by members of their own ethnic group.

The news media, as well, must recognize their powerful role and commanding access to television and radio. Media spokespersons must remain objective, professional and absolutely accurate in reporting only the substantiated facts when investigating and reporting high profile incidents without slanting or demeaning, intentionally or unintentionally, anyone or any group. On February 26, 2012, George Zimmerman, a neighborhood watch coordinator, fatally shot Trayvon Martin. Initial news broadcasts reported that Zimmerman was white and had shot Martin, an unarmed African-American youngster. This irresponsible reporting only served to inflame a situation unnecessarily. Later, after significant unrest in the African-American community, in large part due to this reported misinformation, the media corrected the reported ethnicity of Zimmerman accurately as mixed race Hispanic.

Just as my experience has shown me, consistent with research statistics, the vast majority of police officers never deprive suspects of their rights, but perform their dangerous duties day and night seeking to help those they serve. A recent study conducted by researchers at Bowling Green State University looked at the crime committed by police officers between the years of 2005 to 2011. A police population between 850,000 and 950,000 was cited during the years of the study. The study concluded police officers are not committing crimes anywhere the near the rate of civilian population, citing police officers having an arrest rate of 1.7 arrests per 100,000 population whereas civilians showed an arrest rate of 3,888 per 100,000 population. Much of the credit for this finding is a stringent screening process in hiring police officers. In my personal experiences I have seen arrests of judges, legislators, clergy, attorneys, doctors, and members of all other occupations as well. After all, people, no matter what their station in life or ethnic background, are subject to human frailties and are capable of committing crimes.

Recently, to protest oppression of people of color, Colin Kaepernick, quarterback for the San Francisco 49'ers, sat rather than stood, during the playing of the national anthem. Before pro and con comments fill the air, it might be helpful to remember that in this country we have a right to express our views and responses so long as they are lawful. Kaepernick's actions were lawful and it was his right to so respond. However, I ask if the United States or the national anthem was to blame for Kaepernick's perceived oppression of persons of color? I only ask that before misplaced action is taken, seek to understand all of the facts, attempt to understand opposing viewpoints on the issue, express your words or actions in a lawful manner, and direct them to the proper venue rather than at an innocent party.

Near the end of the Summer Olympics this year, I was impressed and moved by an interview with Carmelo Anthony, New York Knicks basketball star, after the U.S. men's basketball team won the gold medal. He acknowledged that there are problems in the United States with racial issues, but he advocated understanding, restraint and working together to resolve these issues. That is what I have tried to show in *Tuebor. My experiences have also shown me that although most of us have opinions and positions on most topics, attempts to understand opposing opinions and positions go a long way in resolving most issues. Learning and understanding the true facts surrounding any given situation further aids in making sound decisions to guide future actions. I believe this will go a long way in helping to heal and move forward as Carmelo Anthony so eloquently stated.*

ABOUT THE AUTHOR

Bob Muladore began his police career in June of 1976 with the Bridgeport Township Police Department in Bridgeport, Michigan. As the first full-time patrolman and with no police academy training behind him, lessons were learned "on the fly". The author would like to thank Chief Louie Robinson for giving him his start in the sometimes mysterious career of policing. He also wishes to thank Dave Heterick, the part-time Bridgeport Township police officer who taught him the basic skills necessary that allowed him to safely negotiate his first 14 months of policing with the township police department that allowed him to go home each night to his family. Without Dave's early guidance, the author's life might have been much different.

The author spent 25 years with the Michigan State Police initially assigned to the Northville Post in Northville, Michigan, where he learned the methods of effective patrol and investigation. State troopers in Michigan handle most of their own investigations unlike many other police departments where the road officers turn over many, if not all of their cases, to the detectives. A great deal is learned from handling an investigation from beginning to end. Other troopers, post detectives and local police officers generously shared their knowledge along with the State Police crime lab personnel in helping the author learn how to effectively perform his job. Investigative skills were honed to a fine edge, but it was the people skills that were learned and refined that became an indispensable tool in his array of options to effectively deal with the variety of situations thrown at him on a daily basis.

While working as a trooper, the author attended the Detroit College of Law in the evenings, (now Michigan State University School of Law in East Lansing, Michigan) earning his Juris Doctorate Degree (commonly known as a law degree). That knowledge greatly assisted him in his career with the MSP. He instructed criminal and civil law courses to MSP, local and tribal police officers for over 18 years. He rose through the ranks in various positions including, the Uniform Division, Training Division, Narcotics Division, Executive Division, Fire Marshal, and Technical Solutions Division before retiring from the department, having attained the rank of Inspector. He maintained a steadfast goal of working to assist others rather than seeking personal gain or recognition.

Upon retiring from the MSP the author earned his Ph.D. degree, in Public Affairs and Administration, from Western Michigan University. He was certified as a public safety officer and worked with the Northern Michigan University Public Safety Department providing legal training to police academy recruits. *Tuebor* is the author's second book, the first being a criminal law overview that was used by police academy students in Michigan. He is currently working on a book about his work as an attorney.